Art and Architecture
of the World's Religions

Art and Architecture of the World's Religions

Volume 1

LESLIE ROSS

GREENWOOD PRESS
An Imprint of ABC-CLIO, LLC

A B C C L I O

Santa Barbara, California • Denver, Colorado • Oxford, England

Library of Congress Cataloging-in-Publication Data

Ross, Leslie, 1956–
    Art and architecture of the world's religions / Leslie Ross.
        p. cm.
    Includes bibliographical references and index.
    ISBN 978-0-313-34286-8 (hard copy set : alk. paper) — ISBN 978-0-313-34288-2 (hard copy v. 1 : alk. paper) — ISBN 978-0-313-34290-5 (hard copy v. 2 : alk. paper) — ISBN 978-0-313-34287-5 (ebook set) — ISBN 978-0-313-34289-9 (ebook v. 1) — ISBN 978-0-313-34291-2 (ebook v. 2)
    1. Art and religion.   2. Architecture and religion.   3. Religions.   I. Title.
N7790.R67   2009
203'.7—dc22   2009014590

13   12   11   10   09   1   2   3   4   5

This book is also available on the World Wide Web as an eBook.
Visit www.abc-clio.com for details.

ABC-CLIO, LLC
130 Cremona Drive, P.O. Box 1911
Santa Barbara, California 93116-1911

To my parents

Contents

Volume 1

Volume 2

Contents

Acknowledgments

Many colleagues, friends, and acquaintances have, during the two to three years since these volumes have been in preparation, expressed either great sympathy or total disbelief about this project. How could one possibly even begin to think about composing a book or two dealing with such a large topic as the art and architecture of the world's religions? This is a question I have regularly asked myself too. And, in reply to queries about how long I have been working on this book, I have simply had to say that I have been working on this study, in some form, for *many* decades now.

I need to give great credit to my editor at Greenwood Press, Debra Adams, for her consistent enthusiasm and helpful guidance, as ever. Debby has invited and assisted me enormously in shaping and defining my previous several book projects for Greenwood Press, and her support for and enthusiasm about this current project has been deeply cherished indeed.

A number of other staff members of Greenwood Press deserve copious thanks too. Liz Kincaid is to be greatly thanked for her assistance with the final details of image acquisition, and Sandy Windelspechts's creation of the excellent graphics (diagrams and floor plans) found in these volumes deserves more than great thanks indeed. Many thanks to the staff at Apex CoVantage for overseeing the final production stages of these volumes. It has been a pleasure, as always, to have worked with Greenwood Press.

My research and writing also relied most significantly on the library staff at Dominican University of California. I want to express my deepest gratitude to the Dominican Sisters of San Rafael for their founding, in the late 19th century, an institution that continues to support scholarship in a wide range of fields and with excellent library resources to do so. The many decades of library collection development policies of Sister Marguerite Stanka have been continued in recent years by Alan Schut, who has been most instrumental in continuing to acquire titles in the arts and humanities for the Dominican Library. Any books and journal articles that I needed for this current research, not available in the Dominican University Library, were happily and gladly obtained for me via Interlibrary Loan, by library staff members, Kenneth C. Fish, Jr., A. J. Real, and Shaun Barger. In spite of my periodic and often great demands on their time, all Dominican Library staff members have been of great assistance to me— I sincerely thank them again.

I also want to heartily thank several esteemed colleagues who have read and made suggestions on my chapters. These include: Maureen O'Brien, Sister Barbara Green, Neal Wolfe, Peter Flagg, Heidi Chretien, Victoria Sheridan, Janet Giddings, Bergen Kirk, and Diana and John Harrington. These colleagues have been very generous with their time and of enormous assistance in offering suggestions on specific sections of the text. Their support overall is deeply cherished.

There is no doubt that this project could never have been completed without the ongoing inspiration and support offered by my dear parents—to whom these volumes are dedicated.

Introduction

A friendly study of the world's religions is a sacred duty.
—Mahatma Gandhi, *Young India*, September 2, 1926

SCOPE AND PURPOSE

This book is designed to provide an introduction to the major religions of the world, with special focus on the art and architectural forms associated with these belief systems. The study is divided into two volumes with a total of 16 chapters. Each chapter concentrates on a major world religion and includes sections on: (1) the origins and development of the religion, (2) the principal beliefs and key practices, (3) the traditional art and architectural forms, and (4) selected and illustrated examples of art and architecture.

The religions covered in these volumes include belief systems of very ancient origin as well as religions whose development is, relatively speaking, more modern. Some of the ancient religions discussed in these volumes are not currently practiced today in their original form. The evidence for these ancient belief systems is primarily archaeological, art historical, or textual. The reader will thus find information on prehistoric belief systems, ancient Mesopotamian, Egyptian, and classical Greek and Roman religions in volume 1. Religions that continue to be practiced today in various forms, such as Judaism, Christianity, Islam, Hinduism, and Buddhism are covered primarily in volume 2. The reader will also find chapters on the indigenous belief systems of Africa, Oceania, Australia, and the Native Americas in volume 1, and discussions of Shintoism, Taoism, and Confucianism in volume 2.

World map.

Asia

Middle
East

Pacific
Ocean

Indian
Ocean

Australia

Of necessity, even given the scope of these volumes, readers will doubtless find that several world religions as well as several regions of the world are not included in this study. A full and completely comprehensive coverage of all of the world's religions and the religious art and architectural forms associated with all geographic regions of the globe would require a far greater number of volumes. Such comprehensive coverage is not the goal of this present study. These two volumes are simply designed to present an introduction to the richness, vastness, and diversity of this material, with the hope that readers will be encouraged and inspired to delve further. It is assumed that readers will recognize that the materials presented in these volumes represent carefully selected examples of the religious art and architecture traditionally associated with a diversity of faith traditions and practices. Readers are encouraged to understand that any gaps they may perceive in the coverage of world religions or world regions in these volumes are not intended to either maximize or diminish the status and importance of any world religions or regions.

Further details and suggestions about how to use this book most effectively are found at the end of this introduction. In the interim, some definitions will usefully serve to explain the goals and parameters of this study. Before proceeding further, it will be helpful to define what we mean by "religion" and what we mean by "religious art and architecture."

WHAT IS RELIGION?

Religion can be (and has been) defined in many different ways. Religion can be seen as the inherent human impulse to seek meaning in life and death, to develop and maintain a relationship with the transcendent, to explain or justify why certain things happen in life, to connect or communicate with higher and nonhuman forces, to receive guidance on correct attitudes and ethical behaviors, and to provide and promote community among cultural groups. All of these factors have played significant roles, to a greater or lesser extent, in the development, promulgation, rise, and transformation of the world's religions. The questions traditionally posed by humans, and diversely answered by the world's religions, address the same issues and concerns.

> Is there something "greater than us" that we identify as deity? If there is, who or what is this divine entity? . . . What is the nature of the world and the heavens? Did they emanate from the divine, were they created by the divine, or are they unrelated to anything divine? . . . What is humanity's place both within the world and in relation to the divine? . . . What does the divine expect or demand of us? What actions are good, and what actions are bad? Is there life beyond death? If there is, how is it gained or received? What will it be like? Where will it happen? How shall we get there?[1]

These are some of the fundamental questions that are addressed by the world's religions and to which these religions have responded in diverse ways. Of course, it should be noted that many scholarly and popular studies have been devoted to the question-asking process itself—why, where, when, and in what circumstances do religious beliefs arise? Are religions invented by humans simply to provide meaning in life, to understand and control their circumstances? Or, are religious beliefs firmly based on the awareness or revelation of divine, cosmic, suprahuman forces? Much intriguing—and often contentious—discussion about the origins of religion has been undertaken by many writers.[2] Although these topics are certainly touched on in these present volumes, this study is less concerned with the meanings, purposes, and origins of religion overall but is instead focused on the visible manifestations of diverse beliefs via the evidence in art and architectural forms. In other words, this study assumes (1) that religious beliefs have played a central role in the lives of humans through history and (2) that this fact is exceedingly well demonstrated in humanity's attention to the creation of religious art and architecture, past and present.

WHAT IS RELIGIOUS ART?

For purposes of this study, religious art is defined as any and all visible manifestations of belief. Such a broad definition is necessary because, throughout history and across the world, religious beliefs and practices have been, and continue to be, visually manifested in a great diversity of forms. These forms, of course, include the tangible and traditionally enduring monuments of architecture, sculpture, and painting, customarily studied by art historians. Readers will thus find much coverage devoted to these generally familiar categories of art, albeit in culturally diverse varieties. The forms of religious architecture discussed in these volumes include temples, shrines, synagogues, mosques, churches, and other worship environments constructed by humans. Numerous works of painting and sculpture are also discussed, such as stained glass windows, icons, statues of holy figures, pictorial narrative scenes, and so on. Many of these examples of painting and sculpture are closely associated with religious architectural structures, while other examples are less closely tied to specific architectural contexts.

However, our broad definition of religious art—as any and all visible manifestations of belief—also extends to forms of art that do not necessarily fit neatly into the traditional art historical categories of architecture, painting, and sculpture. Religious art is also performative; it involves actions and attitudes. Much attention in these volumes is thus devoted to the context and usage of religious art—not simply its appearance. Dance, music, song, ceremony, ritual actions, prayer, and the performance of individual or collective worship are all integral aspects of the religious nature of religious art. This study thus delves into areas of investigation most often associated with the disciplinary fields of archaeology, anthropology, and ethnographic studies. What the creators and users of religious art do and say (or do not say) about their beliefs and practices are critical factors in any efforts to understand the visual culture of past and present societies.[3] The ongoing dialogues between art historians, anthropologists, archaeologists, and scholars of visual and popular culture are reflective of a broader approach to the study and definition of religious art, from which this own work has benefited.

Indeed, it can be said that religious art not only reflects, but also creates, the primary symbols of meaning for humans and societies. In this sense, the diverse forms of religious art (from small to large scale, monumental to ephemeral, sophisticatedly crafted to more rustic) all function as activating agents as well as reverberations of humankind's ultimate concerns. A respectful approach to the world's religions, and attentive study and analysis of their visible manifestations can be seen as "itself a deeply religious act."[4]

THE IMPORTANCE OF ART IN RELIGIOUS STUDIES

While the specific beliefs and practices associated with the world's religions vary greatly, all religions can be said to share an interest in creating or acknowledging a sense of the sacred in visible or symbolic form. Humans have expressed their religious impulses from prehistory to the present day in visible forms. Whether these forms are simple or elaborate, small or large scale, permanent or temporary, religious art and architecture serves to make beliefs visible and tangible in ways that sacred texts, writings, and scholarly commentaries do not. Indeed, it can be argued, that it is far more likely to be the visual forms of religious expression that impress and resonate most profoundly with believers and nonadherents alike. The visual expression of religious beliefs in art and architectural forms may be seen as the unity in diversity among the world's religions. It is this shared artistic impulse that provides the primary lens for this study of the world's religions.

> Across time, space, and culture, in all of humanity's wrestling with life and its meaning, the issues have been the same. Recognition of this bond with peoples of the past can give rise within us to an empathy capable of transcending our theological and liturgical particularities, an empathy that permits us to value another people's answers, another people's religion.[5]

When one first enters a medieval cathedral filled with the colorful glow of stained glass windows, or when one first stands in front of a Hindu temple replete with complex and elaborate sculptural carvings, the very special power of the visible expression of belief impresses one with extreme directness and tangibility. Whether this sensation is one of awe, or fright, or confusion, or attraction combined with a desire to know more, it can be said that religious art and architecture serves a critical function as the primary visible entrance or doorway into the belief systems of the world.

Entrances and doorways may be actual physical structures. They may also be seen as more symbolic passages into the realms of religious beliefs. In either case, these entrances are often evoked and assisted by their visual forms. On the literal level, the design of religious architecture functions to create and signal sacred space—space that, in various ways, is differentiated, or set apart, from nonsacred space. One may enter a physical structure of faith (whether a temple, a church, a shrine, or a mosque, for example) by passing through a physical doorway. The entrance to the structure represents a transition from the exterior to the interior—from the world outside to the interior world of the sanctified space. The creation of physical and often permanent forms of sacred space can be (and often has been, historically and presently) a massive architectural undertaking. Many of the most visibly impressive architectural structures created by humans through the ages and around the world have been and continue to be designed for religious purposes.

However, sacred space can be (and often has been, historically and presently) created via other means. Sacred spaces can be created by an event, a temporary acknowledgment of the confluence or presence of sacred forces or powers, a performance, a ritual, or a recognition of preexisting sacredness in the world or in specific natural landscape features. Whether sacred space involves an imposing or humble architectural construction, major or minor manipulation of the environment by humans, or simply involves an acknowledged orientation to, or focus on, a ritual action or landscape feature, it can be argued that visuality, in some form, always plays a critical role in serving as an entrance/doorway/passage into belief systems, and also in directing and inspiring belief.

These closely related functions, of directing, promoting, and inspiring belief, are the fundamental grounds for religious art and architecture through the ages. Art plays an especially didactic and faith-directing role in some religious traditions, specifically in serving to teach adherents about the primary tenets of the religion in the form of visual narratives or symbols. It is often the case that these visual images are actually and physically located at the literal entrances to sacred buildings. These images, such as paintings and sculptures, which may show the events and stories from the sacred texts or may visually narrate the lives and deeds of holy figures, are common in many religious traditions. The appearance of these visual images on the exteriors of sacred structures often reinforces the transition from the secular and worldly to the sanctified and holy interior space.

Of course, the function of visual imagery as an entrance or passage into faith traditions is by no means restricted to the form of physical doorways on the exteriors of buildings. Visual imagery very often enriches the interiors of sacred spaces as well, and in this location serves the same function as doorways into the faith. Regardless of scope, location, and portable or nonportable format, visual images can serve as directing doorways into faith traditions by providing information and inspiration.

The inspiring function of religious art and architecture takes on a variety of different forms as well. The directive and edifying presentation of visuals (especially those involving figural imagery) is not demonstrated or shared by all faith traditions. Islamic religious art, for example, maintains an extremely rich visual tradition but one that generally avoids figural, narrative imagery in sacred spaces. Even so, the primary aim of Islamic religious art is to inspire, and to assist adherents in their experience of the faith. One will not, for example, find visual illustrations of the life of Muhammad in a traditional Islamic mosque, whereas in traditional Eastern Orthodox churches one will often be overwhelmed by the abundance of visual imagery on all available surfaces—walls and ceilings—plus the holy icons placed throughout the church and on towering icon screens. Many protestant Christian denominations avoid visual imagery to a greater or lesser extent, whereas Buddhism and Hinduism are, in general, faith traditions that, in their various branches, significantly rely on visual imagery to teach and to inspire.

Whether in abundant and colorful presence or in determined and sparing absence, visual imagery plays a critical role as an entryway into all faith traditions. The creation and usage of sacred space also serves to provide a fundamental and shared passageway into the belief systems of the world. The study of the art and architecture associated with the world's religions is the guiding gateway through which we truly must enter in our goals of understanding and appreciating this unity and diversity.

> What distinguishes sacred art from other varieties is the window it opens onto another world—a world that is vaster, stranger, more real, and more beautiful than the world we normally encounter. . . . What makes art sacred is not what it depicts, but the way it opens onto transcendence and carries the viewer into it.[6]

It is the hope that this current publication will serve to convey and highlight to readers some sense of the brilliant diversity and shared fundamental importance of the visible in the study of the world's religions.

HOW TO USE THIS BOOK

Readers will find that each chapter, in each of the two volumes of this book, has the same structure. Each chapter includes the same four parts (the origins and development of the religion, the principal beliefs and key practices, the traditional art and architectural forms, and selected and illustrated examples). This is deliberate. In visualizing and planning these volumes, the author has taken great care to ensure that each religion (or related sets of religions) discussed in the book is given the same coverage as all of the others, in the sense that each chapter is approximately the same length.

At the same time, this carefully designed structure has created some significant challenges for the author and will doubtless do so for readers as well. Not all materials ever fit neatly into any scholarly structure, as this book also hopes to demonstrate. Although it is quite sensible to begin discussions of many world religions with a section on the origins and development of the belief system, this model works especially well for religions that can be traced to specific historical founders (such as Muhammad for Islam, Jesus for Christianity, and the Buddha for Buddhism). But, more than a great many other religions of the world cannot be traced to specific founders, and the origins of these belief systems cannot be so easily identified using the historical and chronological model, which assumes some type of starting point before which the religion was not revealed, known, developed, or practiced. Indeed, many of the world's belief systems are of unknown origin and reflect very ancient cultural traditions of diverse groups in a variety of different world regions. One can trace the historical origins of the religion of Islam to Muhammad, for example. One can discuss the cultural context in which he lived; one can describe the importance of his received revelations and the differences his message posed to then-current and previously practiced belief systems in the Arabian peninsula. But one cannot do so with religions such as Shinto and Hinduism, for example, nor for a great many other religions whose origins cannot be traced to a specific founder, although developments can often be traced through a series of later influential figures. In these cases, the origins and development chapter sections are far less relevant scholarly constructs, as the text hopes to point out as well.

Discussions of the principal beliefs and key practices of the religions covered in these volumes have also been fraught with a number of challenges. Several of the world's belief systems are quite clear about what their adherents are expected to believe and to do. Many religions have creeds, dogmas, or detailed descriptions of beliefs deemed to be correct. However, even within religious systems that are highly dogmatic, many variations and practices may exist. Not all Catholics attend Mass, and not all Jews adhere to the dietary regulations suggested in the ancient Hebrew scriptures. When Buddhism arrived in Japan in the sixth century CE, many of the ancient Shinto deities were given new names or developed other shared correlations with Buddhist deities. Islam recognizes the Hebrew and Christian traditions of prophetic revelation. Many Hindus regard the Buddha as one of many divine or divinely inspired beings. Some Protestant Christian groups maintain rites and rituals that are very akin to Roman Catholicism, whereas other Protestant Christians are extremely concerned to avoid any forms of worship practice that resemble those of Catholic or Orthodox Christians. Attempts to define the principal beliefs and key practices of a vast diversity of world religions will always run the danger of generalization. It is hoped that the present study manages to avoids this to some extent.

The traditional art and architectural forms associated with various belief systems also vary widely. In many cases, monumental architecture (temples, churches, synagogues, and mosques) are the most obvious examples, and the reader will appropriately find many discussions of these forms of sacred structures in several chapters of these volumes. Apart from these diverse architectural forms, and the arts of painting and sculpture often associated with them, the reader will also find discussions of how the sacred buildings were and continue to be used for the specific purposes of different faiths. How buildings appear—as well as how they function—are both extremely important considerations in any discussion of religious art. However, the creation of permanent architectural structures (of large or smaller scale) does not characterize the arts traditionally associated with all religions or regions of the world. This fact is acknowledged and embraced in this study, so readers can expect to find a great diversity of forms of art described or illustrated in different chapters.

Each chapter includes a number of accompanying illustrations as well as several selected examples that are described in fuller detail. Although approximately the same overall number of illustrations are included in each chapter, readers will find that the number of examples chosen for more detailed discussion varies somewhat per chapter. It is hoped that this slight divergence in format between chapters will be welcomed and understood by readers as reflective of the richness of these materials overall as well as the potential for any one example to inspire additional research and consideration. In some cases, longer discussion of several illustrated examples will be found. In other cases, the number of examples signaled out for more detailed discussion is fewer. In some chapters, several groups of images are discussed together as examples of different forms that share the same general subject matter but that may demonstrate different dates, styles, and interpretations of traditional imagery. In all cases, the more focused discussion of specific examples is designed to complement and expand on the materials explored in each chapter, and in no cases is it designed to maximize the importance of selected monuments or diminish the importance of others not included.

At the conclusion of each chapter, readers will find a section titled "Bibliography and Further Reading." At the end of volume 2, readers will also find a selected bibliography. The chapter bibliographies—although fairly lengthy—in all cases necessarily represent only a sampling of the materials available for study of the art and architecture of specific religions or world regions. These listings are, of course, not comprehensive by any means, but may, at least, alert students to some of the major sources and the names of important scholarly specialists. Much additional scholarship exists, and continues to be avidly created, on any number of aspects of the world's religious art and architecture. Indeed, the bibliography on particular monuments (such as the Parthenon in Athens) would, in itself, at least fill a complete volume. Specialists might find the bibliographic listings in these present volumes rather eclectic in their inclusion of not only magisterial overall studies but also more arcane articles in highly specialized journals. This too is deliberate. It is hoped that the bibliographies and suggestions for further reading include samples of the vast range of works that demonstrate the ongoing and lively discussion into which students are encouraged to delve further.

The visual arts play an extremely important role in how religions and faith adherents self-define as groups and as individuals. In all cases, and in more than many ways, all faith traditions seem to require art (or at least an artful presentation of actions), and it is on this basis that this study rests.

NOTES

1. Byron Shafer, ed., *Religion in Ancient Egypt: Gods, Myths, and Personal Practice* (Ithaca, NY: Cornell University Press, 1991), 4–5

2. For example, Daniel Dennett, *Breaking the Spell: Religion as a Natural Phenomenon* (New York: Viking, 2006); Barbara King, *Evolving God: A Provocative View of the Origins of Religion* (New York: Doubleday, 2007); David Lewis-Williams, *The Mind in the Cave: Consciousness and the Origins of Art* (New York: Thames and Hudson, 2002); Steven Mithen, *The Prehistory of the Mind: A Search for the Origins of Art, Religion, and Science* (London: Thames and Hudson, 1996); John Pfeiffer, *The Creative Explosion: An Inquiry into the Origins of Art and Religion* (Ithaca, NY: Cornell University Press, 1985); and John Super and Briane Turley, *Religion in World History* (New York: Routledge, 2006).

3. "Visual culture" is a relatively recent term as well as academic discipline. It refers to the broad-ranging analysis of many forms of visual evidence and is especially concerned with acknowledging and including materials not covered in traditionalist art historical studies. Visual culture studies argue that all forms of visual evidence, from high to low—from the traditional art historical hierarchy of architecture, sculpture, and painting—to forms such as film, television, advertising, fashion, and popular visual ephemera are all important indicators of the values and concerns of diverse cultures. The applicability of this approach to religious art is obvious, as much religious art comes in forms that reside outside the traditional art historical arenas and styles. For example, see Margaret Dikovitskaya, *Visual Culture: The Study of Visual Culture after the Cultural Turn* (Cambridge, MA: The MIT Press, 2005); James Elkins, *Visual Studies: A Skeptical Introduction* (New York: Routledge, 2003), W.J.T. Mitchell, "What Is Visual Culture?" in *Meaning in the Visual Arts: Views from the Outside*, ed. Irving Lavin (Princeton, NJ: Institute for Advanced Study, 1995), 207–17; and David Morgan, *The Sacred Gaze: Religious Visual Culture in Theory and Practice* (Berkeley: University of California Press, 2005).

4. John Dixon, "Art as the Making of the World: Outline of Method in the Criticism of Religion and Art," *Journal of the American Academy of Religion* 51, no. 1 (1983), 34.

5. Shafer, 4.

6. Huston Smith, *The Illustrated World's Religions* (San Francisco: Harper San Francisco, 1986), 6.

BIBLIOGRAPHY AND FURTHER READING

Adams, Doug, and Diane Apostolos-Cappadona, eds. *Art as Religious Studies*. New York: Crossroad, 1987.

Dennett, Daniel. *Breaking the Spell: Religion as a Natural Phenomenon*. New York: Viking, 2006.

Dikovitskaya, Margaret. *Visual Culture: The Study of Visual Culture after the Cultural Turn*. Cambridge, MA: The MIT Press, 2005.

Dixon, John. "Art as the Making of the World: Outline of Method in the Criticism of Religion and Art." *Journal of the American Academy of Religion* 51, no. 1 (1983): 15–36.

Dixon, John. "What Makes Religious Art Religious?" *Cross Currents* 43, no. 1 (1993): 5–25.

Eliade, Mircea. *Symbolism, the Sacred, and the Arts*. Edited by Diane Apostolos-Cappadona. New York: Crossroad, 1985.

Elkins, James. *Visual Studies: A Skeptical Introduction*. New York: Routledge, 2003.

King, Barbara. *Evolving God: A Provocative View of the Origins of Religion*. New York: Doubleday, 2007.

Lavin, Irving, ed. *Meaning in the Visual Arts: Views from the Outside*. Princeton, NJ: Institute for Advanced Study, 1995.

Lewis-Williams, David. *The Mind in the Cave: Consciousness and the Origins of Art*. New York: Thames and Hudson, 2002.

Mitchell, W.J.T. "What is Visual Culture?" In *Meaning in the Visual Arts: Views from the Outside*, ed. Irving Lavin, 207–17. Princeton, NJ: Institute for Advanced Study, 1995.

Mithen, Steven. *The Prehistory of the Mind: A Search for the Origins of Art, Religion, and Science*. London: Thames and Hudson, 1996.

Morgan, David. *The Sacred Gaze: Religious Visual Culture in Theory and Practice*. Berkeley: University of California Press, 2005.

Morgan, David. "Visual Religion." *Religion* 30, no. 1 (2000): 41–53.

Pfeiffer, John. *The Creative Explosion: An Inquiry into the Origins of Art and Religion*. Ithaca, NY: Cornell University Press, 1985.

Prown, Jules. *Art as Evidence: Writings on Art and Material Culture*. New Haven, CT: Yale University Press, 2001.

Shafer, Byron, ed. *Religion in Ancient Egypt: Gods, Myths, and Personal Practice*. Ithaca, NY: Cornell University Press, 1991.

Smith, Huston. *The Illustrated World's Religions*. San Francisco: Harper San Francisco, 1986.

Super, John, and Briane Turley. *Religion in World History*. New York: Routledge, 2006.

–1–

Prehistoric Belief Systems

ORIGINS AND DEVELOPMENT

The term *prehistory* is used to refer to time periods before written records exist or during which written records were not created. It is a rather controversial and problematic term, however, because writing systems were invented or came into use at different times in various areas of the world, so the chronological time span for prehistory can vary a great deal between different world regions.[1] Prehistory can refer not only to time periods before specific cultures developed their own writing systems, but also to time periods before written records were produced by other people about these world regions and cultures. In that sense, in some regions of the world (such as parts of the Americas, Oceania, and Africa), the prehistoric period can be said to have lasted well into the modern era and to have concluded only via contact with Europeans or other writing-producing outsiders.

Although it is clear that the term *prehistory* cannot and does not mean that no history existed before writing systems were invented or used in different world regions, the designations *prehistory* and *prehistoric* were first used by scholars in the 19th century who placed a great deal of emphasis on the presence of written language as an indication of cultural advances. More recent scholarship has questioned the assumptions that written language is a more important source of information about cultures than nonwritten oral traditions, and that the presence of a developed writing system is a necessary indicator of cultural development. It is always wise to remember that not all of the world's writing systems have been deciphered and also that our perceptions of what constitutes writing are challenged by seemingly illegible texts. In particular, there is some intense scholarly disagreement about the interpretation of a number of ancient artifacts, primarily incised clay tablets and other examples of pottery, found in southeastern Europe, dating to ca. 5000 BCE, which bear what appear to be graphic markings or protowriting systems. The fact that these symbols or signs remain undeciphered by no means indicates their lack of meaning or possible function as conveyors of information. Whether or not these prehistoric signs can be seen as prewriting, or as complete (but as yet undeciphered) writing systems is a matter of debate.[2]

Nevertheless, in spite of these definitional issues, the term *prehistory* is generally understood to refer to a number of different eras of human habitation on earth, the evidence for which comes primarily from archaeological material, not from any decipherable written records produced at the time. "Prehistory is a kind of floating scale that refers in any given region to the period of human occupation before which there is literacy, and thus textual records."[3] The study of prehistory thus involves some special challenges that are rather different from those encountered in studies of time periods for which contemporary written, documentary evidence exists. It is also wise to remember that prehistory (no matter how defined) actually encompasses a substantial and vast time span of human presence on earth—many, many millennia longer than is covered by historical eras.

The archaeological material that exists to indicate human presence on earth varies widely in type as well as presumed dating range from region to region of the world, although it is generally believed that humankind originated in Africa some millions of years ago. The evolution of humans is often traced through a series of phrases (*Homo habilis, Homo erectus*) ultimately resulting in *Homo sapiens*, the ancestor of modern humans. The vast periods of prehistory are often divided up into several phases: The Stone Age (Paleolithic, Neolithic and Mesolithic), Bronze Age, and Iron Age (with dates differing from region to region of the world).[4] The terms *Stone Age, Bronze Age*, and *Iron Age* were developed by early archaeologists to refer primarily to the use of tools and metal production techniques developed during these periods, although as is more commonly understood now, this varies greatly between different world regions.

Because the evidence for prehistoric humans is primarily archaeological and not supported by contemporary written documents, any discussion of prehistoric belief systems tends to be extremely speculative. Some areas of the world (see chapters 6, 7, and 8 in this volume) are populated by cultures that still appear to retain vestiges of very ancient primal (or first) traditions.[5] Information about prehistoric religious beliefs may indeed be gleaned from studies of these traditional cultures, but caution in interpretation needs to be exercised too. "Scholars continue to use ethnographic analogies to explain possible belief systems . . . without the necessary critical distance. As a result, the presumed religion in Paleolithic times partly resembles the mentality of arctic peoples, and partly resembles the beliefs of Australian aborigines, according to the experience and research interests of the scholar."[6] Ethnographic study of the current religious beliefs and practices of various indigenous cultures may provide a useful lens with which to study the prehistoric past, but care must be taken care in the comparative analyses of these materials as well.

PRINCIPAL BELIEFS AND KEY PRACTICES

One of the greatest challenges facing scholars of prehistory involves the interpretation of visual material evidence. Although there is absolutely no lack of material to be analyzed (ranging from paintings and engravings on rock, large- and small-scale carvings, and architectural constructions as well), questions about the meaning, functions, and symbolism of this material have provided copious fodder for diverse approaches and interpretative strategies.[7] This is especially the case with objects to which religious meanings have been attributed. One common assumption is that peoples of the Paleolithic period (or Stone Age, approximately 40,000–10,000 BCE) were occupied or motivated by religious concerns to some significant degree and that this is evidenced in the visual arts produced by these ancient peoples. Many scholars agree "that prehistoric art is not unmotivated: it responds to religious preoccupations, it is the expression of, or in support of, myths."[8]

Scholarly attention has been devoted especially to the numerous examples of engraved and painted rock surfaces found in areas of Africa and Europe. Some of these examples have recently been dated to as early as 28,000 BCE.[9] In this period when humans were largely occupied with hunter-gatherer activities (basic subsistence modes), they also appear to have taken a significant amount of time to paint and carve images on rock surfaces, often deep within the caves in the entrances of which they may or may not have dwelled.

The prehistoric paintings and engravings found in caves in southern France and northern Spain have been especially often featured in discussions of prehistoric religion (see Plate 1). The naturally occurring geological cave formations were generally not physically altered in any way (by digging deeper, adding more passages, or enlarging the interior spaces) but were very richly embellished with paintings and carvings in often very deep spaces, extremely difficult to access.[10] It would seem clear that the creation of these prehistoric cave paintings and engravings represented an extremely significant activity for these early peoples. But what, exactly, do the subjects and symbols mean?

The most common subjects found in hundreds of examples of prehistoric cave art are animals, such as horses, bison, deer, and other species including the ibex and mammoth. Many of these animals feature in smaller-scale objects as well, such as carved or engraved objects of stone and horn (see Figure 1.1). Sometimes human figures are found, as are figures that combine both human and animal features. Additionally, other nonfigurative signs or markings are extremely common: geometric shapes, ladder designs, and various other symbols. Some

Figure 1.1   Incised reindeer antler ca. 11,000 BCE. London: British Museum. Werner Forman / Art Resource, NY.

images seem easily recognizable to modern viewers, as specific types or species of animals, whole other forms are extremely difficult to decipher. The animals are generally represented in profile; some show varying degrees of realism and detail; others are presented in more abstract or schematized fashions. The irregular contours of the rock surfaces also played an important role in the placement and forms of the images. The process of simply identifying the images has occupied scholars for many decades.[11]

> There are different levels of interpretation . . . the identity of the image; its literal meaning; and its symbolic meaning. The assumptions involved in each of these categories are cumulative. Naturally, all guesses at meaning depend upon the validity of the initial identification of the motifs—which, for the most part, we are unable to verify. What modern humans—whether rock art researchers or indigenous people—think is depicted in prehistoric art is always interesting, but reveals more about the interpreters than about the art.[12]

Several theories have been proposed to explain the meaning of the subjects and symbols depicted in these prehistoric caves. Very few scholars believe that these images have no meaning at all. Some scholars believe that the creation of this animal imagery represented a magical attempt to ensure and increase the number of animals for the food supply necessary for these peoples, that is to say, that the depiction of animals would guarantee their continued presence. Other scholars believe that the paintings and carvings were actively employed in pseudo-hunting rituals, that they were used as religio-magical-pedagogical teaching devices in which ancient peoples enacted hunting activities in a ritualistic fashion. But, because some evidence shows that several of the species of animals depicted in cave art were not, in fact, primary or common sources of food for ancient humans, this theory has been subject to debate. Some scholars believe that the animals served as totems—symbolizing the ancestors of families, clans, or groups. Other scholars have proposed that the cave art was used for initiation ceremonies, providing information about critical survival skills to members of clans, tribes, or family groups. Much recent scholarship has linked the cave art to shamanistic practices—attempts to control, communicate with, and deal with the shared life forces of humans, animals, and the natural world.[13]

Not one of these many theories can be proven. The function of the caves and their art may have varied greatly between regions and time periods. Determining the specific meaning and intentionality of much prehistoric art is extremely challenging. Although it seems logical to assume that a meaning must be inherent—that there is no doubt that the caves and the subjects depicted within them represented extremely significant aspects of the lives and belief systems of prehistoric peoples—what these beliefs actually were remains a matter of great speculation.

> Because caves appear mysterious and menacing places to us, there has long been a tendency to associate their art with secret, esoteric, exclusive rites redolent of fear and awe. . . . Why should art have been placed in such inaccessible locations? Deep caves are strange environments . . . To enter a deep cave is to leave the everyday world and cross a boundary into the unknown—a supernatural underworld. It is easy to imagine that caves therefore symbolized transitions in human life and could be used for rituals linked with those transitions . . . Or perhaps it was felt that by entering this world one could better communicate or summon up the supernatural forces which dwelt there, and hence the images were made to reach and compel those forces. Cave decoration certainly requires strong motivation, since it involves negotiating such obstacles and taking both equipment and illumination into the site.[14]

Small figurines, carved from stone, bone, antler, ivory, and clay are also frequently found during the Paleolithic and later periods. Many have been found within caves and pits; others are clearly associated with burials. Both animal and human (male, female, and non-gender-specific) figurines are common. Among the most well-known and frequently reproduced as illustrations in both scholarly and popular texts are the so-called Venus figurines, which are clearly female. They are often, but not always, depicted with exaggerated indications of female sexual features and reproductive abilities (see Figure 1.2). Much scholarship has been devoted to these ancient objects, and highly lively debates continue to take place today regarding their purpose and function, who made them, and what motivated their creation.[15] Most agree that the child-bearing and life-giving significance of the female logically appears to have been of some importance for prehistoric peoples. This, in turn, has also led many scholars to identify a wide-spread devotion to a general goddess figure in prehistory.

Figure 1.2 The Vestonice Venus ca. 32,000 BCE. Brno, Czech Republic: Moravske Museum. Werner Forman / Art Resource, NY.

The scholarly as well as popular literature devoted to the goddess of prehistory has burgeoned dramatically in the later 20th century, reflective of the feminist movement generally and the resultant academic reassessment of the ways in which history and prehistory have been written about and understood. Viewpoints range widely—if not sometimes wildly—from those desiring to boldly reinstate the mother-goddess figure (and her nurturing matriarchal values) to her rightful position in not only prehistory but also the modern world,[16] to those who take a more cautious view about the assessment and interpretation of evidence.[17] It is an ongoing and very lively debate—and one which will doubtless continue to be transformed with new viewpoints reflective of the decades to come. For many, there seems little doubt that worship of a goddess/earth mother/fertility figure is indicated by the archaeological evidence from prehistory, although the exact nature and identification of the goddess or goddesses and the rituals carried out for worship remain somewhat speculative. Indeed, much disagreement exists about the motivations behind the creation of the figurines, as well as the use of the term "fertility figures" to describe these varied objects.

At different periods in prehistory, it appears that peoples in various world regions began to shift gradually from the hunter-gatherer mode to the agricultural mode or to combine hunting-and-gathering with more settled farming practices. Again, the dates for the adoption of agricultural practices, and the degree to which these replaced or supplemented previous modes of subsistence, vary greatly. Nevertheless, the development of agricultural practices certainly resulted in a more settled lifestyle among many ancient cultural groups and seems also to have resulted in even greater attention being paid to the construction of larger and permanent architectural monuments. Religious significance has been attached to many of these monuments, including the early temple/shrine structures of the Maltese islands (see Figure 1.9), as well as the numerous megalithic (large stone) constructions of virtually worldwide distribution. Many believe that the impressive carved megaliths at the site of Göbekli Tepe in southeastern Turkey date to as early as ca. 10,000 BCE and thus represent the very earliest example of a human-built religious center, constructed by nomadic peoples in a largely pre-agricultural period. All of these examples provide important materials for study and assessment of prehistoric belief systems, especially as manifested in the form of human-built architectural constructions.

In particular, the many ancient examples of standing stones (or menhirs) that appear in circles, pairs, short single rows, and multiple avenues have long attracted scholarly and popular attention because of their frequently impressive size and enigmatic function.[18] Some of the best-known examples occur in the British Isles and on the European continent, such as the multiple row alignments at Carnac in Brittany (northern France), which have been dated to ca. 3000–2000 BCE (see Figure 1.3). The site of Stonehenge in England is also one of the most well-known and oft-studied of these examples (see Figure 1.10 and Plate 2). While the motivations for the placement and erection of these types of large stone monuments remain unknown, many theories have been advanced as to their purpose and function.

Large stones capped or roofed with stone slabs (often called dolmens) also exist in great numbers and are generally understood to have functioned as prehistoric tombs. This certainly seems to indicate that death—and some means of recognizing and enshrining the deceased—were important concerns in later prehistory. More monumental tombs, such as the one impressively large passage grave at Newgrange in Ireland (ca. 3000–2500 BCE) also include examples of extensively decorated carved stones both on the interior and exterior. Circles, lozenges, triangles, and spiral motifs are dominant; many have speculated that the designs have astronomical significance or otherwise refer to cycles of life and time (see Figure 1.4).

Although we lack contemporary written documents from the prehistoric periods, it does seems clear, from the archaeological evidence, that ancient peoples were concerned with issues of life, death, food, and health—and that they approached these concerns in ways that were not always or exclusively utilitarian. The animals painted and carved in prehistoric caves may indeed

Figure 1.3 Menhirs at Carnac, Brittany, France ca. 3000–2000 BCE. Clodio / Dreamstime.com.

Figure 1.4 Newgrange passage grave, Ireland, carved stone ca. 3000–2000 BCE. The Art Archive / Gianni Dagli Orti.

represent or symbolize some of the basic food sources for early peoples, but the extreme care, attention to detail, and physical difficulties surmounted by prehistoric people to visually embody these animals in the interiors of deep and dark caves seem evidence of—if not a codified belief system—at very least an attempt to honor, placate, assuage, or encourage the forces of the natural world that surrounded them. Survival and food sources are closely related concerns, which also appear to be evidenced by the early fertility or goddess figurines as well as the later large stone monuments that may have been designed to chart seasons of the year for the planting and tending of crops. The attention given by later prehistoric peoples to human death (via burials, cremations, and grave goods interred at burial sites) also seems to indicate that early people regarded death (as well as birth) as a significant event too, and one that was due some attention in a ritual format.

Nevertheless, "the question of the origin of religion is still unsolved."[19] Although many scholars believe that religion was "a part of human nature from the very beginning,"[20] others feel that the archaeological evidence simply does not support this claim. Even so, "the opinion that Paleolithic man already had a complicated religion, with certain notions of the holy and various rituals, can be found in nearly every religious reference work."[21] It is wise to remember that the span of prehistory is extremely vast and that while evidence of religious belief is indeed indicated during the late Paleolithic period (especially in the form of burials, assumed to be evidence of a belief in the afterlife or spirit world), one must exercise caution in reading too far back into prehistory for the origins of practices that developed later.

TRADITIONAL ART AND ARCHITECTURAL FORMS

Because the span covered by prehistory is so great, and varies so widely in different world regions, prehistoric art exists in many different forms and materials. It must be immediately noted, however, that the definition of art is among the many terminological challenges faced by students of prehistory. This is especially the case when dealing with extremely ancient materials—such as the painted images and carved objects that provide the very earliest evidences of what appear to be art-making activities by humans. Much intriguing scholarship has been devoted to analyses of the minds of ancient humans, the cognitive and creative processes that resulted in the initial creation of visual images.[22] But because the meanings and functions of these very ancient images and objects are often elusive, many scholars caution against the use of the term *art* to describe them. For modern audiences, art may have a variety of meanings—ranging from the expression of personal creativity on the part of specially gifted individuals, to works which express the community values and concerns of groups of people at different periods, to objects that are created for sale or display in galleries and museums.

It is always important to be reminded that *art* is not a strictly defined term that concisely and consistently refers only to specific forms of visual expression, such as the traditional categories of architecture, painting, and sculpture, as generally studied by art historians, or nonpermanent forms of artistic expression such as dance, masking performances, and music, such as studied by anthropologists and ethnographers. The term *art* can encompass an enormous range of forms—and can be used for objects or experiences that range from the permanent to the transitory, from the utilitarian to the seemingly unnecessary. If we accept that art—in its widest definition—involves the creation of visual and performance modes that express the values and concerns of groups of people at different periods in time, we may be somewhat better positioned in our attempts to understand the surviving art of prehistoric periods.

Of course, it is also critical to recall that the surviving material evidence from prehistory, although copious, is doubtless only a very small fraction of what once existed. The surviving objects of study are only those that were created from relatively durable materials, whereas the objects produced of more ephemeral or organic materials have long perished. It is thus quite impossible to reconstruct a complete picture of prehistoric art or religion simply based on the surviving material.

Durable rock carvings (petroglyphs) and paintings on rock (pictographs) provide a major portion of the materials available for scholars of prehistory. The animals, other figures, and graphic symbols characteristic of prehistoric rock art were created by engraving, carving, and painting with mineral-based pigments. The painting may have been done with brushes made of animal hair, or by spraying the pigments (through a tube or by mouth) directly onto the rock surfaces. Ladders or some forms of scaffolding must have been used to reach the upper wall levels and ceilings of caves and upper level wall surfaces.

The most ancient examples of prehistoric rock art have been found in Africa, Europe, and Asia. Relatively much more recent examples exist also in copious numbers in the Americas, in Africa, and in Australia especially, where many aboriginal peoples continue to closely guard their heritage and practice this form of art. The ancient peoples (from Africa, via Asia) who arrived to and populated Australia in the Paleolithic period are the ultimate ancestors of the many Australian aboriginal groups today. The old rock paintings of Australia, and the recorded accounts about their origins and meanings, are important to consider here. According to some traditions, the sprit beings who created the earth in the Dreamtime (see chapter 7) also created the first examples of visual imagery. So the images found in rock art, as well as more modern bark painting, in Australia reflect these ancient guidelines and symbols that were set down in the long-ago past.

Images of spirit beings often feature in many examples of Australian rock art, such as the Wandjina figures depicted in the example shown in Figure 1.5, from the Kimberly region of northwestern Australia, which probably dates originally to ca. 1300 BCE. The Wandjina "are said to have come out of the sea and the sky, to have created features of the landscape and then to have been absorbed into the walls of rock shelters in the territories of different clans."[23] These beings are generally depicted with extremely large eyes, no mouths, and with haloes surrounding their heads. Although these images are of great antiquity, the aboriginal clans with whom specific examples are associated have continued to tend and care for the images over the centuries by regular repainting, "making the paintings equally part of the present and the past."[24] Thus, in some regions of the world, such as Australia, it could be said that prehistoric religious art is still being produced today.

Rock engravings and paintings of even more modern antiquity in Africa and the Americas also bespeak these ancient roots. Rock paintings created by the San (or Sandawe) peoples of southern and southeastern Africa are generally agreed to have ancient origins but are notoriously hard to date, as is generally the

Figure 1.5 Rock painting of Wandjina figures, Kimberly region, Australia ca. 1300 BCE. The Art Archive / Global Book Publishing.

case with much prehistoric art (see Figure 1.6). Although the images of hunters and prey found in many of these ancient Paleolithic, and more recent, African examples have been avidly studied especially within the context of San shamanistic practices of more modern times, the ultimate antiquity of these symbols and forms as well as the antiquity of beliefs surrounding them is challenging to determine.[25] Some of the most ancient examples of African rock art have been dated to ca. 25,000 BCE, whereas other examples are relatively much more recent. Much rock art from the Americas is similarly difficult to date and contains elusive meanings that are not necessarily explicated by the oral traditions surrounding these works.[26] Important examples of prehistoric rock art abound in many world regions.[27] Scholars continue to explore these challenging and intriguing arenas.

Figurines and larger sculptural works from the prehistoric periods were shaped and carved, via sawing or grinding with stone or metal tools (as developed by various dates), further enriched (via incision or engraving or painting), and appear in both relief and three-dimensional forms. Many works of terracotta (clay) were produced in the

Figure 1.6 Rock painting, Tanzania, Africa ca. 15,000 BCE?. Dar es Salaam: Tanzania National Museum. Werner Forman / Art Resource, NY.

ancient Mediterranean world, such as the modeled clay figurines from Cyprus (see Figure 1.7). Many works were also produced in stone, such as the carved marble figures from the Cycladic islands (see Figure 1.8).

The terracotta statuette illustrated here from the eastern Mediterranean island of Cyprus has been dated to ca. 1450–1200 BCE. Several such examples have been found, especially within tombs. Large-hipped female figures are frequent and often show exaggerated eyes and prominent beak-like noses. They are thus generally described as "bird-headed women" or "women with bird faces."[28] They may be shown with arms crossed or placed on their hips or torsos, with laterally projecting hairdos or enlarged ears enriched with looped terracotta earrings. Several examples depict the women carrying or cradling babies. Many scholars have associated these figures with fertility and regeneration, thus their placement within tombs is believed to indicate concerns with renewal of life, if not also a belief in the afterlife. Other evidence from ancient Neolithic and Bronze Age Cyprus, in the form of terracotta models of shrines/sanctuaries, plus materials from tomb excavations, appears to indicate a religious preoccupation with fertility and renewal, including practices of animal sacrifice and other ceremonial offerings. The terracotta works from ancient Cyprus demonstrate a

Figure 1.7   Terracotta statuette from Cyprus ca. 1420–1200 BCE. New York: The Metropolitan Museum of Art / Art Resource, NY.

distinctive style and "show what today appears to be a playfulness and pleasure in creating complex forms with elaborate decoration."[29]

The older Cycladic example shown here has been dated to ca. 2700–2500 BCE and is typical of many other ancient marble figurines from this Aegean region. These early Cycladic figures, as well, show a highly distinctive and immediately recognizable style, the development of which took place over many centuries during the Neolithic period and early Bronze Age.[30] Several different types of statues were produced, including seated male figures playing harps and other musical instruments, voluptuous and rounded female figures, violin-shaped figures, as well as the relatively slim and schematized nude female figures most often featured in studies of Cycladic art. These range in size from small figurines of 8 to 10 inches in height to larger statues of many feet tall. Typically, the figures show flattened faces with long, vertical, projecting noses, elongated necks, small breast mounds, and triangular pubic areas indicated by carved incisions. The legs may be joined together or partially separated, and the arms are often positioned across the torsos.

A religious significance is generally assumed for these statues. They have often been termed "idols" or "fertility figures." Many have been found in association with graves, while taller examples (too large for typical burial practices) may have functioned as cult statues in shrines or other venues. Their exact purpose and use is unclear. It is wise to remember that, lacking written records,

> It is virtually impossible for us to comprehend the intent of the prehistoric carvers . . . we can only hypothesize about the language of the ancient Cycladic islanders, how they perceived themselves, their world, and their cosmos, and the meaning or significance they attributed to the marble artifacts they left behind. What is certain, however, is that these objects were important to the Bronze Age people in and around the Cyclades, as excavated examples come from contexts spanning more than six hundred years.[31]

The geometric abstraction and clarity of these minimal, schematic forms has had special appeal to many modern viewers, and much has been written about their remarkable visual impact, artistic restraint, and formal technique. Indeed, a number of important early 20th-century artists were much inspired by their encounters with "the clean lines and supple, abstract, but still human forms" of early Cycladic art.[32] "For many modern viewers, the stark, unadorned surfaces of nearly all of the objects seem consistent with the minimal definition of their forms, leading to the supposition that their modern appearance closely resembled their original state."[33]

Figure 1.8 Cycladic figurine ca. 2700–2500 BCE. London: The Trustees of The British Museum / Art Resource, NY.

Several recent researchers have, however, shifted the focus of scholarship on these ancient Cycladic works by drawing particular attention to the traces of mineral and vegetable pigments frequently found on these examples. Although this painted evidence has always been visible to some degree, modern scientific analysis techniques have greatly increased the awareness of the extent to which these objects were originally painted. Rather than being stark, unadorned, proto-modern works, it seems now clearer that these figures were originally much more richly embellished with boldly painted eyes and other facial features, plus details of jewelry and costume.

> Many, if not most, Cycladic figures were decorated with one or more colors, in patterns that do not necessarily emphasize or enhance their sculptural forms. And just as the idea of bright colors applied to the sculptures and architecture of Archaic and Classical Greece was at first difficult to accept, so elaborate painting on the smooth forms of Early Cycladic sculpted marbles definitely changes the way one thinks about these objects and the people who created them.[34]

This again provides an extremely useful reminder of the many challenges involved with the study and interpretation of prehistoric art. Modern viewers of these ancient objects may simply not be seeing, or accurately imagining, their original appearances. This may hamper the interpretative understanding of the meaning, context, and purpose of the objects. At the same time, this is also a very exciting reminder of how continued scholarship serves to ever change, augment, and increase our knowledge and perceptions of prehistory.

EXAMPLES

Mnajdra Temple complex, Malta, ca. 3300–2500 BCE

The Maltese archipelago consists of several islands located in the Mediterranean Sea between Italy and north Africa. The islands are extremely rich in remarkable prehistoric remains, some dating from as early as the fifth and fourth millennia BCE. These remains include pottery and sculpture as well as numerous architectural structures, generally described as temples (see Figure 1.9). These ancient temples are believed to be among the earliest free-standing examples of religious architecture in the world. Some of the structures are single buildings; others are architectural complexes that include several temples. In all, there are over 20 temples on the islands, including major examples such as Mnajdra, Hagar Qim, and Tarxien on the island of Malta, and Ggantija on the island of Gozo.

Although much scholarly attention has been devoted to the Maltese temples, especially since the mid-19th century, early archaeologists were unclear as

Figure 1.9 Mnajdra Temple complex, Malta ca. 3300–2500 BCE. Mccarthy-studio / Dreamstime.com.

to the date of the structures, and most believed them to have been constructed by the Phoenicians, who were active in the Mediterranean world during the first millennium BCE and who were present on the Maltese islands in the seventh century BCE. Further archaeological work in the mid- to late 20th century, however, has determined the much greater antiquity of these important and unique structures. They are now dated largely to the mid-fourth through mid-third millennia BCE.

The monuments are unusual in that they appear not to have been influenced by other cultures or to have significantly influenced the architectural constructions of later cultures in the Mediterranean world. They are built of large limestone slabs using post-and-lintel as well as corbel construction techniques (layering projecting stones to form arches and vaults.) Most of the temples have enclosed courtyards with entrances leading into central areas from which three or more semicircular lobes or apselike chambers project. This lobed, trefoil, or cloverleaf plan is uniquely typical of Maltese temples. Several scholars have proposed that their shape mirrors the bulbous forms seen in numerous carved stone female figures also associated with the temples.

Free-standing carved stone blocks found in the temples are believed to have been used as altars. Animal bones found in excavations have led scholars to assume that animal sacrifices were practiced. The structures appear not to have served as burial sites because human bones have customarily not been found in the excavations. Cemeteries and funerary complexes also have been excavated on the Maltese islands, but they are generally separate and removed from the temples.[35] Some of the temples include relief carvings of animals (goats, sheep, pigs, fish, and bulls) plus various spiral designs. Several include interior benches and hearths. "The interiors of temples are relatively small, and it is thought that they were used mostly by religious specialists and officials, with larger congregations of the community taking place outdoors on the paved courtyards in front of temples."[36]

The architectural complexity, unique floor plans, and dominance of carved stone female figures found in association with these temples have led many to believe that prehistoric religion on Malta centered on goddess worship, a theme that many feel permeated Neolithic cultures in other world regions as well.[37] "Central to this culture is veneration of the Goddess-Creator in all her aspects, the major aspects being the birth-giver, the fertility-giver, the life- or nourishment-giver and protectress, and the death-wielder."[38] Others, however, are far less convinced that the Maltese temples give evidence of ancient goddess worship.

Overall, responses to the Maltese temples and their related art may be seen as intriguing reflections of the changing interpretative strategies that have been, and continue to be, employed in studies of prehistoric art. It is always wise to remember that "any interpretation of the past is a social product which has more to do with the historical moment in which it is produced than the period to which it refers."[39] The Maltese temples provide an especially fascinating study of such reinterpretation. The temples today have become important centers of tourism, especially for goddess pilgrims who visit in great numbers to reconnect with the ancient matriarchal past.[40] The popular and archaeological discourses about the Maltese temples thus tend to diverge in some significant ways, reflecting different agendas and variant modes of understanding prehistory. For adherents of the goddess movement, the Maltese temples and their related art stand as signal proof of the prepatriarchal harmony of ancient female-centered cultures. Others, opposed to this view, see "no conclusive evidence that Malta was ever [a] a matristic Goddess-worshiping utopia."[41] Even so, the antiquity and importance of the temples themselves is not a matter of dispute, and "whatever other agendas each group has, a crucially important shared agenda is the preservation of the sites."[42]

Stonehenge, England, ca. 3000–1500 BCE

Stonehenge, on the Salisbury Plain in Wiltshire in southern England, is certainly one of the most well-known and well-studied examples of a specific type of prehistoric megalithic (large stone) monument[43] (see Figure 1.10 and Plate 2). Scholars have determined that there was a very long process of construction and use of Stonehenge (approximately 3000–1500 BCE), with many additions and alterations made to the site during three distinct phases of building and renovation. The monument consists of a number of large upright standing stones (menhirs), enclosed within a circular ditch (or *henge*) with a series of 56 burial pits on the interior of the ditch. Many archaeologists believe that the stones replaced an earlier timber structure on the site, which served as a type of mortuary chapel for corpses awaiting burial. The large sarcen (sandstone) menhirs, many of which are still upright today, were set up ca. 2000 BCE and arranged in a circle forming a complete ring with a continuous set of lintel stones. Although there are numerous other examples of prehistoric stone circles (widely distributed throughout the world), Stonehenge is unique in the fact that the builders shaped the huge stones with notches/joints in mortise-and-tenon fashion so that the monumental lintel stones fit neatly into slots carved on the tops of the giant uprights. Within the sarsen circle are five trilithons (two upright stones sharing a lintel) arranged in a horseshoe shape. The tallest is about 25 feet in height. In addition, bluestones (so named because they take on a bluish tone when wet) were added in a later phase, and a large altar stone was set up close to the center of the circle. The bluestones were transported to the site from Wales (about 190 miles away) via water and overland dragging, while the sandstones were dragged to the site from about 15 miles away.

Clearly, the efforts entailed to create, maintain, and renovate this monument over thousands of years are evidence that Stonehenge was of extreme significance for the prehistoric peoples of the region. However, interpretations of the function and purpose of Stonehenge have ranged widely, if not wildly, through centuries of scholarship. A number of scholars currently agree that

Figure 1.10 Stonehenge, Wiltshire, England, ca. 3000–1500 BCE, aerial view. National Trust / Art Resource, NY.

Stonehenge primarily, if not originally, served as a monumental observatory for charting the seasons of the year by indicating the summer and winter solstices. The midsummer sun rises over a specific stone, and several stones are also aligned to the midwinter sunset. This archaeo-astronomical aspect of Stonehenge has attracted the greatest attention in late 20th-century technology-based scholarship,[44] although other theories about Stonehenge (as a site for ancient Druid rituals, as a marker of territory, as a solar temple for worship of the sun god) have been proposed.

As with all examples of art and architectural forms from prehistory, the lack of written records makes it difficult to do anything other than purely speculate about purpose and function. The logical tendency is to assume that Stonehenge had a religious or ritual function of some sort—but the exact nature of this will doubtless continue to be explored by generations of scholars and enthusiasts in the future.

Minoan Snake Goddess, ca. 1600 BCE

This small (13½ inches high) glazed earthenware statuette is one of the most frequently reproduced images of ancient religious art (see Figure 1.11).

Figure 1.11 Minoan Snake Goddess ca. 1700–1600 BCE. The Art Archive / Heraklion Museum, Crete / Gianni Dagli Orti.

The object was discovered in the early 20th century during the excavations undertaken by the British archaeologist, Sir Arthur Evans (1851–1941), at the site of the great Palace of Knossos on the island of Crete. Evans's pioneering work at Knossos, his nomenclature of the Minoan civilization (after the legendary King Minos of Knossos), the chronology he developed for the various phases of this civilization (ca. 3500/3000–ca. 1050 BCE), and his theories about and reconstructions of Minoan art and architecture have provided the foundations for subsequent scholarly work as well as intense dispute about this ancient culture.

The Minoans appear to have been a prosperous and peaceful civilization who engaged in trade and commerce with other ancient peoples in the Aegean and Mediterranean world, notably the Egyptian, Syrian, and Cycladic cultures. The Minoans were great builders, and a number of impressive residential and ceremonial centers (or palaces, Knossos being the largest) were constructed beginning ca. 2000 BCE. Frescoes, pottery, metalwork, engraved seals, figurines of animals and humans in clay and ivory, jewelry of gold, bronze, and gemstones all survive in abundance and give evidence of a high degree of sophistication and skill with art production in a wide range of media.

Much scholarship has been devoted to the topic of Minoan religion, based on numerous representations in Minoan art of scenes involving god and goddess figures, priest and priestess figures, worshippers, ritual offerings, and processions. Objects that appear to be cultic/ceremonial in nature have been found in abundance not only in the several palaces but also in caves and sanctuaries located in the hills and mountains.[45] Altars and offering tables, votive figurines, ritual libation vessels, and symbols such as double-axes, bull's horns, and heraldic animals are the most common forms in the artistic vocabulary of Minoan ritual practices. Some scholars believe that Minoan palaces were deliberately laid out and oriented toward the peak sanctuaries in the neighboring mountains where caves devoted to worship of a nature or fertility goddess were located.[46]

Whether as Mistress of the Animals, Goddess of Nature, Fertility Goddess, Bird Goddess, or Water Goddess—solo or accompanied by a Warrior/Hunter God—the female goddess figure dominates the imagery of Minoan religious art.

Whether she is one goddess with several different aspects or several different goddesses is unclear.

The glazed earthenware statuette of the Snake Goddess in the Archaeological Museum in Heraklion, Crete, demonstrates many aspects of her traditional imagery. On engraved seals, wall paintings, and in other media, the same forms appear: the long flounced skirt, narrow waist, tall silhouette, and bared breasts. When the figurine was found in the early excavations at Knossos, it was broken in several places. The head of the figure and the head of the one original snake were missing as well as most of the figure's left arm. These missing pieces were created and attached to the figurine by an early 20th-century artist/conservator employed by Sir Arthur Evans. Although the head is not original, the beret/cap and cat/feline form atop the beret were found in the excavations (although not with the figurine) and were attached to the reconstructed head to make up the ensemble as it exists today.[47]

In spite of the frequency with which this image is reproduced, the Snake Goddess per se is otherwise a relatively rare subject in Minoan art. Several other statuettes do exist of similar figures with outstretched arms twined with snakes, but several of these are modern forgeries loosely based on this one reconstructed example and a few other examples with secure ancient origin. Although there seems "ample archaeological evidence for a predominant female deity (or deities) on Crete,"[48] the attention given to the cult of the Snake Goddess in particular has tended to overshadow and dominate the discussion. It is wise to remember that for the periods of prehistory without written sources, much remains a matter of speculation. Indeed, "until Minoan writing is deciphered, the precise nature of early Cretan religion must remain uncertain."[49]

NOTES

1. In ancient Mesopotamia and Egypt, the writing systems known, respectively, as cuneiform and hieroglyphs, are generally dated to ca. 3000 BCE; writing developed in China about 1500 BCE, and the Maya culture of Mesoamerica developed a writing system ca. 300 CE. See Anne-Marie Christin, ed., A History of Writing: From Hieroglyph to Multimedia (Paris: Flammarion, 2002) and Steven Roger Fischer, A History of Writing (London: Reaktion Books, 2001).

2. The numerous studies by Marija Gimbutas argue for an "old European sacred script" that pre-dates Mesopotamian and Egyptian writing by several millennia. See, for example, Marija Gimbutas, The Living Goddesses (Berkeley: University of California Press, 1999) and Marija Gimbutas, The Goddesses and Gods of Old Europe: Myths and Cult Images (London: Thames and Hudson, 1982.) A differing view is proposed by Shan Winn, Pre-Writing in Southeastern Europe: The Sign System of the Vinča Culture (Calgary, Alberta: Western, 1981) who describes the markings found on European prehistoric artifacts as a "proto" (not fully developed) writing system. A useful overview is provided by James Elkins, On Pictures and the Words That Fail Them (Cambridge, UK: Cambridge University Press, 1998), especially chapter 4, "The Signs of Writing."

3. Randall White, *Prehistoric Art: The Symbolic Journey of Humankind* (New York: Harry N. Abrams, 2003), 8.

4. Traditional dates for the prehistoric eras in Europe, for example, are roughly as follows: the Stone Age (Paleolithic: 40,000–10,000 BCE; Mesolithic: 10,000–7000 BCE; Neolithic: 7000/6000–3000 BCE), Bronze Age: 2500–1500 BCE, and Iron Age: 1500–500 BCE.

5. Göran Burenhult, *Traditional Peoples Today: Continuity and Change in the Modern World* (San Francisco: Harper San Francisco, 1994).

6. Ina Wunn, "Beginning of Religion," *Numen* 47, no. 4 (2000), 418.

7. Margaret Conkey, "Making Things Meaningful: Approaches to the Interpretation of the Ice Age Imagery of Europe," in *Meaning in the Visual Arts: Views from the Outside*, ed. Irving Lavin (Princeton, NJ: Institute for Advanced Study, 1995), 49–64.

8. Jean Clottes, "The Identification of Human and Animal Figures in European Palaeolithic Art," in *Animals into Art*, ed. Howard Morphy (London: Unwin Hyman, 1989), 22.

9. The paintings in the cave of Chauvet, France, just recently discovered in the mid-1990s, are now considered to the oldest examples and have been dated to ca. 28,000 BCE. See Jean Clottes, *Chauvet Cave: The Art of Earliest Times* (Salt Lake City: University of Utah Press, 2003) and Jean-Marie Chauvet, Eliette Deschamps, and Christian Hillaire, *Dawn of Art: The Chauvet Cave: The Oldest Known Paintings in the World* (New York: Harry N. Abrams, 1996.)

10. The following passage by Noel Smith describing his personal experience visiting the cave of Les Trois Frères in France captures this perfectly; he writes: "Many people have commented on the great difficulties that Ice Age people overcame in negotiating some of these caves . . . but one cannot fully appreciate what they endured until traversing a cave like Les Trois Frères. Before entering, one dons high rubber boots, coveralls, knee pads, a hard hat, and, of course, a powerful light. Once in the cave one must alternately crawl through low muddy passages, climb over boulders, cross pools of water and oozing mud, climb or descend muddy inclines and rocky precipices, ease down slippery slopes, and in one case descend a vertical drop at the edge of a pit where one slip could end in tragedy. And in the midst of this, one finds exquisitely drawn animals that vanished from the area ten thousand years ago." Noel Smith, *An Analysis of Ice Age Art: Its Psychology and Belief System* (New York: Peter Lang, 1992), xii.

11. Michel Lorblanchet, "From Naturalism to Abstraction in European Prehistoric Rock Art," in *Form in Indigenous Art: Schematisation in the Art of Aboriginal Australia and Prehistoric Europe*, ed. Peter Ucko (Canberra, Australia: Institute of Aboriginal Studies, 1977), 43–56.

12. Paul Bahn, *The Cambridge Illustrated History of Prehistoric Art* (Cambridge, UK: Cambridge University Press, 1998), 176.

13. See, for example, Jean Clottes and David Lewis-Williams, *The Shamans of Prehistory: Trance and Magic in the Painted Caves* (New York: Harry N. Abrams, 1998) and Miranda Aldhouse-Green and Stephen Aldhouse-Green, *The Quest for the Shaman: Shape-Shifters, Sorcerers and Spirit-Healers of Ancient Europe* (London: Thames and Hudson, 2005.)

14. Bahn, *Cambridge Illustrated History*, 138.

15. LeRoy McDermott's suggestions that these figurines are self-portraits created by women has recently generated much lively discussion. LeRoy McDermott, "Self-

Representation in Upper Paleolithic Figurines," *Current Anthropology* 37, no. 2 (1996): 227–75.

16. For example, see, Carol Christ, *Rebirth of the Goddess: Finding Meaning in Feminist Spirituality* (New York: Routledge, 1997); the numerous works by Marija Gimbutas (see bibliography); and Peg Streep, *Sanctuaries of the Goddess: The Sacred Landscape and Objects* (Boston: Little, Brown, 1994).

17. Margaret Conkey and Ruth Tringham, "Archaeology and the Goddess: Exploring the Contours of Feminist Archaeology," in *Feminisms in the Academy*, ed. Donna Stanton and Abigail Stewart (Ann Arbor: University of Michigan Press, 1995), 199–247; Cynthia Eller, *The Myth of Matriarchal Prehistory: Why an Invented Past Won't Give Women a Future* (Boston: Beacon, 2002); Jo Ann Hackett, "Can a Sexist Model Liberate Us? Ancient Near Eastern 'Fertility' Goddesses," *Journal of Feminist Studies in Religion* 5, no. 1 (1989): 65–76; Kathryn Rountree, "The Politics of the Goddess: Feminist Spirituality and the Essentialism Debate," *Social Analysis* 43, no. 2 (1999): 138–65; Lynn Meskell, "Goddesses, Gimbutas and 'New Age' Archaeology," *Antiquity* 69 (1995): 74–86; and Mary Jo Weaver, "Who Is the Goddess and Where Does She Get Us?" *Journal of Feminist Studies in Religion* 5, no. 1 (1989): 49–64.

18. See Aubrey Burl, *From Carnac to Callanish: The Prehistoric Stone Rows and Avenues of Britain, Ireland and Brittany* (New Haven, CT: Yale University Press, 1993) and John Michell, *Megalithomania: Artists, Antiquarians and Archaeologists at the Old Stone Monuments* (Ithaca, NY: Cornell University Press, 1982.)

19. Wunn, 448.

20. Wunn, 448.

21. Wunn, 433.

22. For example, see David Lewis-Williams, *The Mind in the Cave: Consciousness and the Origins of Art* (New York: Thames and Hudson, 2002); Steven Mithen, *The Prehistory of the Mind: A Search for the Origins of Art, Religion, and Science* (London: Thames and Hudson, 1996); Barbara King, *Evolving God: A Provocative View of the Origins of Religion* (New York: Doubleday, 2007); and John Pfeiffer, *The Creative Explosion: An Inquiry into the Origins of Art and Religion* (Ithaca, NY: Cornell University Press, 1985).

23. Howard Morphy, *Aboriginal Art* (London: Phaidon, 1998), 55.

24. Morphy, 56.

25. Brian Fagan, *From Black Land to Fifth Sun: The Science of Sacred Sites* (Reading, MA: Addison-Wesley, 1998), especially chapter 3, "San Artists in Southern Africa," 51–69; and David Coulson and Alec Campbell, *African Rock Art: Paintings and Engravings on Stone* (New York: Harry N. Abrams, 2001).

26. Among copious sources for this material, a very useful introduction is Polly Schaafsma, *Indian Rock Art of the Southwest* (Santa Fe, NM: School of American Research, 1980).

27. Robert Brooks and Vishnu Wakankar, *Stone Age Painting in India* (New Haven, CT: Yale University Press, 1976).

28. Carlos Picón, Joan Mertens, Elizabeth Milleketer, Christopher Lightfoot, and Seán Hemingway, *Art of the Classical World in the Metropolitan Museum of Art* (New York: The Metropolitan Museum of Art, 2007), 458.

29. Picón et al., 223.

30. Joan Mertens, "Some Long Thoughts on Early Cycladic Sculpture," *Metropolitan Museum Journal* 33 (1998): 7–22.

31. Elizabeth Hendrix, "Painted Ladies of the Early Bronze Age," *The Metropolitan Museum of Art Bulletin* 55, no. 3 (1997–98): 4–5.

32. Hendrix, 6.

33. Hendrix, 4.

34. Hendrix, 6.

35. A. Bonanno, T. Gouder, C. Malone, and S. Stoddart, "Monuments in an Island Society: The Maltese Context," *World Archaeology* 22, no. 2 (1990): 190–205.

36. Kathryn Rountree, "Re-inventing Malta's Neolithic Temples: Contemporary Interpretations and Agendas," *History and Anthropology* 13, no. 1 (2002): 35.

37. Streep, especially chapter 5, "In and of the Earth: Malta," 83–101.

38. Muriel Hilson, "Neolithic Art and the Art History Class," *Studies in Art Education* 32, no. 4 (1991): 235.

39. Rountree, "Re-inventing," 32.

40. Kathryn Rountree, "Goddess Pilgrims as Tourists: Inscribing the Body through Sacred Travel," *Sociology of Religion* 63, no. 4 (2002): 475–96.

41. Rountree, "Re-inventing," 45.

42. Rountree, "Re-inventing," 46.

43. Richard Hayman, *Riddles in Stone: Myths, Archaeology and the Ancient Britons* (London: Hambledon Press, 1997).

44. Gerald Hawkins, *Stonehenge Decoded* (London: Fontana, 1970).

45. Peg Streep, *Sanctuaries of the Goddess*, especially chapter 7, "The Goddess at the Peak: Crete," 130–57.

46. Vincent Scully, *The Earth, the Temple, and the Gods: Greek Sacred Architecture*, rev. ed. (New Haven, CT: Yale University Press, 1979).

47. Kenneth Lapatin, *Mysteries of the Snake Goddess: Art, Desire, and the Forging of History* (Cambridge, MA: Da Capo Press, 2002).

48. Lapatin, 73.

49. Lapatin, 90.

BIBLIOGRAPHY AND FURTHER READING

Aldhouse-Green, Miranda, and Stephen Aldhouse-Green. *The Quest for the Shaman: Shape-Shifters, Sorcerers and Spirit-Healers of Ancient Europe*. London: Thames and Hudson, 2005.

Bahn, Paul. *The Cambridge Illustrated History of Prehistoric Art*. Cambridge, UK: Cambridge University Press, 1998.

Bahn, Paul, and Jean Vertut. *Journey through the Ice Age*. Berkeley: University of California Press, 1997.

Bonanno, A., T. Gouder, C. Malone, and S. Stoddart. "Monuments in an Island Society: The Maltese Context." *World Archaeology* 22, no. 2 (1990): 190–205.

Brooks, Robert, and Vishnu Wakankar. *Stone Age Painting in India*. New Haven, CT: Yale University Press, 1976.

Burenhult, Göran. *Traditional Peoples Today: Continuity and Change in the Modern World*. San Francisco: Harper San Francisco, 1994.

Burl, Aubrey. *From Carnac to Callanish: The Prehistoric Stone Rows and Avenues of Britain, Ireland and Brittany*. New Haven, CT: Yale University Press, 1993.

Chauvet, Jean-Marie, Eliette Deschamps, and Christian Hillaire. *Dawn of Art: The Chauvet Cave: The Oldest Known Paintings in the World.* New York: Harry N. Abrams, 1996.

Christ, Carol. *Rebirth of the Goddess: Finding Meaning in Feminist Spirituality.* New York: Routledge, 1997.

Christin, Anne-Marie, ed. *A History of Writing: From Hieroglyph to Multimedia.* Paris: Flammarion, 2002.

Clottes, Jean. *Chauvet Cave: The Art of Earliest Times.* Salt Lake City: University of Utah Press, 2003.

Clottes, Jean. "The Identification of Human and Animal Figures in European Palaeolithic Art." In *Animals into Art,* ed. Howard Morphy, 21–56. London: Unwin Hyman, 1989.

Clottes, Jean, and Jean Courtin. *The Cave Beneath the Sea: Paleolithic Images at Cosquer.* New York: Harry N. Abrams, 1996.

Clottes, Jean, and David Lewis-Williams. *The Shamans of Prehistory: Trance and Magic in the Painted Caves.* New York: Harry N. Abrams, 1998.

Conkey, Margaret. "Making Things Meaningful: Approaches to the Interpretation of the Ice Age Imagery of Europe." In *Meaning in the Visual Arts: Views from the Outside,* ed. Irving Lavin, 49–64. Princeton, NJ: Institute for Advanced Study, 1995.

Conkey, Margaret, and Ruth Tringham. "Archaeology and the Goddess: Exploring the Contours of Feminist Archaeology." In *Feminisms in the Academy,* ed. Donna Stanton and Abigail Stewart, 199–247. Ann Arbor: University of Michigan Press, 1995.

Conkey, Margaret, and Sarah Williams. "Original Narratives: The Political Economy of Gender in Archaeology." In *Gender at the Crossroads of Knowledge: Feminist Anthropology in the Post-modern Era,* ed. Micaela di Leonardo, 101–39. Berkeley: University of California Press, 1991.

Coulson, David, and Alec Campbell. *African Rock Art: Paintings and Engravings on Stone.* New York: Harry N. Abrams, 2001.

Di Leonardo, Micaela, ed. *Gender at the Crossroads of Knowledge: Feminist Anthropology in the Post-modern Era.* Berkeley: University of California Press, 1991.

Elkins, James. *On Pictures and the Words That Fail Them.* Cambridge, UK: Cambridge University Press, 1998.

Eller, Cynthia. *The Myth of Matriarchal Prehistory: Why an Invented Past Won't Give Women a Future.* Boston: Beacon, 2002.

Fagan, Brian. *Discovery! Unearthing the New Treasures of Archaeology.* London: Thames and Hudson, 2007.

Fagan, Brian. *From Black Land to Fifth Sun: The Science of Sacred Sites.* Reading, MA: Addison-Wesley, 1998.

Fischer, Steven Roger. *A History of Writing.* London: Reaktion Books, 2001.

Gimbutas, Marija. *The Goddesses and Gods of Old Europe: Myths and Cult Images.* London: Thames and Hudson, 1982.

Gimbutas, Marija. *The Living Goddesses.* Berkeley: University of California Press, 1999.

Guthrie, R. Dale. *The Nature of Paleolithic Art.* Chicago: University of Chicago Press, 2005.

Hackett, Jo Ann. "Can a Sexist Model Liberate Us? Ancient Near Eastern 'Fertility' Goddesses." *Journal of Feminist Studies in Religion* 5, no. 1 (1989): 65–76.

Hawkins, Gerald. *Stonehenge Decoded*. London: Fontana, 1970.

Hayman, Richard. *Riddles in Stone: Myths, Archaeology and the Ancient Britons*. London: Hambledon Press, 1997.

Hendrix, Elizabeth. "Painted Ladies of the Early Bronze Age." *The Metropolitan Museum of Art Bulletin* 55, no. 3 (1997–98): 4–14.

Hilson, Muriel. "Neolithic Art and the Art History Class." *Studies in Art Education* 32, no. 4 (1991): 230–38.

King, Barbara. *Evolving God: A Provocative View of the Origins of Religion*. New York: Doubleday, 2007.

Lapatin, Kenneth. *Mysteries of the Snake Goddess: Art, Desire, and the Forging of History*. Cambridge, MA: Da Capo Press, 2002.

Lavin, Irving, ed. *Meaning in the Visual Arts: Views from the Outside*. Princeton, NJ: Institute for Advanced Study, 1995.

Lewis-Williams, David. *The Mind in the Cave: Consciousness and the Origins of Art*. New York: Thames and Hudson, 2002.

Lorblanchet, Michel. "From Naturalism to Abstraction in European Prehistoric Rock Art." In *Form in Indigenous Art: Schematisation in the Art of Aboriginal Australia and Prehistoric Europe*, ed. Peter Ucko, 43–56. Canberra, Australia: Institute of Aboriginal Studies, 1977.

Maringer, Johannes. *The Gods of Prehistoric Man*. London: Phoenix Press, 2002.

McDermott, LeRoy. "Self-Representation in Upper Paleolithic Figurines." *Current Anthropology* 37, no. 2 (1996): 227–75.

McMann, Jean. *Riddles of the Stone Age: Rock Carvings of Ancient Europe*. London: Thames and Hudson, 1980.

Mertens, Joan. "Some Long Thoughts on Early Cycladic Sculpture." *Metropolitan Museum Journal* 33 (1998): 7–22.

Meskell, Lynn. "Goddesses, Gimbutas and 'New Age' Archaeology. *Antiquity* 69 (1995): 74–86.

Michell, John. *Megalithomania: Artists, Antiquarians and Archaeologists at the Old Stone Monuments*. Ithaca, NY: Cornell University Press, 1982.

Mithen, Steven. *The Prehistory of the Mind: A Search for the Origins of Art, Religion, and Science*. London: Thames and Hudson, 1996.

Morphy, Howard. *Aboriginal Art*. London: Phaidon, 1998.

Morphy, Howard, ed. *Animals into Art*. London: Unwin Hyman, 1989.

Pfeiffer, John. *The Creative Explosion: An Inquiry into the Origins of Art and Religion*. Ithaca, NY: Cornell University Press, 1985.

Picón, Carlos, Joan Mertens, Elizabeth Milleketer, Christopher Lightfoot, and Seán Hemingway. *Art of the Classical World in the Metropolitan Museum of Art*. New York: The Metropolitan Museum of Art, 2007.

Rountree, Kathryn. "Goddess Pilgrims as Tourists: Inscribing the Body through Sacred Travel." *Sociology of Religion* 63, no. 4 (2002): 475–96.

Rountree, Kathryn. "The Politics of the Goddess: Feminist Spirituality and the Essentialism Debate." *Social Analysis* 43, no. 2 (1999): 138–65.

Rountree, Kathryn. "Re-inventing Malta's Neolithic Temples: Contemporary Interpretations and Agendas." *History and Anthropology* 13, no. 1 (2002): 31–51.

Ruspoli, Mario. *The Cave of Lascaux: The Final Photographs*. New York: Harry N. Abrams, 1987.

Schaafsma, Polly. *Indian Rock Art of the Southwest*. Santa Fe, NM: School of American Research, 1980.

Scully, Vincent. *The Earth, the Temple and the Gods: Greek Sacred Architecture*, rev. ed. (New Haven, CT: Yale University Press, 1979.)

Skomal, Susan, and Edgar Polomé, eds. *Proto-Indo-Europeans, The Archaeology of a Linguistic Problem, Studies in Honor of Marija Gimbutas*. New York: The Institute for the Study of Man, 1987.

Smith, Noel. *An Analysis of Ice Age Art: Its Psychology and Belief System*. New York: Peter Lang, 1992.

Stanton, Donna, and Abigail Stewart, eds. *Feminisms in the Academy*. Ann Arbor: University of Michigan Press, 1995.

Streep, Peg. *Sanctuaries of the Goddess: The Sacred Landscape and Objects*. Boston: Little, Brown, 1994.

Ucko, Peter, ed. *Form in Indigenous Art: Schematisation in the Art of Aboriginal Australia and Prehistoric Europe*. Canberra, Australia: Institute of Aboriginal Studies, 1977.

Weaver, Mary Jo. "Who Is the Goddess and Where Does She Get Us?" *Journal of Feminist Studies in Religion* 5, no. 1 (1989): 49–64.

White, Randall. *Prehistoric Art: The Symbolic Journey of Humankind*. New York: Harry N. Abrams, 2003.

Winn, Shan. *Pre-Writing in Southeastern Europe: The Sign System of the Vinča Culture*. Calgary, Alberta: Western Publishers, 1981.

Wunn, Ina. "Beginning of Religion." *Numen* 47, no. 4 (2000): 417–52.

—2—

Religion in Ancient Mesopotamia

ORIGINS AND DEVELOPMENT

Geography

Mesopotamia is an ancient Greek term that means "the land between the rivers." This region, the core of which is primarily located in present-day Iraq, roughly between the Tigris and Euphrates rivers, has often been called the cradle of civilization. It is acclaimed for evidencing some of the very earliest human achievements in agriculture and irrigation methods, for the use of the wheel, for the invention of writing methods and of mathematics, and for the early development of urban centers.

Mesopotamia is at the heart of a much larger geographic region often called the fertile crescent. The term *fertile crescent* was first used in the early 20th century by the American scholar James Henry Breasted (1865–1935), the founder of the Oriental Institute of the University of Chicago, to describe the vast geographic region extending from the eastern Mediterranean northwards to the Syrian desert and southeast to the Persian Gulf. Mesopotamia refers to the wide area of the fertile crescent roughly corresponding to all of present-day Iraq, plus sections of southeastern Turkey, eastern Syria, and parts of western Iran.

Chronology

Although human habitation in Mesopotamia can be traced far back into prehistory, it was the cultivation of plants and the domestication of animals, beginning perhaps around 9000 BCE, that provided the early foundations for the eventual and lengthy growth of a series of settled communities and civilizations in this region. The "entangled millennial history" of Mesopotamia involves a series of periods named after, or associated with, a succession of civilizations that came to prominence in particular regions, that overlapped with or conquered earlier civilizations, and that established empires of greater or lesser duration.[1] A basic chronology of these ancient civilizations (spanning ca. 4000 BCE to the second century CE) would include the Sumerians, Akkadians, Babylonians, Hittites, Kassites, Assyrians, Persians, Hellenistic Greeks, and Romans.

The initial transition from small agricultural villages to much larger urban centers took place largely in the fourth millennium BCE in both northern and southern Mesopotamia (Sumeria). These early cities were inhabited by people who had developed, doubtless over many previous centuries, impressive architectural construction techniques, and who lived within a highly stratified society in which emphasis was placed on earthly as well as heavenly/religious concerns.

One of the most substantial of these early cities was Uruk, in southern Mesopotamia. Uruk was the largest of a number of urban centers of the Uruk period (ca. 4000–2900 BCE). The site appears to have been inhabited since the fifth millennium BCE and remained continually occupied up through the seventh century CE. Uruk is especially famous for its remarkable art and architecture and, traditionally also, for the development of the earliest recognized writing system in world history: cuneiform (or wedge-shaped) writing.[2] Cuneiform evolved from the previous system of pictographs used by the early Sumerians and others who scratched small pictures (primarily representing words/objects, mostly inventories of cattle, food, and other goods) into soft clay tablets with reeds or a sharp tool (stylus). This early pictography eventually developed, around 3000–2900 BCE, into the more abbreviated signs of cuneiform and a complex system of grammar that allowed for the creation of much longer texts, documents, legal, and literary works.

Early Sumeria was ultimately composed of a number of independent city-states, which were frequently at war with each other. These Sumerian city states in the Early Dynastic period (ca. 3000–2340 BCE) were ruled by powerful dynasties of leaders, some of whose names are known (such as Gilgamesh, ca. 2700 BCE) and whose deeds and heroic exploits were later recorded. These rulers were understood to have had special relationships with the deities in functioning as their chief servants on earth. Each Sumerian city-state was believed to be under the protection of one or more deities whose presence was symbolized and embodied in the dominant temple complexes that traditionally provided the urban focal points. Major cities such as Ur (the leading city of Sumeria by around 2500 BCE, with a population of over 20,000), Eridu, Kish, Nippur, and Lagash were flourishing centers of commerce and art production.

Following the Early Dynastic centuries, during the third millennium BCE, northern Mesopotamia came under the control of the Akkadians who ultimately, under the leadership of Sargon (r. 2334–2279 BCE), conquered the southern Sumerian city-states. The vast Akkadian empire ultimately comprised most of the regions of the fertile crescent. In the late third millennium BCE, however, the Akkadian empire was overthrown by invading peoples from the northeast. This ultimately ushered in the Neo-Sumerian period (ca. 2125–2025 BCE) with the ancient cities of Ur and Lagash again playing prominent roles. The western Amorites, who began to enter Mesopotamia in the late Neo-Sumerian period, established their capital at the city-state of Babylon. During the early second millennium BCE, Babylonia was the major city-state in the region, notably flourishing during the reign of Hammurabi, who ruled from ca. 1792–1750 BCE. The Babylonians were ultimately supplanted by the Hittites (in the middle of the 17th century BCE), and then by the Kassites (in the middle of the 15th century BCE), who were, in turn, conquered by the Elamites from Iran. The Assyrians became the major power in the region during the late second and early first millennium BCE until the re-ascendance of the Babylonians (in the seventh and sixth centuries BCE), and the Persian Achaemenians (in the sixth through fourth centuries BCE), followed by the Hellenistic Greeks via the conquests of Alexander the Great, who died in Babylon in 323 BCE. Ultimately, sections of Mesopotamia came briefly under Roman rule in the second century CE before the reestablishment of Persian power under the Sassanids (during the third through sixth centuries CE), followed by the Arab Abbasids (of the eighth and ninth centuries CE). These periods, the religions of ancient Persia (e.g., Zoroastrianism), and the later phases of Mesopotamian history lie outside the scope of this present discussion.

Even a brief survey of the exceedingly complex history of ancient Mesopotamia demonstrates that this region was, and indeed continues to be, of signal historical importance for world history. In its position as the birthplace or cradle of Western civilization, this area of the world (bridging Asia and Africa and Europe) has experienced a remarkable and lengthy history, characterized by the rise and fall of a plethora of civilizations and cultural groups whose achievements in science, engineering, literature, and the visual arts continue to serve as extremely impressive testimonials of these ancient peoples.

Our knowledge of ancient Mesopotamian civilizations comes primarily from two sources: archaeological evidence and written documents. Although copious materials of both of these forms still exist, the evidence that survives represents only a tiny sampling, simply shadows of these ancient cultures. The ongoing conflicts and conquests that took place in this region during antiquity, as civilizations succeeded each other in power and control, resulted in the destruction of much archaeological and artistic material. Attempts to destroy the past and shatter its visible monuments by way of ushering in new eras is an all too common event in human history. Many of these destructive actions happened in ancient Mesopotamia, as well as in other ancient world regions. The looting and pillaging of potentially valuable art works has always fueled the past and current market for dealers in and collectors of antiquities.

Nevertheless and without doubt, the looting and destruction of a monumental portion of the collections housed in the Iraq Museum in Baghdad in the wake of the American invasion of 2003—preceded and followed by years of political unrest in the country and the looting of many significant archaeological sites—remain signal tragedies in human history. It is a truly disastrous fact that so many ancient works of art and archaeological sites of ancient Mesopotamia—the cradle of Western history and civilization—have now been irretrievably lost to history and will never be recovered.[3]

Religion

The complex and lengthy history of ancient Mesopotamia—the extent of the geographic region and the many civilizations that have successively inhabited this area of the world—provide many challenges in any attempts to succinctly describe Mesopotamian religion. Although many scholars have confidently undertaken this task, other scholars believe that it is really quite impossible to do so.[4] Any description of religious beliefs in ancient Mesopotamia needs to take into consideration the complicated history of this world region and look carefully at the surviving textual and archaeological evidence from a notably lengthy succession of cultures.

What did the ancient Sumerians believe? Were their religious beliefs and practices different from those of the slightly later Akkadians, or the much later Babylonians, or the Assyrians? "Mesopotamian religion presents itself as a complex, multilayered accumulation," which is additionally complicated by the association of this world region with early Judaic history as well.[5] The ancient biblical patriarch Abraham was born in the Mesopotamian city of Ur; Mesopotamia is often said to have been the location of the biblical Garden of Eden; the biblical stories of the Great Flood are found in ancient Mesopotamian writings as well as in the Hebrew scriptures. The relationship of the Hebrews, who eventually settled in Israel, with their neighbors in Mesopotamia form a significant portion of ancient Jewish historical narratives (see chapter 9, "Judaism"), especially when the Babylonians extended their empire to the east and subsumed the land of Israel, destroyed the preeminent Jewish Temple in the city of Jerusalem, and took the Jews into captivity in Babylon in the sixth century BCE.

Judaism is a monotheistic religion. It developed in the ancient world in—or as—a great contrast to the polytheistic religious beliefs held by numerous other peoples in the fertile crescent. The ancient Sumerians, and their successors (the Akkadians, Assyrians, Babylonians, and other peoples) were polytheistic. They devoted their worship focus not to a single god or goddess, but to many different gods and goddesses. These gods and goddesses were associated with various and critical natural forces—observed in the movements of the sun, the moon, the stars, and the seasons of the year—plus events such as wind, flood, fire, and drought.

The primary deities of the ancient Sumerians were: An (the god of the sky), Enlil (the god of the air and wind), Ninkhursaga (the goddess of the earth), and Enki (the god of the waters.) A vast panoply of other deities were also venerated in, or associated with, various ancient Sumerian city-states. This "older generation" of gods were the ancestors and source of other deities, some of whom became especially prominent under the Akkadians.[6] These include astral deities such as: Nanna, or Sin (the moon god), Utu, or Shamash (the sun god), and Inanna, or Ishtar (the star goddess of Venus and fertility). The deities of the ancient Sumerians actually numbered in the thousands, and successive cultures in Mesopotamia tended to retain, absorb, and modify the pantheon. Ishtar was the most widely worshiped deity of the Babylonians (by the second millennium BCE), whose powerful god Marduk (son of the storm) ultimately derived from the Sumerian wind god, Enlil. The major Assyrian god, Assur, similarly also had many of the attributes of the Sumerian sky god, An (or Anu). Although the names and roles of the deities evolved and were slightly altered in successive phases of history, and some deities were especially prominent and venerated in particular locales during specific periods, in general there appears to be a remarkable sense of similarity and continuity in the beliefs and religious practices among the civilizations of ancient Mesopotamia.

PRINCIPAL BELIEFS AND KEY PRACTICES

Evidence for the principal beliefs and key practices associated with religion in ancient Mesopotamia is based on archaeological and textual sources. Archaeological evidence takes the form of monumental architecture (temples and temple complexes) and numerous examples of small-scale works in various sculptural media (stone, metal, and clay) that depict deities, humans, and ritual actions. Because so much of the surviving art from ancient Mesopotamia seems to be religious in nature, it appears that religion played a critical role in these ancient societies. This impression is also supported by the vast body of textual evidence, myths and epic stories of the creation of the world, tales of the activities of the gods and goddesses, documents that detail temple holdings and goods, and other works containing prayers, hymns, and directions for rituals.

Although it is not always possible to confidently correlate the artistic and textual evidence (for example, the exact identification of specific deities and pictorial narrative scenes on many works of art remains speculative), it appears clear that religion—centered on the powerful deities—was a major component of ancient Mesopotamian life. "Ancient Mesopotamians regarded personal well-being as being tied to correct worship of the gods. If an individual sinned or a community neglected the proper rites, disorder, plague, earthquake, fire, or other evils could befall the entire community."[7] The various deities were thus regarded as active forces in the realms of human life and human endeavors. Pleasing and placating these divine figures, who in turn would protect, nourish, and support humans, is generally seen to be at the core of Mesopotamian religious practices.

Achieving and maintaining the beneficence of the deities was critical, and the enactment of highly formal duties was the primary responsibility of the ruling and priestly members of society. Ordinary people did not play a major role in this but served primarily as distanced onlookers to the formalized rituals that were carried out by the appointed specialists. "For the average person [in ancient Mesopotamia], religion was ceremonial and formal rather than intense and personal."[8] Rituals performed in temples were off limits to ordinary people; however, there were also larger public festivals that the general population could witness and in which they could participate to some degree.

In many ways, the religious practices of ancient Mesopotamian civilizations resemble those of the ancient Egyptians, who similarly developed a highly stratified society in which the formal or state religion was largely in the hands of the upper and priestly classes. Like the temple complexes of ancient Egypt, the temple complexes of ancient Mesopotamia were centers of wealth and power and served as social and economic focal points of the cities and city-states. Unlike the ancient Egyptians, however, Mesopotamian cultures appear not to have developed any extremely detailed beliefs about death and the afterlife, which were matters of such importance to the ancient Egyptians (see chapter 3: "Religion in Ancient Egypt").

Although "many literary texts struggled with the meaning of death and dealt with the fortunes of the dead in the netherworld" (including the *Epic of Gilgamesh* and the *Descent of Inanna to the Netherworld*), the ghostly inhabitants of the netherworld, presided over by various deities and courtly bureaucracies, existed in a pale imitation of life on earth, in a "land of no return."[9] Funerals and burials were often elaborate, especially for the upper classes, and bodies were often buried with grave goods and personal items, but most bodies were buried without any of the preservation or mummification practices associated with ancient Egypt. The concepts of reincarnation, heavenly rewards, or torments in hell for sins on earth do not appear to have been factors in Mesopotamian conceptions of death or the afterlife.[10] "The worst punishment dispensed to a sinner was denial of entry by the gods of the netherworld. In this way, the sinner was sentenced to sleeplessness and denied access to funerary offerings."[11] Funerary offerings were regularly made to the deceased, and again, the degree of elaboration depended on their social standing or family wealth. Proper offerings ensured the favor of the ghosts of the dead, and several times a year celebrations were held during which the ghosts might return briefly to earth. Dangerous and restless ghosts could cause evil for the living, as could demons or evil spirits who were frequently appeased by rituals and incantations or warded off with protective amulets. Priests and sorcerers were often involved with exorcisms or reading omens via several different forms of divination. The richness and complexity of religious beliefs and practices in ancient Mesopotamia is well demonstrated also in the surviving religious art and architecture.

TRADITIONAL ART AND ARCHITECTURAL FORMS

Temples and Ziggurats

Temples—in the form of religious buildings with specific spatial enclosures—appear to have been critical components in ancient Mesopotamian urban centers, serving as focal points for the cities. Scholars believe that each ancient Mesopotamian city was dedicated to a specific god or goddess among the polytheistic pantheon and that the inhabitants of the cities believed that the god/goddess to whom their city was dedicated actually or symbolically resided (or might choose to reside) within the temple complex provided by the people of the city. Temples thus served as the dwelling places for the patron/patroness of the city, but they also served extremely important economic roles as well. "The temple represented the communal identity of each city."[12] They were considered to be the homes as well as the estates of the deities. Temples owned property and engaged in "various productive and commercial activities . . . [such as] cultivation of cereals, vegetables, and fruit trees; management of sheep, goats, and cows; manufacture of textiles, leather, and wooden items; and promotion of trading links with foreign lands. These enterprises necessitated storerooms, granaries, and workshops within the temple enclosure."[13] Surpluses of food and goods were maintained by the temples and distributed to the populace in times of need. Temples also performed other charitable acts (such as caring for poor or orphaned children) and provided a venue for certain legal proceedings (such as the swearing of oaths). Temples could thus be vast complexes of buildings, including buildings outside the city.

At the heart of the temple complex, the religious architectural structure most commonly associated with ancient Mesopotamian belief systems is the ziggurat. Ziggurats are multitiered, stepped monuments, on the tops of which temple structures were raised. The ziggurat form evolved largely in the Neo-Sumerian period (ca. 2150–2000 BCE), ultimately based on earlier practices of erecting temples on large elevated platforms. The elevation of the temple created visual prominence for the monument and also served practical concerns in protecting the temple from floods or attacks during frequent periods of warfare. Many scholars believe that the practice of elevating temples toward the heavens also reflects important symbolism—the desire that the deities would descend from the heavens to reside in a sacred and lofty abode. The description of the infamous Tower of Babel in the Hebrew scriptures is often assumed to have been based on ancient Mesopotamian ziggurats, notably the great ziggurat of Babylon (see Figure 2.1).

Ziggurats were generally constructed of sun-dried brick encased in slightly more durable kiln-fired brick. Ziggurats were constructed by the Sumerians, Babylonians, Assyrians, and Persians with some variations and modifications in style. The ziggurat of Ur (ca. 2100 BCE) is one of the most famous of these early ancient monuments.

Figure 2.1   Model of the Marduk sanctuary at Babylon with the Tower of Babel. From the time of Nebuchadnezzar II, 604–562 BCE. Berlin: Vorderasiatisches Museum. Bildarchiv Preussischer Kulturbesitz / Art Resource, NY.

Deities and Devotees

The gods and goddesses of ancient Mesopotamia were frequently depicted in art and are generally recognizable because of distinctive attributes and symbols. By and large, Mesopotamian divinities were represented in anthropomorphic form, that is, in the guise of human figures. This poses a contrast to many of the deities of ancient Egypt who often combined human and animal attributes, in zooanthropomorphic forms. With rare exceptions, Mesopotamian deities were conceived with human attributes and "were regarded as an aristocracy of great landowners, the country's powerful upper class. . . . the gods and their world were modeled on the world of humans."[14] The deities had spouses, children, servants, and a royal entourage "similar to a human ruler, but without human boundaries."[15]

Statues of the deities were installed in the temples, and these images were profoundly significant in that they were believed to be inhabited by the divinities.[16] Textual and visual evidence indicates that these sanctified images, or cult statues, were fed, clothed, and entertained by priests and other temple personnel.[17] Very few, if any, of these cult statues have survived, but images of the deities appear in many other media.

The deities are frequently identifiable due to their garments and especially their elaborate headgear or crowns. For example, the moon god Nanna is

Figure 2.2 The Ur-Nammu stele, ca. 2100 BCE. Philadelphia: University of Pennsylvania Museum of Archaeology and Anthropology. Bildarchiv Preussischer Kulturbesitz / Art Resource, NY.

believed to be the deity represented on an early limestone stele that was discovered during the excavations of ancient Ur in the 1920s[18] (see Figure 2.2). Known as the Ur-Nammu stele, this well-studied monument, which originally stood over 10 feet in height, contains numerous relief scenes carved in horizontal registers on both sides, representing male and female deities, and kingly figures carrying building tools and making offerings to the deities. Although the specific identification of the figures and activities shown are matters of some scholarly dispute, the scene illustrated in the reconstruction shown is traditionally believed to depict the great Sumerian king and builder Ur-Nammu (ca. 2112–2095 BCE) making a libation offering to the moon god Nanna. Nanna presents Ur-Nammu with a staff and coils of rope, symbols of power and authority as well as references to architectural construction tools and measuring devices. The deity wears an elaborate tufted robe and a tall crown that consists of several tiers of horns. He is seated on a throne that resembles a temple structure with a series of recessed doorframes, partially covered by a scalloped canopy.

The iconography of the Ur-Nammu stele, with a seated deity approached by a standing figure of a worshiper, is often repeated throughout ancient Mesopotamian art. Another especially famous example showing this imagery is the stele with the law code of the Babylonian ruler, Hammurabi, ca. 1780 BCE (see Figure 2.3). "One of the most remarkable treasures of the ancient world," this tall black basalt stele contains the cuneiform text of Hammurabi's law code, the earliest to have survived in great detail (earlier law codes of rulers such as Ur-Nammu survive only in part).[19] The cuneiform text of 3,500 lines, detailing close to 300 laws, is surmounted by a carved relief scene depicting the standing figure of Hammurabi respectfully approaching the seated sun god, Shamash. The stele was probably originally placed in the temple of Shamash at Sippar. The god Shamash wears a flounced robe, necklaces and bracelets, and is seated on a throne with architectural motifs similar to that depicted on the Ur-Nammu stele. Flames, or sun rays, surround his shoulders, and he wears an elaborate tiered horned headdress and a square, curled beard. He presents the symbols of authority—a staff and ring—to Hammurabi, who raises his hand in a gesture of respect and deference to the divine figure. Unlike the Ur-Nammu stele, where the king offers a libation, on the stele of Hammurabi, "the space between the king and the deity has been freed, allowing the two figures to be closer and emphatically gaze into each other's eyes."[20]

The tufted or flounced robes (sometimes referred to as *kaunakes*—although scholars dispute the use of this term) and the horned headdresses worn by the deities in these examples contrast with the relatively plainer garments and caplike headgear (often termed *polos*) worn by the kingly figures. Although these garments and headdresses do not always, or exclusively, indicate either divine or human status, a Sumerian cylinder seal from ca. 2000 BCE shows figures also wearing these distinctive garments and hats. Cylinder seals survive in great numbers from ancient Mesopotamia and are among the most important and traditional forms of Mesopotamian art.[21] Normally made of stone and shaped like spools, they were used to create clay stamps to seal, protect, validate, or identify documents, storage jars, and other objects. Many cylinder seals contain both cuneiform texts and images, such as the example shown in Figure 2.4. In this case, the seated figure, wearing the flounced robe and *polos*-style hat, has been identified as the deified ruler Ibbi-Sin (ca. 2028–2004 BCE). He holds a cup and is seated on a low stool.[22] Approaching him are two standing figures; the central figure wears a flounced robe and horned headdress that identify her as a goddess. She grasps the arm of a male figure who raises up his right hand, mirroring the goddess's gesture of greeting to the divine ruler. The standing male figure is hatless and wears a long fringed robe. The inscription identifies him as the owner of the seal, Ilum-bani. Traditionally identified as a presentation scene, the worshiper/petitioner is led by the goddess into the divine royal presence.

Figure 2.3 Stele of the law code of Hammurabi, ca. 1792–1750 BCE. Paris: Louvre. Réunion des Musées Nationaux / Art Resource, NY.

Figure 2.4 Cylinder seal, ca. 2000 BCE. New York: The Metropolitan Museum of Art / Art Resource, NY.

Figures of worshipers also feature prominently in other media from ancient Mesopotamia. Among the most famous are the group excavated in the 1930s from the site of the temple of the god Abu at Eshnunna (modern Tell Asmar) (see Plate 3). The figures, which have been dated to ca. 2700 BCE, are carved out of gypsum and stand anywhere from nine inches to two feet tall. Both male and female figures were found, and the majority are portrayed standing upright with their hands folded across their chests. Many of the men are bearded and wear belts and long fringed skirts. The women also wear long robes. All of the figures have extremely large staring eyes, inlaid with shell and black stone. They are traditionally described as votive statues and are believed to have represented worshipers in perpetual prayer to the deity venerated in the temple. Many such examples have been found at various sites, and some are identified with inscriptions, telling the name of the person who offered the statue or naming the deity worshiped.

Statuettes of royal figures were also frequently placed within temple complexes, indicating their authority and close relationship with the deities. The great Neo-Sumerian ruler of Lagash, Gudea (ca. 2150?–2125? BCE) was represented in a remarkable series of close to 30 examples of both seated and standing statues, some of which survive intact while others are in more fragmentary form[23] (see Figure 2.5). Many are carved from the costly stone, diorite, and are enriched with inscriptions detailing Gudea's piety and his dedication to the deities he served, for whom he had many temples newly built or restored. Evidence suggests that these royal statues were, like the cult statues of the deities, believed to be animated (via ritual consecration ceremonies) and thus able

Figure 2.5 Seated statue of Gudea, ca. 2150–2100 BCE. New York: The Metropolitan Museum of Art / Art Resource, NY.

to communicate directly with the gods and goddesses.[24]

EXAMPLES

The Warka Vase, ca. 3500–3000 BCE

The Warka Vase (or Uruk Vase) is one of the most significant examples of ancient Mesopotamian religious art (see Plate 4). It was discovered in the 1930s during excavations at the ancient site of Uruk (the modern city of Warka) in Iraq. The tall alabaster vessel stands about a yard tall and is enriched with low relief carvings in several registers, showing some "of the first illustrations of the ritual and religious practices that were the basis of Mesopotamian society."[25] One of the greatest treasures of the Iraq Museum in Baghdad, this object was taken from the museum during the disastrous looting and destruction of the museum's collections in 2003. It was eventually returned to the museum and has undergone restoration and repair.

The vase was originally excavated from the site of the temple of Inanna, the patron goddess of Uruk, and so is considered to have had a ritual function. Indeed, two vessels of similar format are illustrated in the top register of the relief carvings, among the numerous other gifts being presented to the goddess. Scholars generally agree that the scenes carved on the vase illustrate the highly important annual New Year festival of the city in which offerings to the temple were made to ensure the continued protection of the patron goddess, who symbolized fertility and fruitfulness. "At a time when the survival of individual humans was still so very precarious, and when organized agriculture and cattle breeding were still fairly novel, the gifts of life and food were the most serious concerns of the people."[26]

The bottom register of the vase depicts water (indicated by rippling lines) from which two varieties of plants or trees sprout healthily. (These are variously identified as barley and palms, or flax.) The next register shows an orderly line of alternating male and female sheep. The middle register depicts a procession of plump, naked male figures carrying baskets, ceramic vessels, and pots filled with food. The top register (a portion of which was damaged in antiquity) depicts the goddess (or a priestess) standing outside the temple (symbolized by two curving reed poles) who is approached by an offering-bearer, similar to the figures in the register below. The missing/damaged section is believed to have illustrated the priest-king (or En) of Uruk. Only a section of his long, fringed belt, held up by an attendant, survives. The priest-king is understood to be at the head of the offering-bearing procession, presenting gifts to the temple in the annual festival. Some scholars believe this also represents the symbolic marriage of the deity and ruler, a ritual that took place during the New Year celebrations.[27]

Although scholarly descriptions and identifications of some of the specific objects and actions depicted on the vessel diverge slightly, it is generally agreed that "the vase itself narrates, perhaps for the first time in the history of humans . . . a complexly organized society with spiritual, moral, and practical functions."[28] The protection of the patron deity, the role of the temple in receiving and storing food and gifts for the benefit of the population, and the role of the ruler (priest-king) in serving as leader and intercessor between the human and divine realms are illustrated in a significantly early, clear, linear, and sequential narrative fashion.[29]

The Ziggurat at Ur, Iraq, ca. 2100 BCE

The ziggurat at Ur was constructed under the direction of the important and influential king, Ur-Nammu (ca. 2112–2095 BCE), whose "piety and attention to building and restoring shrines led to his posthumous deification."[30] Ur-Nammu ruled over a significant territory in Sumeria and directed the construction of ziggurats at the cities of Eridu, Uruk, and Nippur as well. The ziggurat at Ur has been called "the first proper ziggurat" and is one of the few examples of these type of ancient structures to remain standing today, albeit in an incomplete and only partially restored state[31] (see Figure 2.6).

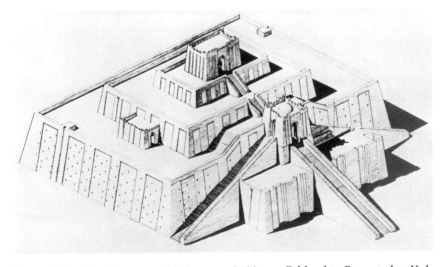

Figure 2.6   The Ziggurat at Ur, Iraq, ca. 2100 BCE. Bildarchiv Preussischer Kulturbesitz / Art Resource, NY.

The reconstruction drawing shows the monument as it would have originally appeared. It consisted of three successively smaller, inward-sloping platforms on a base of over 200 by 140 feet. It is estimated to have been well over 70 feet tall. The very top terrace was occupied by the temple structure itself—an enclosed, rectangular building (none of which survives.) The temple was dedicated to the patron deity of Ur, the moon god, Nanna. This impressive edifice was approached by three long flights of stairs that met at a tower gate on the first terrace level. Two smaller flights of stairs led from there up to the second and third platforms. Only priests were allowed to visit the upper levels and enter the temple to perform rituals and make offerings to the deity.

It is extremely important to realize that the ziggurat at Ur was the nucleus of a much more extensive religious/economic complex. Excavations have revealed numerous other structures, including storerooms, smaller buildings, courtyards, and a shrine dedicated to the goddess Ningal (the partner of Nanna). The whole of the sacred precinct was surrounded by a wall and was located at the core of the ancient walled city. Several residential quarters have also been excavated at Ur. Cities such as ancient Ur were highly organized economic centers in which the highly visible elevated temple/ziggurat represented the life source of the community.

Clay Mask of the Demon Humbaba, ca. 1800–1600 BCE

This intriguing object references several significant aspects of ancient Mesopotamian religious beliefs, practices, and mythology (see Figure 2.7). Found at the city of Sippar in southern Iraq, this small clay mask represents the demon Humbaba (or Huwawa, or Khumbaba), a major character in the *Epic of Gilgamesh*. The face is formed of coiling lines representing the internal organs of a sacrificial animal. Study of the entrails of animals was practiced in ancient Mesopotamia as a form of divination, a means to foretell the future.[32] The ancient Mesopotamians "believed that the gods disclosed their intentions to humans by signs in natural phenomena and world events. These signs could be interpreted through prolonged observation and deep study. The most common forms of divination were examination of the entrails of sacrificial animals (extispicy) and observation of the stars and planets (astrology)."[33]

Diviners, who were usually scholars associated with the royal governments or military, solicited and received omens from the gods and often recorded these communications in texts or handbooks and other forms, such as this clay example. A cuneiform inscription on the back of the piece identifies the maker of the mask as Warad-Marduk, a diviner who was active in the city of Sippar. The city of Sippar was dedicated to the sun god Shamash, who was often associated with powerful omens. The mask is formed of a continuous coiled line in configurations that are believed to have symbolized a revolution or upheaval to come.

Figure 2.7   Clay Mask of the Demon Humbaba, ca. 1800–1600 BCE.
London: British Museum. Erich Lessing / Art Resource, NY.

The demon Humbaba is also mentioned in the cuneiform inscription on
the back of the mask. According to the *Epic of Gilgamesh*, Humbaba was a
monstrous demon who guarded the Cedar Forest. He was eventually conquered
and killed by the hero Gilgamesh and his friend and companion, Enkidu. Ultimately, the chief god Enlil punished and killed Enkidu for this deed, demonstrating that all life depends on the favor (or disfavor) of the gods.

The *Epic of Gilgamesh* is doubtless the most famous and well-studied work
of ancient Mesopotamian literature.[34] The saga recounts the heroic deeds and
adventures of Gilgamesh and Enkidu in their search for immortality.

> It is a work of adventure, but it is no less a meditation on some fundamental issues
> of human existence. The Epic explores many issues; it surely provides a Mesopo-
> tamian formulation of human predicaments and options. Most of all, the work
> grapples with issues of an existential nature. It talks about the powerful human
> drive to achieve, the value of friendship, the experience of loss, the inevitability
> of death.[35]

Gilgamesh was an actual person, king of the Sumerian city of Uruk in the early
third millennium BCE. However, the epic itself, which exists in several versions

from the early to mid-second millennium BCE, represents variations and elaborations of legends associated with his name. Gilgamesh, "like King Arthur . . . is a historical figure, though better known in legend than history."[36] And, like the Arthurian tales much later in Western Europe, scenes from the *Epic of Gilgamesh* are often seen in ancient Mesopotamian art, especially on cylinder seals. Many of these scenes include Gilgamesh battling with great beasts and encountering numerous deities who play major roles in the tale, although exact iconographic identification of several motifs remain subjects of scholarly speculation.[37]

Section of the Facade of the Eanna Temple from Uruk, ca. 1415 BCE

During the second millennium BCE, the Kassites came to power in southern Mesopotamia and occupied numerous ancient sites such as Uruk. The temple in Uruk constructed by the ruler Karaindash (or Kara-Indash), dedicated to the goddess Ishtar (Inanna or Eanna), in many ways typifies the continuity of religious beliefs and practices in ancient Mesopotamia (see Figure 2.8). The

Figure 2.8   Section of the facade of the Eanna Temple, Uruk, Iraq ca. 1415 BCE. Berlin: Vorderasiatisches Museum. Bildarchiv Preussischer Kulturbesitz / Art Resource, NY.

Kassites appear to have "very deliberately perpetuated Babylonian culture and civilization in the political, religious, and intellectual fields [and] continued the policy of building and maintaining sanctuaries."[38] The goddess Ishtar is one of the most ancient of Mesopotamian deities, and "one can speculate that by building a temple at the already ancient and storied city of Uruk, to a goddess whose importance stretches back for more than a millennium, the Kassite king was attempting to not only exploit the important natural power of such gods but to also demonstrate his legitimacy in the eyes of the local population."[39]

The molded and baked clay reliefs—a Kassite innovation—represent elongated figures of male and female deities standing frontally in recessed niches. Wearing typical horned headdresses and long robes, the figures hold overflowing vessels with parallel streams of water descending onto rounded forms (mountains?) The scalelike pattern on the robes of the male deities, and the undulating pattern on the robes of the female deities may identify them as divinities who "embody natural forces—earth and water—which underlie those of the fertility goddess Inanna, to whom the temple is dedicated."[40]

The goddess Inanna plays an important role in the *Epic of Gilgamesh* as well as in the ancient work (early to mid-second millennium BCE) known as the *Descent of Inanna to the Netherworld*, which tells of her journey to, imprisonment in, and eventual release from the realm of the dead.[41] One of the most ancient and widely venerated deities, Inanna is frequently depicted in Mesopotamian art.

Relief from the Palace of Sargon II at Khorsabad, Late Eighth Century BCE

The Assyrians came to dominance in northern Mesopotamia in the first millennium BCE and established an extensive empire controlled by powerful rulers based in several impressive cities. The city of Khorsabad (ancient Dur Sharrukin) constructed by Sargon II (r. 721–705 BCE) is an especially good example of the prestige and ambitions of these powerful rulers. The walled city, which measured about a square mile, included a ziggurat, sanctuaries for at least six deities, residential areas, and a vast elevated royal palace enriched with magnificent art works.

These include numerous relief carvings of the king and his great deeds, as well as massive guardian figures of winged human-headed bulls (*lamassu*) and winged human figures generally identified as genies, or beneficent celestial beings. One such genie is shown in Figure 2.9, a gypsum relief about 10 feet tall. The figure wears a long tufted robe, a horned headdress, armlets and bracelets, and carries a small bucket (or *situla*). The pineconelike object he holds in his right hand is customarily identified as a sprinkler, used to scatter drops of sanctified liquid in rituals of purification and immunization against evil forces.

Figure 2.9 Relief from the Palace of Sargon II, Khorsabad, Iraq, late eighth century BCE. Baghdad: Iraq Musuem. Scala / Art Resource, NY.

Numerous such relief carvings appear in Sargon's palace in Khorsabad as well as in other great Assyrian fortress citadels such as Nimrud and Ninevah. While distinctively Assyrian in style and iconography, these works also demonstrate the continuity of ancient Mesopotamian beliefs in the necessary favor of the divine forces for human well-being and success.

NOTES

1. Leo Oppenheim, *Ancient Mesopotamia: Portrait of a Dead Civilization* (Chicago: University of Chicago Press, 1977), 175.

2. C.F.B. Walker, *Cuneiform* (Berkeley: University of California Press, 1987).

3. See Milbry Polk and Angela Schuster, eds., *The Looting of the Iraq Museum, Baghdad: The Lost Legacy of Ancient Mesopotamia* (New York: Harry N. Abrams, 2005).

4. Oppenheim, especially 171–83: "Why a 'Mesopotamian Religion' Should Not Be Written."

5. Oppenheim, 180.

6. Karen Rhea Nemat-Nejat, *Daily Life in Ancient Mesopotamia* (Westport, CT: Greenwood Press, 1998), 182.

7. Nemat-Nejat, 178.

8. Nemat-Nejat, 178.

9. Nemat-Nejat, 141, 144.

10. See Alan Bernstein, *The Formation of Hell: Death and Retribution in the Ancient and Early Christian Worlds* (Ithaca, NY: Cornell University Press, 1993).

11. Nemat-Nejat, 145.

12. Nemat-Nejat, 187.

13. Nemat-Nejat, 188.

14. Nemat-Nejat, 180.

15. Nemat-Nejat, 180.

16. Victor Hurowitz, "The Mesopotamian God Image, from Womb to Tomb," *Journal of the American Oriental Society* 123, no. 1 (2003): 147–57.

17. Eiko Matsushima, "Divine Statues in Ancient Mesopotamia: Their Fashioning and Clothing and Their Interaction with the Society," in *Official Cult and Popular Religion in the Ancient Near East,* ed. Eiko Matsushima, 209–19 (Heidelberg, Germany: Universitätsverlag C. Winter, 1993).

18. Jeanny Canby, *The "Ur-Nammu" Stela* (Philadelphia: University of Pennsylvania Museum of Archaeology and Anthropology, 2001).

19. Polk and Schuster, 6.

20. Denise Schamdt-Besserat, *When Writing Met Art: From Symbol to Story* (Austin: University of Texas Press, 2007), 94.

21. The literature on cylinder seals is voluminous. Useful sources are Dominique Collon, *First Impressions: Cylinder Seals in the Ancient Near East* (London: The British Museum Press, 2005) and Edith Porada, "Why Cylinder Seals? Engraved Cylindrical Seal Stones of the Ancient Near East, Fourth to First Millennium B.C.," *The Art Bulletin* 75, no. 4 (1993): 563–82.

22. Irene Winter, "The King and the Cup: Iconography of the Royal Presentation Scene on Ur III Seals," in *Insight through Images: Studies in Honor of Edith Porada*, ed. Marilyn Kelly-Buccellati, 253–68 (Malibu, CA: Undena Publications, 1986).

23. Flemming Johansen, *Statues of Gudea—Ancient and Modern* (Copenhagen, Denmark: Akademisk Forlag, 1978).

24. Irene Winter, "'Idols of the King:' Royal Images as Recipients of Ritual Action in Ancient Mesopotamia, "*Journal of Ritual Studies* 6, no. 1 (1992): 13–42.

25. Diana McDonald, "The Warka Vase," in *The Looting of the Iraq Museum, Baghdad: The Lost Legacy of Ancient Mesopotamia*, ed. Milbry Polk and Angela Schuster (New York: Harry N. Abrams, 2005), 80.

26. McDonald, "The Warka Vase," 80.

27. Jerrold Cooper, "Sacred Marriage and Popular Cult in Ancient Mesopotamia," in *Official Cult and Popular Religion in the Ancient Near East*, ed. Eiko Matsushima, 81–96 (Heidelberg, Germany: Universitätsverlag C. Winter, 1993).

28. McDonald, "The Warka Vase," 80–81.

29. See Schamdt-Besserat, especially 41–46.

30. Nemat-Nejat, 188.

31. Nemat-Nejat, 188.

32. See John Matthews, *The World Atlas of Divination* (Boston, MA: Bulfinch Press, 1992) and Robert Temple, "An Anatomical Verification of the Reading of a Term in Extispicy," *Journal of Cuneiform Studies* 34, no. 1–2 (1982): 19–27.

33. Nemat-Nejat, 198.

34. Many translations and commentaries exist including: Andrew George, trans., *The Epic of Gilgamesh: The Babylonian Epic Poem and Other Texts in Sumerian and Akkadian* (London: Penguin, 2003), Stephen Mitchell, trans., *Gilgamesh: A New English Version* (New York: Free Press, 2004) and N. K. Sanders, trans., *The Epic of Gilgamesh* (London: Penguin, 1972).

35. Tzvi Abusch, "The Development and Meaning of the *Epic of Gilgamesh*: An Interpretive Essay,"*Journal of the American Oriental Society* 121, no. 4 (2001): 614.

36. John Gray, *Near Eastern Mythology* (London: Hamlyn, 1969), 39.

37. Wilfrid Lambert, "Gilgamesh in Literature and Art: The Second and First Millennia," in *Monsters and Demons in the Ancient and Medieval Worlds*, ed. Ann Farkas, Prudence Harper, and Evelyn Harrison, 37–52 (Mainz, Germany: Phillip von Zabern, 1987).

38. Jean-Daniel Forest and Nathalie Gallois, "Mesopotamian Art from c2000 to 330 BC," in *The Art and Architecture of Ancient Mesopotamia*, ed. Giovanni Curatola (New York: Abbeville Press, 2007), 72.

39. Diana McDonald, "From the Kassite Temple of Karaindash," in *The Looting of the Iraq Museum, Baghdad: The Lost Legacy of Ancient Mesopotamia*, ed. Milbry Polk and Angela Schuster (New York: Harry N. Abrams, 2001), 144.

40. McDonald, "Kassite Temple," 144.

41. Bernstein, 5–11, and Stephanie Dalley, *Myths from Mesopotamia: Creation, the Flood, Gilgamesh, and Others* (Oxford: Oxford University Press, 1989).

BIBLIOGRAPHY AND FURTHER READING

Abusch, Tzvi. "The Development and Meaning of the Epic of Gilgamesh: An Interpretive Essay."*Journal of the American Oriental Society* 121, no. 4 (2001): 614–22.

Aruz, Joan, and Ronald Wallenfels, eds. *Art of the First Cities: The Third Millennium B.C. from the Mediterranean to the Indus.* New Haven, CT: Yale University Press, 2003.

Bernstein, Alan. *The Formation of Hell: Death and Retribution in the Ancient and Early Christian Worlds.* Ithaca, NY: Cornell University Press, 1993.

Bertman, Stephen. *Handbook to Life in Ancient Mesopotamia.* New York: Facts on File, 2002.

Black, Jeremy, and Anthony Green. *Gods, Demons, and Symbols of Ancient Mesopotamia.* Austin: University of Texas Press, 1992.

Canby, Jeanny. *The "Ur-Nammu" Stela.* Philadelphia: University of Pennsylvania Museum of Archaeology and Anthropology, 2001.

Collon, Dominique. *Ancient Near Eastern Art.* Berkeley: University of California Press, 1995.

Collon, Dominique. *First Impressions: Cylinder Seals in the Ancient Near East.* London: The British Museum Press, 2005.

Cooper, Jerrold. "Sacred Marriage and Popular Cult in Ancient Mesopotamia." In *Official Cult and Popular Religion in the Ancient Near East,* ed. Eiko Matsushima, 81–96. Heidelberg, Germany: Universitätsverlag C. Winter, 1993.

Curatola, Giovanni, ed. *The Art and Architecture of Ancient Mesopotamia.* New York: Abbeville Press, 2007.

Dalley, Stephanie. *Myths from Mesopotamia: Creation, the Flood, Gilgamesh, and Others.* Oxford: Oxford University Press, 1989.

Downey, Susan. *Mesopotamian Religious Architecture.* Princeton, NJ: Princeton University Press, 1988.

Fairservis, Walter. *Mesopotamia, The Civilization That Rose out of Clay.* New York: MacMillan, 1964.

Farkas, Ann, Prudence Harper, and Evelyn Harrison, eds. *Monsters and Demons in the Ancient and Medieval Worlds.* Mainz, Germany: Phillip von Zabern, 1987.

Forest, Jean-Daniel, and Nathalie Gallois. "Mesopotamian Art from c2000 to 330 BC." In *The Art and Architecture of Ancient Mesopotamia,* ed. Giovanni Curatola, 65–96. New York: Abbeville Press, 2007.

Frankfurt, Henri. *The Birth of Civilization in the Near East.* Bloomington: Indiana University Press, 1951.

George, Andrew, trans. *The Epic of Gilgamesh: The Babylonian Epic Poem and Other Texts in Sumerian and Akkadian.* London: Penguin, 2003.

Gray, John. *Near Eastern Mythology.* London: Hamlyn, 1969.

Hurowitz, Victor. "The Mesopotamian God Image, from Womb to Tomb." *Journal of the American Oriental Society* 123, no. 1 (2003): 147–57.

Johansen, Flemming. *Statues of Gudea—Ancient and Modern.* Copenhagen, Denmark: Akademisk Forlag, 1978.

Kelly-Buccellati, Marilyn, ed. *Insight through Images: Studies in Honor of Edith Porada.* Malibu, CA: Undena Publications, 1986.

Lambert, Wilfrid. "Gilgamesh in Literature and Art: The Second and First Millennia." In *Monsters and Demons in the Ancient and Medieval Worlds,* ed. Ann Farkas,

Prudence Harper, and Evelyn Harrison, 37–52. Mainz, Germany: Phillip von Zabern, 1987.

Lloyd, Seton. *The Art of the Ancient Near East*. London: Thames and Hudson, 1961.

Margueron, Jean-Claude. *Mesopotamia*. New York: World, 1965.

Matsushima, Eiko. "Divine Statues in Ancient Mesopotamia: Their Fashioning and Clothing and Their Interaction with the Society." In *Official Cult and Popular Religion in the Ancient Near East*, ed. Eiko Matsushima, 209–19. Heidelberg, Germany: Universitätsverlag C. Winter, 1993.

Matsushima, Eiko, ed. *Official Cult and Popular Religion in the Ancient Near East*. Heidelberg, Germany: Universitätsverlag C. Winter, 1993.

Matthews, John, ed. *The World Atlas of Divination*. Boston: Bulfinch Press, 1992.

McDonald, Diana. "From the Kassite Temple of Karaindash." In *The Looting of the Iraq Museum, Baghdad: The Lost Legacy of Ancient Mesopotamia*, ed. Milbry Polk and Angela Schuster, 144–45. New York: Harry N. Abrams, 2001.

McDonald, Diana. "The Warka Vase." In *The Looting of the Iraq Museum, Baghdad: The Lost Legacy of Ancient Mesopotamia*, ed. Milbry Polk and Angela Schuster, 80–81. New York: Harry N. Abrams, 2001.

Mitchell, Stephen, trans. *Gilgamesh: A New English Version*. New York: Free Press, 2004.

Nemat-Nejat, Karen Rhea. *Daily Life in Ancient Mesopotamia*. Westport, CT: Greenwood Press, 1998.

Oates, Joan. *Babylon*. London: Thames and Hudson, 1979.

Oppenheim, Leo. *Ancient Mesopotamia: Portrait of a Dead Civilization*. Chicago: University of Chicago Press, 1977.

Parrot, André. *The Arts of Assyria*. New York: Golden Press, 1961.

Polk, Milbry, and Angela Schuster, eds. *The Looting of the Iraq Museum, Baghdad: The Lost Legacy of Ancient Mesopotamia*. New York: Harry N. Abrams, 2005.

Porada, Edith. "Why Cylinder Seals? Engraved Cylindrical Seal Stones of the Ancient Near East, Fourth to First Millennium B.C." *The Art Bulletin* 75, no. 4 (1993): 563–82.

Roaf, Michael. *Cultural Atlas of Mesopotamia and the Ancient Near East*. New York: Facts on File, 1990.

Sanders, N.K., trans. *The Epic of Gilgamesh*. London: Penguin, 1972.

Schamdt-Besserat, Denise. *When Writing Met Art: From Symbol to Story*. Austin: University of Texas Press, 2007.

Temple, Robert. "An Anatomical Verification of the Reading of a Term in Extispicy." *Journal of Cuneiform Studies* 34, no. 1–2 (1982): 19–27.

Van de Mieroop, Marc. *A History of the Ancient Near East, ca. 3000–323 BC*. Malden, MA: Blackwell, 2004.

Walker, C.F.B. *Cuneiform*. Berkeley: University of California Press, 1987.

Winter, Irene. "'Idols of the King:' Royal Images as Recipients of Ritual Action in Ancient Mesopotamia." *Journal of Ritual Studies* 6, no. 1 (1992): 13–42.

Winter, Irene. "The King and the Cup: Iconography of the Royal Presentation Scene on Ur III Seals." In *Insight through Images: Studies in Honor of Edith Porada*, ed. Marilyn Kelly-Buccellati, 253–68. Malibu, CA: Undena Publications, 1986.

−3−

Religion in Ancient Egypt

ORIGINS AND DEVELOPMENT

Evidence for the development of civilization in ancient Egypt dates at least back to the fourth and fifth millennium BCE. From these early origins, and for close to 3,000 years thereafter, ancient Egyptian civilization developed and maintained a remarkable degree of continuity. Religion consistently played a central, critical role in society. When the Greek historian Herodotus visited Egypt in the middle of the fifth century BCE, he was extremely impressed by the ancient monuments and expressed his opinion that the ancient Egyptians must have been exceedingly, if not excessively, religious. The importance of religion is abundantly demonstrated in the surviving art and architectural monuments of ancient Egypt, the majority of which were designed for, or which can be seen to reflect, religious purposes. "Egypt is an outstanding example of a religious tradition pervading a civilization continuously for well over 3000 years, the inner cohesion being supported by the geography and by long periods of relative isolation."[1]

The history of civilization in ancient Egypt, centered around the fertile and longest river in the world, the Nile, is traditionally divided into a series of distinct but continuous periods. Although specific dating for ancient Egyptian history is extremely problematic and often disputed, it is generally thought that what is termed the Pre-Dynastic period began ca. 3500 BCE. Toward the end of this era the separate civilizations of upper (southern) and lower (northern) Egypt were geographically and politically united under single rulership. This marked the beginning of the Dynastic period (ca. 2920 BCE) when political leadership was held by a series of supreme rulers, or pharaohs. The 31 dynasties of ancient Egyptian history began in the Early Dynastic period (ca. 2920–2575 BCE) with the first three dynasties of rulers. The subsequent long centuries of Egyptian civilization are then traditionally divided into the Old, Middle, and New Kingdoms, with intermediate periods between these eras. The exact chronology is a matter of scholarly divergence.[2] The Old Kingdom (ca. 2575–ca. 2134 BCE), of the fourth through eighth dynasties, is often considered to be the critical foundational period during which belief systems were developed in a codified form and the classic, traditional styles of religious art and architecture evolved. The Middle Kingdom (ca. 1240–1640 BCE), of the 11th through 14th dynasties, was followed by the period of the New Kingdom (ca. 1550–1070 BCE), of the 18th through 20th dynasties. During the subsequent later eras, Egyptian civilization entered a Late Dynastic period, was eventually conquered by the Persians in the mid-sixth century BCE, by Alexander the Great in 332 BCE, and by the Romans in 30 BCE. Needless to say, this brief outline hardly does justice to the length and complexity of Egyptian history, which includes periods of prosperity and stability as well as times of social and political upheaval, internal conflicts among rival rulers, periods of foreign control (for example by the Asiatic peoples known as the Hyksos from ca. 1630–1540), and periods of territorial conquests and warfare waged by numerous Egyptian rulers (for example with the Nubian kingdoms in the south.)

The history, art, and religion of ancient Egypt have intrigued and fascinated scholars for many centuries. An important and early summary of the overall chronology of ancient Egyptian history, which provided the basis for the division into periods and dynasties used today, was composed in the late third century BCE by an Egyptian historian and priest named Manetho. His major work, written in Greek, is known as the *Aegyptiaca* (*History of Egypt*) and, like the much earlier king-lists found inscribed in temples or on papyrus scrolls, provides a selected chronology of Egyptian rulers from the very ancient period to the fourth century BCE. Manetho's division of Egyptian rulers into dynasties has had an enormous impact on later historians, although it should be noted that his use of the term *dynasty* includes groups of rulers not necessarily related by birth.

A few centuries before Manetho, the Greek historian Herodotus visited Egypt and recorded his descriptions and impressions in the second book of his *Histories*. Later Greek and Roman historians, such as Strabo and Diodorus Siculus, visited Egypt in the middle of the first century BCE, and their writings are significant sources of information about the ancient monuments and customs surviving into the late period of Egyptian history. Ultimately, as part of the vast territory of the Roman Empire, Egypt became Christianized, and then later (during the seventh century CE), came under Arab Islamic domination. "Eventually, Egypt's temples and other monuments of her pharaonic past became as mysterious to the Egyptians themselves as they were to the outside world."[3]

Very significantly also, as the spoken and written languages of ancient Egypt were replaced by Coptic, which became the language of the Egyptian

Christian church, and later by Arabic, knowledge of the writing systems of old Egypt was entirely lost. "The evidence suggests that by the end of the fifth century (CE) knowledge of how to read and write the old scripts was extinct. . . . The break in knowledge was complete. The hieroglyphs were fully surrendered to the larger myth of ancient Egypt—the land of strange customs and esoteric wisdom."[4] Although important attempts were made by some medieval Arabic scholars to decipher the hieroglyphic writings,[5] throughout the Middle Ages Egypt was "a source of little more than stories and legends, which grew ever more fabulous as they spread."[6] The European rediscovery, in the early 15th century, of a manuscript known as the *Hieroglyphica*, attributed to Horapollo (an author of the mid-fifth century CE, purportedly one of the last members of the ancient Egyptian priesthood, or a scholar/grammarian) resulted in a great surge of interest in ancient Egypt among Renaissance scholars.[7] Printed editions of the *Hieroglyphica* were first produced in the early 16th century, followed by numerous later editions and translations. This text, "combining a distinctly Greek point of view with a smattering of knowledge of the Egyptian language and culture . . . was taken up by early typographers and printers. . . . whose extrapolation of the hieroglyphic tradition led to investigation of the symbolic properties" of the ancient symbols.[8] Hieroglyphs (the term itself comes from Greek for "sacred writing"; the ancient Egyptians used the term *medu netcher*: "the gods' words") were thus associated with magical symbols of highly esoteric meaning and complexity.[9]

Greater advances in knowledge and study of ancient Egypt date only to the 18th and 19th century with a series of European scholars who traveled extensively in Egypt specifically to document and describe the ancient monuments. The military campaigns of Napoleon Bonaparte (1769–1821) in the late 18th and early 19th century mark a critical point in the growth of Egyptology as an academic field. Napoleon's "scholars systematically studied and recorded monuments and artifacts in a manner which was truly unprecedented . . . [ultimately resulting in] nothing short of a mania for all things Egyptian, and adventurers, antiquarians, artists and scholars began to travel to Egypt in increasing numbers."[10]

A major breakthrough came in the early 19th century with the work of the French scholar Jean-François Champollion (1790–1832). His successful decipherment, in 1822–24, of the three parallel texts inscribed on the late first century BCE Rosetta Stone (discovered in 1799) paved the way for the continued burgeoning of Egyptian studies through the 19th and 20th centuries, up to the present day. "With Champollion's decipherment of the hieroglyphs . . . Egyptology changed dramatically from a speculative exercise to a scholarly discipline."[11]

Egyptology (or the study of ancient Egypt) is a distinctive and multidisciplinary academic field whose chief adherents have been and continue to be archaeologists, art historians, historians, historians of religion, linguists, epigraphers, and paleographers, among others. Scholarship on ancient Egypt continues to flourish; even so, there is still much to be discovered and learned about the history, religion, art, and culture of this ancient civilization.

PRINCIPAL BELIEFS AND KEY PRACTICES

Abundant visual and textual materials exist for the study of ancient Egyptian religion, and copious scholarship has been devoted to defining and understanding the beliefs and practices of this civilization, which endured and flourished for so many millennia. Religion was an absolutely fundamental aspect of Egyptian civilization throughout its lengthy history, influencing and reflecting all aspects of life from politics to social structure to daily routine. A concern for stability, the performance of proper actions to maintain the cosmic and earthly order (*maat*), belief in an afterlife, and the veneration of a multitude of diverse deities all characterize religious beliefs and practices in ancient Egypt. Ancient Egyptian religion has been described as being stable and conservative but at the same time also highly fluid and flexible. "Religious beliefs did not remain constant over the three millennia but were continually reinterpreted."[12] Nevertheless, in general it may be said that the core beliefs of the ancient Egyptians were centered around the concept of life after death, the veneration of multiple deities, and the role of the rulers (pharaohs) in relationship to these deities. Egyptian religion represents "a very complicated and sophisticated set of . . . beliefs . . . a highly developed concept of the divine."[13]

The complexity of ancient Egyptian religion is perhaps best demonstrated by the fact that there exists no one standard theological text or set of scriptures that provides consistent and fundamental details about their ideas and beliefs. "Egyptian religion was not one of revelation; its doctrines were not ascribed to any one divinely inspired intermediary and teacher akin to Christ, Mohammed, or the Buddha."[14] Thus, a variety of texts, popular during different eras and promulgated in different regions of ancient Egypt, include diverse creation myths, different cosmologies, and different pantheons of major and lesser deities. This only "serves to emphasize the interconnected and yet seemingly contradictory system of beliefs referred to as ancient Egyptian religion."[15]

Gods and Goddesses

Egyptian religion was polytheistic, but it is important to always bear in mind that "what we categorize as polytheism was for the ancients a way of seeing all forms of life and nature as sacred."[16] Some Egyptian deities were closely associated with natural phenomena such as air, water, earth, darkness, the sun, moon, and various stars. Other deities were associated with abstract ideas such as divine speech, divine energy, and divine knowledge. Some gods and goddesses were worshiped in specific regions, whereas others were of more widespread or national veneration. Some were associated with specific cult centers, such as the temples of Thebes, Memphis, Edfu, and Heliopolis. Others deities became prominent because of their veneration by specific pharaohs or dynasties. Some deities were associated with events in human life, such as birth and death. Funerary deities such as Anubis (overseer of embalming rituals) and Osiris (lord of the underworld) were especially important. Some deities were associated with specific professions (such as Thoth, the patron of scribes) or with events such as farming and the harvest. Other deities were worshiped in households or as personal protectors. The associations of the multitude of Egyptian deities were vast and diverse.

Egyptian deities were frequently visualized in human (anthropomorphic) form, in animal (zoomorphic) form, in the form of composite animals (combining features of more than one animal), and in zooanthropomorphic form (combining human and animal features and qualities.) As the deities were seen as symbols or manifestations of divine forces and powers, and the "Egyptians believed that some mystery was necessary to preserve the dimensions of divine power, their visual images and written descriptions of the gods pointed only to some aspects of the deities and were not intended to detail every aspect."[17] Moreover, the attributes and forms of various deities were often blended, or syncretized, representing a process of ongoing transformation. Many deities shared their roles and associations with other deities.

Egyptian society was highly stratified, and religious practices reflect this as well. The "religious practices of the privileged classes differed markedly from those of the mass of ordinary people. . . . Egyptian temples were intended not for popular worship but to provide a place where the king could commune with the gods . . . The abstract religious concepts associated with large temples would have been incomprehensible to the majority of ordinary people."[18] Yet the state religion (represented by the temple, priests, and pharaohs) and popular religion (represented by the day-to-day practices of the common people) were closely interrelated. "The two existed side by side in harmony, as the various minor deities worshiped by the people were believed to be local manifestations of either the overall state god or a god of one of the major cults."[19]

Although Egyptian religion was generally characterized by a polytheistic embrace of diverse cults, attempts to change these traditions were dramatically and briefly undertaken during the reign of the pharaoh Amenhotep IV—better known as Akhenaten (ca. 1352–ca. 1336 BCE). During this time, often known as the Armana period (after the modern name of the city he founded as his capital, Akhetaten), the ruler promoted sole worship of Aten, the god of the sun. Aten was one of the several forms of the sun god previously venerated in Egypt; however, Akhenaten disallowed worship of any other deities in favor of the supreme Aten. He took on the name Akhenaten ("Beneficence of the Aten") and called his new capital Akhetaten ("Horizon of the Aten"). This revolutionary form of monotheism represented a dramatic break with the past as well as a notable dismantling of the priestly offices. Akhenaten declared himself to be the sole priest of Aten and the only intermediary through whom the deity could be approached. There is much speculation about the nature of what surely were both complex theological and political motivations on the part of Akhenaten.

His era also represents a brief change in style in Egyptian artistic traditions. New facial and figural types appear in art, especially in representations of the pharaoh himself, as well as his family. Akhenaten appears to have had a unique physiognomy, with an elongated head, paunchy stomach, and enlarged hips. He is often portrayed in scenes with the sun disk, Aten, from which issue multiple light rays terminating in hands holding ankh symbols (a T-shaped form with a looped top—the symbol of life) (see Figure 3.1). Akhenaten's new religion was short-lived, and of little lasting influence. Soon after his death, the ancient traditions quickly returned.

The Pharaoh and the Priests

Akhenaten's declaration of himself as the sole priest of the one god, Aten, was certainly a revolutionary break with previous Egyptian practices. Even so, throughout the lengthy history of civilization in Egypt, secular and spiritual authority were always closely intertwined. This is perhaps best seen in the prominent role played by the pharaohs, who functioned not only as earthly authorities but also as critical links to the divine realms. It is often said that the Egyptian pharaohs were venerated as living divinities, as gods resident on

Figure 3.1 Pharaoh Akhenaten and Queen Nefertiti with their daughters, limestone relief, ca. 1345 BCE. Berlin: Agyptisches Museum. Bildarchiv Preussischer Kulturbesitz / Art Resource, NY

earth. In some periods, this was certainly the case. Particular pharaohs, such as the extremely powerful and long-lived Ramses II, often called Ramses the Great (ca. 1279–ca. 1212 BCE) were especially directive in promoting their divine status. Ramses II actively encouraged worship of himself, based at his cult temple in Abu Simbel, which was adorned with numerous impressive images of himself as the living god (see Figure 3.2).

Nevertheless, the Egyptians' perception of the pharaohs and their status underwent several changes during the millennia of their history. It would probably be most accurate to say that kingship, in itself, was regarded as a divine office. The pharaohs were clearly mortal human beings like all others, but in holding the divine office of ruler, they had a unique relationship with the gods and a critical role to play in maintaining stability and order in the earthly realms as well. The pharaohs combined human and divine attributes and associations while on earth, and they were believed to become fully identified with the divine after death. This is well attested throughout Egyptian history by the vast number of tombs and mortuary temples created for the afterlife well-being of the rulers.

The pharaoh was also considered to be "nominally the high priest of every god in every temple throughout the country."[20] Pharaohs thus functioned simultaneously as the head of the state and of the church. "It was the role of the king to ensure the beneficence of the gods and thereby ensure peace, harmony, and prosperity in Egypt. The king was essential to universal order, and it was his duty to maintain *maat* at all times."[21] Functionally however, the pharaoh

Figure 3.2   Great Temple of Ramses II, Abu Simbel, Egypt, ca. 1279–1213 BCE. 2009 Jupiterimages Corporation.

could not be present at all temples and ritual sites, so priests were needed to carry out the many rites associated with Egyptian religious practices.

The word *priest* is customarily used to translate the ancient Egyptian term *hem netjer,* which more accurately means "servant of the god." Temples in ancient Egypt were often extremely vast complexes and involved the employ-ment of hundreds of people as servants of deities. Many of these people were involved with various duties required to maintain the prosperity and security of the temples. Temples served as important economic centers for their regions. Workshops, storerooms, libraries, and schools were often associated with tem-ples. The rituals specifically involved with tending to the needs of the god, such as the daily rites and offerings, were carried out only by the elite and specially trained among the many priests. In addition, each temple had a high priest, an office that was usually held by royal appointment. High priests acted on behalf of the pharaoh and they

> had closer contact with the cult statue of the god than anyone else in the tem-ple complex. It is likely that only the High Priest would have been allowed to stand before the image of the god in the shrine. Temple reliefs illustrate what was expected of the High Priest, but because the presence of the king was still consid-ered necessary in the temple, even if only symbolically, it was the ruler who was shown performing the rituals.[22]

Although fewer in number than men, women also served as priestesses in the temples. The title *hemet netjer* ("wife of the god") was used to describe these important women. They were often married to priests, and some women also served as high priests, especially in association with the worship of the goddess Hathor, a fertility deity.

Death and the Afterlife

Some of the oldest surviving archaeological evidence from ancient Egypt indicates that concerns for proper burial and hopes for life after death devel-oped extremely early. A belief in the afterlife is a key component in under-standing Egyptian religion and a factor that is consistently demonstrated in visual and textual evidence throughout the millennia. To some modern minds, it might seem as if the Egyptians had an almost morbid fascination with death, but it may be far more accurate to see this within the context of the unique geographic situation of this civilization based on the banks of the Nile river. In ancient times, the yearly floods of the Nile brought renewed fertility to the land, and represented a cycle of hoped-for regeneration of resources after periods of inundation. Witnessing these cycles surely must have inspired the ancient Egyptians to regard the processes of birth and death as consistently renewed and naturally occurring events, operative in all related arenas of human, plant, and animal life. Just as the fertile soil of the Nile was refreshed yearly, so could humans and animals expect to be renewed in the afterlife.

It is important to note, however, that the Egyptian belief in the afterlife is not the same as the concept of reincarnation. Other ancient world religions (such as Hinduism) visualize the cycle of death and rebirth as being repeatable through a series of potential stages in a progressive (or digressive) sequence. The ancient Egyptians, in contrast, appear to have believed that one's life on earth was followed by an eternal afterlife, which ideally mirrored the finest aspects of one's earthly life. Appropriate and ethical behavior in one's earthly life would ensure one of successful passage to the eternal afterlife.

It appears that the ancient Egyptians, regardless of social class, believed in the afterlife. However, the elite members of the society were those who were best able to afford grand burials and make elaborate preparations for their after-life experiences. It was believed that "the journey into the Afterlife was no mean feat—all manner of demons and hazardous obstacles had to be bypassed and overcome."[23] Thus, much textual and visual evidence demonstrates the importance of proper preparation for death as well as the challenges to be faced in the passage to the afterlife. The afterlife was visualized as an idyllic version of life on earth, a realm in which individuals would become closer to the gods. The pharaohs, of course, were necessarily expected to enter into a happy afterlife in eternal communion with the deities with whom they were already closely associated, thus continuing to ensure order and balance in the world and cosmos.

The practice of mummification (embalming and wrapping the bodies of the deceased) was an important aspect of Egyptian funerary religion, afforded primarily by the wealthy classes.

> In very early times, the Egyptians buried their dead without coffins in simple pit graves dug into the desert sands. The hot, dry sand, which came into contact with the bodies, desiccated them and acted as a natural preservative. The remarkable preservation of these natural "mummies" must have been observed by the ancient Egyptians and may have contributed to early religious beliefs in survival after death.[24]

The concern for preserving the body to ensure the afterlife ultimately developed into the elaborate process of mummification, which involved specific rituals and a series of stages of purification. For those able to afford the most elaborate techniques, the process often involved removal of selected internal organs (subject to decay and putrefaction), which were embalmed separately and placed near the body in special vessels, known as canopic jars. These were often decorated with images of the deities associated with these internal organs, the human headed Imset (for the liver), the baboon-headed Hapy (for the lungs), the jackal-headed Duamutef (for the stomach), and the falcon-headed Kebehsenuf (for the intestines) (see Figure 3.3).

The body of the deceased was believed to serve as a vessel for the spirit, soul, or "etheric double" of the body, the ka.[25] "The ka was thought to come into being at the birth of an individual. . . . ka is often translated as 'spirit' or 'vital

Figure 3.3   Painted wooden canopic jars, ca. 700 BCE. London: The Trustees of The British Museum / Art Resource, NY.

force,' as in the creative life force of an individual . . . It was believed that the *ka* required food and drink, so offerings were made to it for as long as possible after death."[26] Additionally, the *ba* (often translated as "soul") and the *akh* (often translated as "spirit") were closely related components in the afterlife of the deceased. The *ba* "was considered more mobile than the *ka* and it enabled the dead person to move about in the Afterlife."[27] The *akh* was also believed to fly to the otherworld in the form of a human-headed bird. Great care was taken to ensure that all elements of the spirit or soul of the deceased were acceptably prepared and would thus continue to exist in the afterlife.

TRADITIONAL ART AND ARCHITECTURAL FORMS

A vast majority of the surviving art and monumental architecture produced in ancient Egypt was designed for religious purposes. The hierarchical nature of the society, the emphasis on death and the afterlife, and the importance of maintaining the cosmic order permeated all aspects of Egyptian society. The great tombs built for the pharaohs, the massive temples built for the major gods and goddesses, and the shrines created for local deities all give evidence of the pervasive nature of Egyptian religion. The many surviving works of art from ancient Egypt more than indicate that "the role of representational art was closely interwoven with the religious beliefs of the ancient Egyptians and often the one cannot be understood without reference to the other."[28]

Even so, to modern eyes, the arts of ancient Egypt can often seem impenetrable, confusing, and conventionally stylized. Most all figures of gods or humans or animals are presented in profile; they appear to follow standard conventions but at the same time may include "an embarrassment of iconographic riches," in the form of signs and symbols, which are difficult to decipher and understand, even for specialists.[29] The Egyptians appear to have developed their artistic conventions very early (in the Pre-Dynastic period) and maintained them—with slight divergence—throughout their lengthy history. This is not to say that Egyptian art is static and unchanging, but it surely is the case that the forms of visual presentation demonstrate a remarkable coherency.

Tombs and the Funerary Arts

Surely, among the most well-known monuments from ancient Egypt are the pyramids at Giza (see Figure 3.4). These remarkable structures, which date to the Old Kingdom period (ca. 2500 BCE) have fascinated travelers and scholars for centuries. They were considered to be one of the Seven Wonders of the ancient world, and to the present day continue to be a powerful symbol of the achievements of ancient Egyptian civilization.

The architectural form of the pyramid actually represents the culmination of a series of earlier stages. Rectangular stone or brick structures known as mastabas (from the Arabic word for "bench") were originally erected over grave sites. A series of these platforms placed atop each other in diminishing sizes

Figure 3.4 The Pyramids at Giza, Egypt, ca. 2500 BCE. 2009 Jupiterimages Corporation.

led to the stepped pyramid form. The smooth sides of the pyramids at Giza (originally encased in gleaming white limestone) also mimic the shape of the *ben-ben* stone, a symbol of the sun god, Ra. "Both ben-ben and pyramid may have symbolized the rays of the sun . . . the pyramid is thus the immaterial made material. . . . a simulacrum of both the mound of primeval earth and the weightless rays of sunlight, a union of heaven and earth that transforms the divine king and ensures the divine rule."[30]

The pyramids at Giza took about 75 years to construct. They served as tombs for the pharaohs Khufu (r. ca. 2551–2528 BCE), Khafre (r. ca. 2520—2494 BCE), and Menkaure (r. ca. 2490–2472 BCE). They also served as symbols for the sun god Ra. The pharaohs were considered to be sons and incarnations of Ra; thus their monumental tombs with attached mortuary temples (for offerings and rituals) were the centerpieces of a vast complex of other related structures, ramps, causeways, smaller pyramids, and mastabas of other royals and nobles as well.

The conspicuous nature of the pyramids and the vast amounts of treasures contained deep within them, in the tomb chambers of the pharaohs, provided immediate temptations for grave robbers. This was such a serious problem that although pyramids on a smaller scale continued to be constructed periodically through ancient Egyptian history, new forms of tombs became popular after the Old Kingdom period. Most notable are the rock-cut tombs tunneled deep into cliffs in the Valley of the Kings near Thebes.[31] Thebes became an important city especially during the New Kingdom period, and the remote Valley of the Kings contains the burial sites of numerous rulers. These take the form of chambers and corridors tunneled into the rocky cliffs. Although great efforts were often made to conceal the entrances to these tombs, they were ultimately robbed of all, if not major portions of, their grave goods with the exception of the Tomb of Tutankhamun (ca. 1336–ca. 1327 BCE).

The discovery and excavation of the Tomb of Tutankhamun in the early 1920s was a major event in 20th-century archaeology and caused another great revival of interest in all things Egyptian. The wonderful things discovered within this tomb yet again demonstrate the surpassing concern of the ancient Egyptians in making provisions for the afterlife, guaranteeing that the deceased would continue to enjoy the comforts of earthly life, and ensuring the preservation of the deceased body.

King Tut (as he is known popularly today) was buried with immense riches in spite of the fact that he was a short-lived and relatively minor ruler. His mummy was placed within an elaborate sarcophagus in a gold coffin, within two other gilded wooden coffins. A golden mask was placed over the face of the mummy (see Figure 3.5). Richly decorated furniture (beds, chairs, couches, and stools), lamps, torches, musical instruments, swords, daggers, shields, archery equipment, food containers, wine vessels, and writing and gaming equipment were all found in the tomb. The colorful wall paintings depict Tut's journey to the afterlife and his meetings with numerous deities. A vast amount of outstanding and lavish jewelry was also provided for the ruler in the afterlife. Many of these examples are enriched with symbols and images that reinforce the message of his kingly divinity and rule, such as the elaborate pectoral (large pendant) of gold and precious stones (see Plate 5). The king is shown in a disk at the top being crowned by two deities. This moon disk is supported by the lunar crescent, which sits atop a boat holding the symbolic eye of Horus. This in turn is supported by a winged scarab (symbol of the sun god) holding the lotus and papyrus symbols of upper and lower Egypt. Two cobras wearing solar disks symbolize Egypt's strength. The overall impression given by the many objects enshrined with this deceased ruler is one of power and confidence, themes that are repeated in Egyptian art generally.

Figure 3.5 Gold Mask of Tutankhamun, ca. 1336–1327 BCE. Cairo: Egyptian Museum. Scala / Art Resource, NY.

Temples

Ancient Egyptian temples fall into two main and related categories: mortuary temples and temples dedicated to the worship of specific deities. Mortuary temples functioned as places where rituals were performed and offerings were made to deceased rulers, whereas temples dedicated to specific deities functioned as cult centers and dwelling places for the gods. It has been remarked that "the traditional division of temples into the categories of 'mortuary' and 'divine' is a false one [because] the functions and symbolic characteristics of all Egyptian temples were both too varied and too intertwined to support this distinction," thus, it is wise to see these two types of temples as closely related aspects of ancient Egyptian religious beliefs and practices.[32]

"The beginnings of the temple in Egypt are as shrouded in mystery as any aspect of that civilization's ancient origins."[33] Recent excavations at the site of Heirakonpolis (ca. 3500 BCE) have revealed evidence of an enclosed rectangular structure and shrine for the falcon god Horus, a deity closely associated with the later pharaohs. Horus was also worshiped at the Early Dynastic site of Abydos, where ancient festivals in honor of the rulers appear to have taken place as well. This demonstrates the early and close association of the pharaohs with the deities, as is also shown, for example, in the mortuary temples of the Old Kingdom rulers who were entombed in the great pyramids at Giza as incarnations of the sun god Ra.

Hundreds of Egyptian temples were constructed through the long duration of the civilization, and study of these structures is often complicated by the fact that many continued in use for centuries, and were progressively altered and enlarged by successions of pharaohs whose relationship with the deities required their continued attention to these structures.

> As the interface between the divine and human spheres, the Egyptian temple served as a theatre in which symbolic ritual dramas were enacted. Here the myriad gods and goddesses of Egyptian belief were fed, clothed and reassured that justice, order and balance were being preserved through the ritual services performed by the pharaoh and the priests who functioned as his appointed agents. In return, the gods gave life to the land and upheld Egypt's ordained place in the cosmos. In one sense, the Egyptian temple was the source of power by which all of Egyptian society ran.[34]

EXAMPLES

The Temples of Amun at Luxor and Karnak

The related temples at Luxor and Karnak are extremely impressive testimonials to the significance and continuity of religious beliefs and practices in ancient Egypt (see Figures 3.6, 3.7, and 3.8). Located on the east bank of the Nile River less than two miles distant from one another, both temples were begun during the Middle Kingdom period but underwent centuries of rebuilding and additions so that the majority of what can be seen today at these vast complexes primarily dates to the New Kingdom period and especially to the prosperous era of the 18th Dynasty (ca. 1550–ca. 1295 BCE). Typical of Egyptian temple complexes, the many buildings were designed to provide not only facilities for the worship of the sun god Amun (or Amun-Ra) but also facilities for scholarship and priestly training, workshops for art production, libraries and archives, store rooms, and provisions for the various economic functions performed by temples. A series of pharaohs contributed to the enlargement and enrichment of these temples over the centuries, adding courtyards, obelisks, shrines, corridors, gates (pylons), numerous statues and relief carvings, and halls (some with multitudes of columns known as hypostyle halls) so that the effect of these monumental complexes is quite awesome in scale and extent. Indeed, the temple at Karnak is said to be the largest temple complex ever constructed in human history, covering close to 250 acres.

Both temples were designed to function as residences for the sun god and to facilitate veneration of this deity. The much larger temple at Karnak was considered the official residence of the god, while the more compact temple at Luxor was a site that the god visited symbolically, once a year, in a grand pageant known as the Opet festival, in which the cult statues of Amun, his wife, Mut, and their son, Khonsu, were taken out of the temple and placed in highly decorated boats for their ceremonial journey on the Nile to the temple

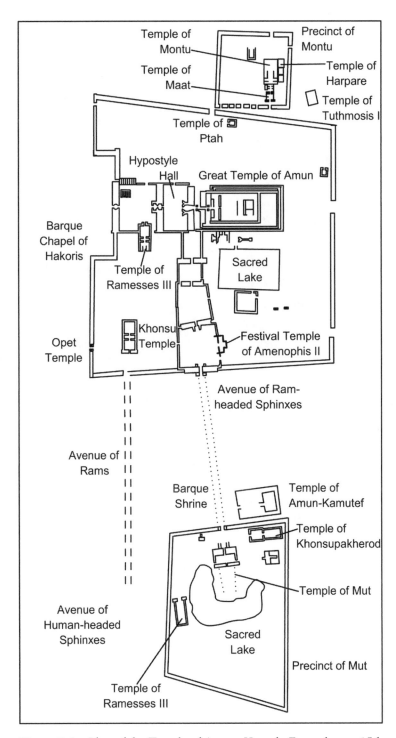

Figure 3.6 Plan of the Temple of Amun, Karnak, Egypt, begun 15th century BCE. Courtesy of Ricochet Productions.

Figure 3.7 Temple of Amun, Karnak, Egypt, 14th to 13th century BCE. Holgs / Dreamstime.com.

Figure 3.8 Temple of Amun, Karnak, Egypt, 14th century BCE. Cmvsm / Dreamstime.com.

at Luxor, where they resided for a short period. The two temples are also linked by an avenue of sphinxes that was used for ceremonial and processional purposes as well.

The Opet festival became especially popular in the New Kingdom period and could last up to several weeks. Festivities included processions, dancing, singing, music, acrobatics, sacrificial gifts, and offerings, all for the enjoyment of the gods. The festival was associated with birth, renewal, and divine vitality, critical for the prosperity and stability of the country. Occasions such as these grand festivals were opportunities for the public to witness and participate in some capacities; however, the high degree of stratification in Egyptian society is also reflected in the religious practices and temple layouts. As dwellings for the gods, the temples mirrored the hierarchy of the society. Access to the inner areas and private shrine rooms, where the gods actually resided, was possible only for the pharaohs and the priests.

The Pharaoh-Queen Hatshepsut

Most Egyptian pharaohs were men. Although the ancient Egyptians worshiped many female deities, and women appear to have been highly esteemed and played significant roles in Egyptian society—they functioned as priestesses and are frequently illustrated in art in positions of prominence—the role of the pharaoh was traditionally a male office.[35] A notable exception to this took place during the reign of Queen Hatshepsut (ca. 1479–ca. 1458 BCE), who ruled Egypt for over 20 years, first as regent for her young nephew/step-son (Tuthmosis III, ca. 1479–1425 BCE), and, after declaring herself king, co-ruling with him for another 14 years while maintaining the position of supreme royal authority.

Early in her reign, she began to supervise the construction of an impressive mortuary temple for herself, which also served as a site for her to worship the gods during her lifetime (see Figure 3.9). Work on this impressive monument took upwards of 15 years. It stands at the base of the cliffs at Deir el-Bahari, opposite the Nile from the Temple of Amun at Karnak. It is one of the best preserved of New Kingdom royal funerary temples and includes shrines to Amun, Hathor, and Anubis, as well as memorials of Hatshepsut and her father, Thutmose I (r. 1524–1518 BCE). Distinctive in some elements of style and layout, it was designed in multiple ascending levels with three broad colonnaded courtyards linked by ramps, and was originally approached along a causeway lined with sphinxes. The queen stated that she built the temple as a garden for the god Amun, hence, in her time the courtyards would have been lovely garden areas filled with exotic and fragrant shrubs and trees.

Numerous statues, paintings, and reliefs depict the queen and her achievements, with an emphasis on her rightful and divinely ordained position as pharaoh. In some instances, she is shown in male form, wearing all the traditional

Figure 3.9 Mortuary Temple of Queen Hatshepsut, Deir el-Bahari, Egypt, ca. 1479–1458 BCE. 2009 Jupiterimages Corporation.

Figure 3.10 Queen Hatshepsut with the Goddess Seshat, relief, Red Chapel of Hatshepsut, Karnak, Egypt ca. 1479–1458 BCE. Werner Forman / Art Resource, NY.

regalia of male kingship (including an elaborate headdress and official false beard) and engaging in all the official activities associated with pharaonic duties. She was a great patron of the arts and added her contributions to the temple at Karnak as well, including several obelisks and a chapel containing reliefs depicting her as a crowned male ruler accompanied by various deities (see Figure 3.10). The close relationship of the rulers and the gods, the importance of maintaining power and stability, and the concern for perpetuity in the afterlife are all traditional themes in Egyptian art well demonstrated by the works associated with the remarkable queen-pharaoh Hatshepsut.

The *Papyrus of Ani* (*Book of the Dead*), ca. 1275–1250 BCE

The *Papyrus of Ani* is an excellent and well-studied example of a funerary scroll containing text and illustrations to the Egyptian *Book of the Dead*. It is made of papyrus—the typical writing material of ancient Egypt—created from the stalks of the reedlike papyrus plant commonly found on the banks of the Nile. The scroll is slightly more than 1 foot high and was originally about 78 feet long; it was cut into 37 sheets in the late 19th century after its discovery in Thebes and its purchase by the British Museum (where it remains today) (see Plate 6).

Various versions of the *Book of the Dead* became extremely popular in ancient Egypt during the New Kingdom period. These illustrated scrolls were customarily placed within the coffin or tomb of the deceased and contain texts and pictures offering guidance for the afterlife. The *Book of the Dead* represents a very lengthy tradition of funerary literature in ancient Egypt. During the Old Kingdom era, pyramid texts were inscribed in royal tombs giving directions to the ruler and his family for proper conduct and what to expect in the afterlife. Later on, from about 2100 BCE, coffin texts became popular, inscribed within sarcophagi. By the New Kingdom period, coffin texts were gradually replaced by the *Book of the Dead*. The *Papyrus of Ani* dates to the New Kingdom period, ca. 1275–1250 BCE, and was produced for an important scribe of Thebes, named Ani (or Any). It is written in cursive-style hieroglyphs and extensively illustrated with painted scenes showing Ani's after-death experiences.

The vignette shown represents a critical moment in Ani's journey. He and his wife Thutu (or Tutu) are depicted on the left side, reverently approaching the central scene of the jackal-headed god Anubis who is weighing Ani's heart. For the ancient Egyptians, "the heart was considered to be the seat of the emotions and the intellect . . . the Egyptian equivalent of the mind."[36] The weighing of the heart represents "the judgment of a person's moral worth as the balancing of his heart against the feather of Maat, the goddess who personified truth, justice and order."[37] In this significant moment of Ani's transition from this world to the afterlife, "the delicacy of the necessary equipoise of moral worth contained in the heart meant that one's sins must be feather-light."[38] Successful passing of this test ensured that the deceased would be allowed to enter the afterlife, rather than dying a second death and becoming nonexistent, by being fed to the hybrid creature on the right side of the scene. This is Ammit ("who swallows the dead")—with attributes of a crocodile, lion, dog, and hippopotamus. Ammit sits behind the ibis-headed god Thoth, who oversees the rituals and records the judgment. Thoth is also symbolized by the small baboon sitting on top of the scales. Numerous other symbolic figures appear in the scene. By the base of the scales appears Shai, above his head the prone figure of Meskhenet is depicted, and two female figures (Meskhenet and Renenutut) stand behind Shai. All of these are various personifications of fate. The human-headed bird standing on a small shrine, eagerly watching the weighing scene, represents Ani's soul. A row of seated deities appear in a horizontal register at the top of the scene. This is the great tribunal of gods and goddesses, including Ra, Nut, Isis, Horus, and Hathor. They all hold scepters, representing strength and good fortune. The surrounding hieroglyphic texts enjoin Ani's heart to be peaceful and truthful "so that it will not act as a witness against Ani in the weighing ceremony."[39] While further trials await Ani in the afterworld (illustrated in copious other vignettes of the scroll) this judgment scene is among the most significant events customarily illustrated in the *Book of the Dead* and other media.

The Sacred Cat (Goddess Bastet), Bronze Statuette, after 600 BCE

Images of cats appear frequently in ancient Egyptian art, in hieroglyphs, wall paintings, and relief carvings in tombs and temples. The earliest feline images have been dated to the Old Kingdom period, during which time cats were domesticated in Egypt. By the second millennium BCE, it appears that domestic cats had become important members of Egyptian households in all levels of society. They were useful for their roles as catchers of snakes, rodents, and other vermin, and they were cherished for their companionship.

Animals of all sorts played a role of supreme significance in ancient Egyptian life and thought. "Just like humans, they were one of the fundamental elements of creation. And they were also the visible signs of primeval forces that it was essential both to recognize and to propitiate."[40] For the ancient Egyptians, the human and animal realms were regarded as a largely harmonious continuum in which neither was dominant or of greater importance than the other. "It is precisely in this context that animals assume their omnipresent nature, as the receptacles and visible signs of formidable and largely inexplicable powers, as the expression of an aspect—alongside rocks, plants and human beings—of the universal life force."[41]

Typically, the ancient Egyptian deities were linked and associated with animals. The solar deity Horus often appears with the head of a falcon; the god Sobek may have the head of a crocodile; Anubis is often shown with the head of a jackal; and the goddess Sekhmet was associated with the lioness—a symbol of great strength and power. The cat goddess, Bastet, represents an evolution in this feline imagery. First shown with the head of a lioness, eventually her form became that of a female cat. Unlike the dangerous and unpredictable Sekhmet, Bastet's nature was generally seen as more peaceful and gentle. Her worship became especially popular in the later periods of Egyptian history and was particularly centered in the city of Bubastis (or Basta), an ancient site in the eastern Nile delta. Although the foundations of the city and the cult of Bastet have been dated back to the Old Kingdom period, her worship flourished during the late and Ptolemaic periods (eighth through first century BCE) when "the festival of the goddess Bastet at Bubastis became one of the largest and most popular in the country" with hundreds of thousands of worshipers attending the annual event.[42] The cult of Bastet was not restricted to Bubastis; she was also celebrated in Thebes, Memphis, and elsewhere.

During these centuries, enormous quantities of small bronze statuettes depicting the cat goddess were produced (see Figure 3.11). Many of these were given by devotees to Bastet shrines and temples. "It was a common custom in late Egypt to present a small monument to a temple, perhaps to commemorate a pilgrimage made on the occasion of a religious festival or as an expression of gratitude to the god for past favours or in expectation of such favours in the future."[43]

The example illustrated is one of the largest and most well-known among the thousands that survive.[44] It stands slightly over 16 inches tall and depicts a slim, alert, and elegantly bejeweled cat wearing a gold nose ring and gold earrings (which may be

Figure 3.11 The Sacred Cat Goddess Bastet, bronze statuette, after 600 BCE. London: British Museum. Werner Forman / Art Resource, NY.

later replacements of original jewelry) and an elaborate collar with a pendant showing the *wedjat* or *wadjit* eye—the eye of Horus. This symbolic eye with drop and spiral pattern imitates the markings of a falcon and was one of the most popular protective motifs in ancient Egypt. A winged scarab beetle (symbol of the sun god and regeneration) is inscribed in silver on the chest of the cat. The eye sockets would have originally been fitted with glass or stone eyes. Although much repaired and restored, this graceful statuette serves as an excellent example of ancient Egyptian artistic sophistication and the veneration of the divine in nature.

NOTES

1. Albert Moore, *Iconography of Religions: An Introduction* (Philadelphia: Fortress Press, 1977), 66.

2. K. Kitchen, "The Chronology of Ancient Egypt," *World Archaeology* 23, no. 2 (1991): 201–8.

3. Richard Wilkinson, *The Complete Temples of Ancient Egypt* (New York: Thames and Hudson, 2000), 29.

4. W. V. Davies, *Reading the Past: Egyptian Hieroglyphs* (Berkeley: University of California Press, 1987), 47.

5. Okasha El Daly, *Egyptology: The Missing Millennium: Ancient Egypt in Medieval Arabic Writings* (London: UCL Press, 2005), especially 57–73.

6. Wilkinson, *Complete Temples*, 30.

7. George Boas, *The Hieroglyphics of Horapollo* (Princeton, NJ: Princeton University Press, 1993.)

8. Johanna Drucker, *The Alphabetic Labyrinth: The Letters in History and Imagination* (London: Thames and Hudson, 1995), 24.

9. Erik Iversen, *The Myth of Egypt and Its Hieroglyphs in European Tradition* (Princeton, NJ: Princeton University Press, 1993).

10. Wilkinson, *Complete Temples*, 31.

11. Ogden Goelet, *The Egyptian Book of the Dead: The Book of Going Forth by Day* (San Francisco: Chronicle Books, 1994), 13–14.

12. Jaromir Malek, *Egyptian Art* (London: Phaidon, 1999), 17.

13. David Silverman, "Divinity and Deities in Ancient Egypt," in *Religion in Ancient Egypt: Gods, Myths, and Personal Practice*, ed. Byron Shafer (Ithaca, NY: Cornell University Press, 1991), 7.

14. Goelet, 14.

15. Lorna Oakes and Lucia Gahlin, *Ancient Egypt: An Illustrated Reference to the Myths, Religions, Pyramids and Temples of the Land of the Pharaohs* (London: Hermes House, 2002), 268.

16. Moore, 66.

17. Silverman, 28.

18. Malek, *Egyptian Art*, 16–17.

19. Clive Barrett, *The Egyptian Gods and Goddesses: The Mythology and Beliefs of Ancient Egypt* (London: Diamond, 1996), 37.

20. Oakes and Gahlin, 345.

21. Oakes and Gahlin, 345.

22. Oakes and Gahlin, 364.

23. Oakes and Gahlin, 391.

24. Sue D'Auria, Peter Lacovara, and Catharine Roehrig, *Mummies and Magic: The Funerary Arts of Ancient Egypt* (Boston: Museum of Fine Arts, 1988), 14.

25. Barrett, 152.

26. Oakes and Gahlin, 393.

27. Oakes and Gahlin, 393.

28. Richard Wilkinson, *Reading Egyptian Art: A Hieroglyphic Guide to Ancient Egyptian Painting and Sculpture* (New York: Thames and Hudson, 1992), 9.

29. Moore, 67.

30. Mark Lehner, *The Complete Pyramids* (New York: Thames and Hudson, 1997), 35.

31. Nicholas Reeves and Richard Wilkinson, *The Complete Valley of the Kings* (New York: Thames and Hudson, 1996).

32. Wilkinson, *Complete Temples*, 25.

33. Wilkinson, *Complete Temples*, 16.

34. Wilkinson, *Complete Temples*, 8.

35. Barbara Lesko, *The Great Goddesses of Egypt* (Norman: University of Oklahoma Press, 1999); Barbara Lesko, "Women's Monumental Mark on Ancient Egypt," *Biblical Archaeologist* 54, no. 1 (1991): 4–15.

36. Goelet, 151.

37. Goelet, 13.

38. Goelet, 13.

39. Goelet, 155.

40. Philippe Germond, *An Egyptian Bestiary: Animals in Life and Religion in the Land of the Pharaohs* (London: Thames and Hudson, 2001), 8.

41. Germond, 16.

42. Jaromir Malek, *The Cat in Ancient Egypt* (London: British Museum, 1993), 98.

43. Malek, 100.

44. Neal Spencer, *The Gayer-Anderson Cat* (London: The British Museum, 2007).

BIBLIOGRAPHY AND FURTHER READING

Barrett, Clive. *The Egyptian Gods and Goddesses: The Mythology and Beliefs of Ancient Egypt*. London: Diamond, 1996.

Boas, George. *The Hieroglyphics of Horapollo*. Princeton, NJ: Princeton University Press, 1993.

Clayton, Peter. *Chronicle of the Pharaohs*. New York: Thames and Hudson, 1999.

Daly, Okasha El. *Egyptology: The Missing Millennium: Ancient Egypt in Medieval Arabic Writings*. London: UCL Press, 2005.

D'Auria, Sue, Peter Lacovara, and Catharine Roehrig. *Mummies and Magic: The Funerary Arts of Ancient Egypt*. Boston: Museum of Fine Arts, 1988.

Davies, W. V. *Reading the Past: Egyptian Hieroglyphs*. Berkeley: University of California Press, 1987.

Drucker, Johanna. *The Alphabetic Labyrinth: The Letters in History and Imagination*. London: Thames and Hudson, 1995.

Germond, Philippe. *An Egyptian Bestiary: Animals in Life and Religion in the Land of the Pharaohs*. London: Thames and Judson, 2001.

Goelet, Ogden. *The Egyptian Book of the Dead: The Book of Going Forth by Day*. San Francisco: Chronicle Books, 1994.

Hollis, Susan. "Women of Ancient Egypt and the Sky Goddess Nut." *The Journal of American Folklore* 100, no. 398 (1987): 496–503.

Iversen, Erik. *The Myth of Egypt and Its Hieroglyphs in European Tradition*. Princeton, NJ: Princeton University Press, 1993.

Kitchen, K. "The Chronology of Ancient Egypt." *World Archaeology* 23, no. 2 (1991): 201–8.

Lehner, Mark. *The Complete Pyramids*. New York: Thames and Hudson, 1997.

Lesko, Barbara. *The Great Goddesses of Egypt*. Norman: University of Oklahoma Press, 1999.

Lesko, Barbara. "Women's Monumental Mark on Ancient Egypt." *Biblical Archaeologist* 54, no. 1 (1991): 4–15.

Malek, Jaromir. *The Cat in Ancient Egypt*. London: British Museum, 1993.

Malek, Jaromir. *Egypt: 4000 Years of Art*. London: Phaidon, 2003.

Malek, Jaromir. *Egyptian Art*. London: Phaidon, 1999.

McDermott, Bridget. *Decoding Egyptian Hieroglyphs: How to Read the Secret Language of the Pharaohs*. San Francisco: Chronicle Books, 2001.

Moore, Albert. *Iconography of Religions: An Introduction*. Philadelphia: Fortress Press, 1977.

Oakes, Lorna, and Lucia Gahlin. *Ancient Egypt: An Illustrated Reference to the Myths, Religions, Pyramids and Temples of the Land of the Pharaohs*. London: Hermes House, 2002.

Reeves, Nicholas, and Richard Wilkinson. *The Complete Valley of the Kings*. New York: Thames and Hudson, 1996.

Robins, Gay. *The Art of Ancient Egypt*. Cambridge, MA: Harvard University Press, 1997.

Shafer, Byron, ed. *Religion in Ancient Egypt: Gods, Myths, and Personal Practice*. Ithaca, NY: Cornell University Press, 1991.

Silverman, David. "Divinity and Deities in Ancient Egypt." In *Religion in Ancient Egypt: Gods, Myths, and Personal Practice*, ed. Byron Shafer, 7–87. Ithaca, NY: Cornell University Press, 1991.

Spencer, Neal. *The Gayer-Anderson Cat*. London: The British Museum, 2007.

Wilkinson, Richard. *The Complete Temples of Ancient Egypt*. New York: Thames and Hudson, 2000.

Wilkinson, Richard. *Reading Egyptian Art: A Hieroglyphic Guide to Ancient Egyptian Painting and Sculpture*. New York: Thames and Hudson, 1992.

Wilkinson, Richard. *Symbol and Magic in Egyptian Art*. New York: Thames and Hudson, 1994.

—4—

Religion in Ancient and Classical Greece and Rome

A great many literary works and examples of visual art and architecture survive today that appear to provide more than adequate, if not copious, material for the study of the religious beliefs and practices of ancient and classical Greece and Rome. Many students of Western civilization are familiar with the names of the major deities revered by the Greeks and Romans, such as: Aphrodite/ Venus—the goddess of love and beauty; Dionysus/Bacchus—the god of wine and revelry; Athena/Minerva—the goddess of wisdom and warfare; and Zeus/ Jupiter—the king of the gods. Epic literary sagas, such as the *Odyssey* and the *Iliad* of the ancient Greek Homeric tradition, and the *Aeneid* of the Roman author Virgil (70–19 BCE), have, for centuries, formed the core of Western and European-focused curriculums devoted to the study of the ancient civilizations of Greece and Rome as representatives of the Western heritage. Examples of religious architecture from ancient Greece (such as the Parthenon in Athens) and examples of Roman religious architecture (such as the Pantheon in Rome) are often presented and studied as exemplars of the achievements, values, and core beliefs of these peoples.

Copious scholarship has been devoted, for centuries, to studies of the art, architecture, history, mythology, religion, and politics of the ancient Greeks and Romans. This leads, not illogically, to the impression that a great deal is securely known about these ancient cultures. On the one hand, this is certainly true. Virtually all—major and minor—aspects of Greek and Roman civilization have been painstakingly scrutinized by scholarly specialists in a vast range of academic disciplines. This work continues to flourish intensely today. It may be the case, however, that the very sense of familiarity and confidence gleaned from this voluminous (and often contentious) scholarship has led to some standardization and repetition of theories and approaches. As research continues to flourish, it is often a wonderful twist of scholarly irony that the more knowledge that appears to be gleaned may actually result in less being truly known—or, at least, less generally agreed on. Such a paradox was much appreciated by the ancient Athenian philosopher Socrates (ca. 470–339 BCE), who claimed that true wisdom ultimately rests in awareness of one's ignorance. Even students who feel already very familiar with the architectural monuments and the epic mythological tales associated with Greek and Roman religious beliefs (as well as students less familiar with this material), may well profit by another look at these ancient and influential cultures.

ORIGINS AND DEVELOPMENT

For purposes of this chapter, the discussion will concentrate largely on the historic eras of ancient Greece and Rome, rather than the prehistoric periods associated with the Cycladic, Minoan, and Mycenaean cultures (some of which material is covered in chapter 1, "Prehistoric Belief Systems").

Following the downfall of Mycenaean civilization in Greece in the 13th century BCE and several subsequent centuries of dark ages, ancient Greek history is traditionally traced in a series of stages from the eighth to first century BCE. These centuries are customarily subdivided into three main phases: the Archaic period (eighth through early fifth century BCE), the Classical period (early fifth through mid-fourth century BCE), and the Hellenistic period (fourth through first century BCE). Each period is associated with several key events, developments, and distinctive art styles.

The Archaic period is characterized by the development of the phonetic Greek alphabet, the creation of the Homeric epics, the development of the city-state (or polis) as the cornerstone of Greek civilization, and the foundation of the Olympic Games (late eighth century BCE). The Classical period is generally regarded as the peak of ancient Greek culture and art, although it was also marked by warfare, notably the Persian War of the early fifth century BCE (when the Greeks battled against the invading Persians) and the Peloponnesian War of the late fifth century BCE (when the city-states of Athens and Sparta fought each other). Toward the end of the Classical period, the Greek city-states were eventually conquered by Philip II of Macedon (382–336 BCE) whose son, Alexander the Great (356–323 BCE) continued expansive territorial conquests until his premature death. The subsequent Hellenistic era, with the division of Alexander's empire into large territories controlled by different (and often conflicting) dynasties, came to an end with the Roman conquest of Ptolemaic Egypt in 30 BCE.

It is important to remember that the geographic range of ancient Greece—or Magna Graecia—far exceeds the confines of the modern day country of Greece.[1] In ancient times, mainland Greece, the Peloponnesus, and the numerous Greek

Aegean islands were only a section of the territories controlled or colonized by the Greek peoples. For example, the colonies of Asia Minor (present-day Turkey) and southern Italy were also extremely important areas of the ancient Greek world.

The civilization of the Etruscans, based in central and northern Italy, overlaps historically with both Greek and Roman cultures. The origin of the Etruscans and their unique, largely still undeciphered language, remain mysterious. Etruscan civilization flourished, in a number of independent cities, during a time roughly corresponding with the Archaic period of the ancient Greeks, with whom they maintained much contact via trade and commerce. The Etruscans emulated many Greek art forms, although they also developed distinctive styles and architectural formats, many of which also provided a heritage for Roman art and architecture.

Rome was initially established as an Etruscan city in the middle of the eighth century BCE. In the late sixth century BCE, the last Etruscan king was expelled from Rome and a new form of constitutional government was established. During the first phase of Roman history (the Republic, 509–27 BCE) Rome eventually conquered all of ancient Etruria and ultimately all of the ancient Greek and Hellenistic territories. This massive expansion continued through the second major phase of Roman history, (the Empire, 27 BCE to late fifth century CE) when the vast Roman empire covered major sections of present-day western Europe, Greece, the Middle East, and Africa.

PRINCIPAL BELIEFS AND KEY PRACTICES

The religious beliefs of the ancient Greeks, Etruscans, and Romans share some fundamental similarities. They were polytheistic and worshiped a number of different deities, both male and female. The ultimate origins of these deities and the beliefs surrounding them are complex matters of much scholarly speculation.[2] As in many other ancient polytheistic cultures, the deities were ultimately associated with elements of nature (such as earth, water, and sky) and observable natural phenomena (such as storms, wind, and rain). The development of specifically named deities, already found in the Mycenaean period, is even more than evident by the Archaic period, notably in the ancient Homeric epics in which the gods and goddesses have distinctive attributes and personalities. In epics such as the *Iliad* and the *Odyssey*, the deities are presented as being quite active in their interest in—as well as their influence on—human lives and events. "In Greek religion, the sacred interpenetrated the world of everyday life to a very high degree."[3] The success or failure of human endeavors was believed to be influenced by divine favor (or disfavor) and, oftentimes, by divine caprice and whimsy as well. The deities who play major and minor roles in the Greek Homeric epics, and who also feature in numerous other later Roman literary works such as the *Aeneid* of Virgil and the *Metamorphoses* of Ovid (43 BCE–17 CE?), ultimately emerge as very humanlike, but immortal, figures whose actions and desires mirror both the best and the worst of human personality traits. The deities "were by no means all good; their distinguishing quality was not goodness, but power."[4] It has been said that "Greek mythology always preferred human modes of expressing the divine."[5]

The aforementioned works are, however, not religious texts per se but rather literary creations in which the deities are described and in which they feature. They give important evidence about ancient religious beliefs, but these are not writings that were understood to be divine revelations (such as the Qur'an for Muslims, and as the Bible is considered to be by many Jews and Christians). "It would be mistaken to conclude that those myths belonged to [ancient] religion as a corpus of beliefs and certainties with the same standing as revelation in the religions that stem from the Bible . . . In no sense did the myths constitute dogmas."[6] There is no single book or set of sacred scriptures on which Greek, Etruscan, and Roman religion can be said to be based. While numerous texts describe the deities and speak of their roles and proper veneration, scholars must use some caution in attempting to understand the realities of ancient religious beliefs and actual practices based on these texts.

Many scholars believe that "before polytheism in Greece there was an era of monotheism" in which veneration of the divine feminine, or Earth/Mother Goddess, dominated.[7] The gradual supplanting of the Neolithic and Bronze Age Mother Goddess by the polytheistic pantheon most often associated with Greek and Roman religion appears to have taken place in the Archaic period of ancient Greece. Important literary works such as the *Theogony* and the *Works and Days* of Hesiod (eighth century BCE) provide "the primary source for our information about the Olympian gods and goddesses who came to form the core of the Greek pantheon."[8]

The Olympian Pantheon

Hesiod's *Theogony* describes generations of deities brought forth from the initial union of the earth/feminine and sky/masculine forces, which ultimately resulted in the 12 major divinities of the Greek pantheon.[9] Six of these deities were feminine, and six were masculine, with the male sky god, Zeus, serving as king of the deities and ruler of the universe.

Zeus was the god of power and generation; his symbol is the lightening bolt. The official wife of Zeus was Hera, the patroness of marriage and protector of social order. Zeus ruled the heavens while his brother, Poseidon, ruled the seas. Poseidon's symbol is the trident. The sister of Zeus, Demeter, symbolized fertility. Closely linked with the ancient Earth Mother, Demeter was widely worshiped in mystery rituals. Apollo, a son of Zeus, represented law, order, creativity, knowledge, and prophecy. The virginal sister of Apollo, Artemis, was associated with the moon, wild animals, and youthfulness. Ares was the god of war, whereas Aphrodite was the goddess of love, nature, beauty, and fruitfulness. Hermes, another son of Zeus, was the messenger god, associated with spiritual guidance, sleep, dreams, prophecy, and revelation. Athena, a daughter of Zeus, was the goddess of wisdom, purity, and intellect, and she appears in many guises, often as a triumphant warrior maiden. Hestia was the goddess of the hearth, home, and social unity. Sometimes she is replaced in the pantheon by Dionysus (yet another son of Zeus), associated with revelry and lack of constraint. Dionysus was also widely worshiped in mystery/cultic rituals.

Apart from the 12 primary Olympian deities (so named as they were legendarily believed to reside on Mount Olympus), Greek myths are populated by a vast host of additional gods and goddesses, heroes, semidivine beings, centaurs, nymphs, and both beneficent and evil forces. The god of death and the underworld was Hades; the god of healing was Asclepius; Eros, the wanton and youthful love god is associated with Aphrodite; the Fates ruled human destiny, while the Furies served as forces of vengeance; the Muses inspired poetry, music, dance, and other creative achievements, while the three Graces represented beauty, gentleness, and friendship. The exploits and adventures of the semidivine hero Herakles feature prominently in art and literature.

The deities simultaneously and later venerated by the Etruscans and Romans have many counterparts to those of ancient Greece. Although relatively little is very clearly understood about Etruscan religious beliefs and practices, archaeological and later literary evidence indicates that several of the prominent Etruscan deities included gods such as Tinia (Zeus/Jupiter) and Apulu (Apollo), as well as goddesses such as Uni (Hera/Juno), Menvra (Athena/Minerva), and Artumes (Artemis/Diana).

By and large, the Roman pantheon of deities represent borrowings from the Greek and Etruscan plus additional figures as well. Some deities of ancient Greece were less popular among the Romans, whereas other lesser Greek deities became more widely venerated among the Romans. Especially as the vast Roman empire grew and expanded around the Mediterranean world and beyond, the Romans absorbed and assimilated many deities of a wide range of cultural origins. "As the Romans saw it, there were countless gods. They filled the whole known world. Some had made themselves known to the Romans . . . Other deities lived in foreign lands."[10] Many of the myths and legends of the Greeks were retained and augmented by the Romans, and deities such as the ancient Egyptian goddess Isis, and the Persian god Mithra, were widely venerated at various times by certain segments of the Roman population. Roman religion may ultimately be seen as highly eclectic—with both public and private aspects.

A clash between the so-called public and private aspects of ancient Roman religious practices is generally associated with the growth and development of Christianity within the Roman empire in the first through third centuries CE (see chapter 10, "Christianity"). It is traditionally understood that the monotheistic Christians were persecuted by the Roman authorities because of their refusal to engage in public worship of the Roman gods as well as their refusal to accept and acknowledge the deified status of the emperors, a practice that had began in the late first century BCE. Although the reasons for the persecution of Christians are extremely complex, one gains a sense that the maintenance of at least outward conformity to any variety of official/public/state religious practices during the Roman empire was paramount and considered to be an important duty and responsibility of Roman citizens.[11]

The fundamentally civic and communal nature of religious practices both in ancient Greece and Rome must be emphasized. Both Greek and Roman religion have been described as emphasizing *orthopraxy* (correct practice/performance) rather than *orthodoxy* (correct belief/opinion). In the Greek city-states, "it was the task of the noble Greek to [serve] the *polis* as a citizen. His duties were to fight if called upon, to debate the issues of the day, to serve in the assembly or in whatever position the *polis* might assign him, and most of all to support with his wealth the festivals and honors due to the gods."[12] Similarly, "religion as a communal relationship with the gods, and religion as a system of obligations stemming from that relationship" are critical defining features of Roman religion.[13] Both Greek and Roman religious practices were highly ritualistic, based on ceremonies and regularly held public festivals. Festal calendars naturally diverged from place to place and evolved over time. Some festivals were local and others were more widely celebrated. No absolutely universal civic religious calendar existed, although many festivals were held in accordance with natural yearly agricultural and seasonal activities. People also "took an active part in the religious festivals and obligations that concerned them within the context of a domestic cult or of the religions of smaller, local communities with the city."[14] Ritual sacrifices of animals (especially sheep, goats, and cattle), divination practices, the consulting of oracles, offerings of incense and libations, celebrations with feasts, processions, and athletic competitions in honor of the gods all characterize the religious practices of the ancient Greeks and Romans.[15]

Some of the most important festivals of ancient Greece included the regularly held Olympic Games in honor of the god Zeus at the site of Olympia (from the early eighth century BCE) and the Pythian Games in honor of the god Apollo at the great sanctuary at Delphi (from the early sixth century BCE). These were Panhellenic celebrations that took place every four years and were attended by Greeks from many different regions and city-states. The great Panathenaic festival of Athens, celebrated every four years in honor of the goddess Athena (from the middle of the sixth century BCE) was a local city festival of grand proportions that also included games and competitions among athletes from many regions of the Greek world.[16]

Among the vast number of festivals celebrated by the ancient Romans were annual events such as the spring Lupercalia (in honor of Lupa, the she-wolf, who legendarily suckled the infant founders of Rome, Romulus and Remus), the summer Consualia festival (in honor of the god Consus, who protected the harvest), and the extremely popular winter Saturnalia (in honor of the god Saturn—this festival was characterized by great merriment and reversal of traditional social roles).

Priests and priestesses conducted rituals associated with festivals and temples in ancient Greece "but never developed into a class of their own because of the lack of an institutional framework."[17] Indeed, "Greek religion might almost be called a religion without priests; there [was] no priestly caste as a closed group with fixed tradition, education, initiation, and hierarchy."[18] Even so, the leadership roles in Greek religious ceremonies were often assumed by members of various prominent families who traditionally oversaw specific rituals. Some positions were hereditary, others were by appointment or could be purchased. The number of years these positions could or might be held varied widely as well.

Although the roles of women in ancient Greece were largely restricted to domestic and child-bearing duties, "in one crucial area, that of religious practice, the barriers between women and public life were conspicuously breached."[19] Women participated quite fully in religious life in ancient Greece, and many recent studies have been devoted to the importance and prominence of priest-esses.[20] Religious officials in ancient Rome were almost exclusively male, although an important exception to this were the priestesses of Vesta (or the Vestal Virgins) who tended the shrine and sacred fire of Vesta, the goddess of the home and hearth, at a special sanctuary in Rome.[21]

Although there is little doubt that "death was taken very seriously by the ancient Greeks and Romans,"[22] it is also clear that "no one explanation for death encompassed the whole Greco-Roman cultural ambience."[23] The shad-owy underworld of Hades and the ghostly souls roaming netherworld regions such as the Elysian Fields feature prominently in early mythology; there are many literary works describing heroic journeys to (and returns from) the realms of the dead, as well as works describing the return of ghostly shades (both threatening and beneficent) to the realms of the living.[24] Even so, the con-cepts of the afterlife that developed in ancient Greece and Rome vary widely in specificity and detail—including the issues of after-death judgment and reward or punishment for earthly deeds. A concern for proper burial and funeral rites was demonstrated in both Greek and Roman practices, and the dead were commemorated in both private familial rites and larger community festivals. Although some scholars have claimed that the popularity of the mystery cults can be attributed to their offering of greater specificity about the afterlife, this is by no means clear or generally agreed.

Mystery Cults

Supplementing civic religious practices in ancient Greece and Rome were a number of mystery cults in which only initiates were allowed to fully partici-pate.[25] These include the Eleusinian, Dionysian, Orphic, and Mithraic myster-ies. The roots of several of these cults seem to be of very ancient origin, and many scholars believe they reflect practices of the prehistoric Aegean world (the Minoan and Mycenaean periods, if not earlier).

The Eleusinian mysteries, held in honor of the earth goddess Demeter and her daughter Persephone (who was abducted into the underworld by Hades and who returned to earth after several months) celebrated regeneration and fertility, death and rebirth. Centered at the site of Eleusis, near Athens, the mystery rituals took place regularly—at least yearly—and attracted many followers.[26] Eleusis remained an extremely important cult and pilgrimage center under the Romans as well, until the sanctuary was closed under the direction of the Christian Roman emperor Theodosius in the late fourth century CE. Although much scholarship and archaeological work has been devoted to Eleusis and the ancient mystery rituals performed there, the exact nature of these rituals and their intended cathartic or transforming effect on participants remain matters of some speculation. Unlike civic religious ceremonies, the rituals of Eleusis (as other mystery cults) were hidden from noninitiates, and participants were vowed to secrecy. "Those involved in the mystery religions possessed secret knowledge which was transmitted through the special bond of membership."[27]

TRADITIONAL ART AND ARCHITECTURAL FORMS

Temples

In both Greece, Etruria, and Rome, the primary forms of religious architecture were temples dedicated to the gods and goddesses. Some sanctuaries were located in rural areas outside of cities. Cities of any size often had several temples dedicated to different deities. Numerous examples survive to the present day either in well-preserved or more fragmentary form. Major examples such as the fifth-century BCE Parthenon in Athens and the second-century CE Pantheon in Rome represent centuries of development in architectural construction methods and forms.

Many scholars concur that the horizontal, rectangular temple form that is most traditionally seen in both Greek and Roman religious architecture ultimately represents a lengthy development from the ancient Mycenaean Greek type of building known as the *megaron*, which primarily appears to have functioned as a royal audience hall and focal structure in Mycenaean palace-citadels. Excavations of Mycenaean sites such as Mycenae, Tiryns, and Pylos have uncovered the remains of *megaron* structures that, in general layout and format, resemble the later temple buildings of Archaic and Classical Greece.

Sacred sites in the pre-Classical period, with space marked out for religious purposes—often including a tree or grove, source of water, and an altar—have been uncovered in archaeological excavations. The careful siting of sanctuaries within the landscape has often been extolled as one of the most significant and aesthetically symbolic aspects of Greek architecture in general.[28] It is important to remember, however, that the gleaming white marble temples, which stand out with such impressive clarity in their settings today, were originally enriched with color. Traces of pigment found on the architectural and sculptural elements of many temples indicate that they were originally much more color-ful than their present appearance demonstrates.

All Greek temples use a trabeated system of construction with horizontal and vertical members (posts or columns supporting lintels or beams). The majority of Greek and Roman temples constructed in stone employ this format, which is ultimately based on timber (wood) building methods. Etruscan temples were constructed of wood (as the earliest Greek temples presumably were as well), hence evidence for the appearance of Etruscan temples must be gleaned from other sources, such as small clay models that demonstrate their form. Although Greek temples generally were constructed atop low stone platforms with steps surrounding on all four sides, Etruscan and Roman temples generally have sim-ply one flight of steps on the front leading to their entrances. Greek and Roman temples may be dated and categorized as per the appearance of specific details of their vertical columns and capitals (topping the columns) and horizontal entablatures (sections of the structure supported by columns). The develop-ment of different styles or orders of classical architecture took place over many centuries. The traditional style designations of Doric, Ionic, Corinthian, and Composite reflect not only geographic origins or usages but also, to a large extent, the chronological development of these forms (see Figure 4.1).

The Doric order, with plain columns and relatively simple cushionlike capi-tals standing directly on the temple base or platform, was widely employed in early Greek temples such as the several examples at Paestum in southern Italy (see Figure 4.2), and in classical Greek temples such as the Parthenon in

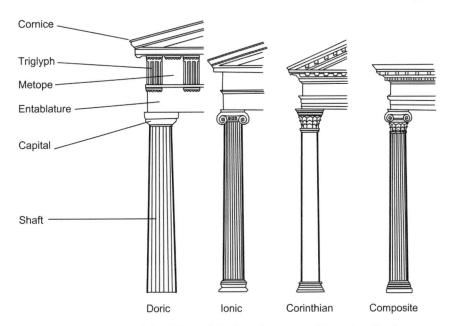

Figure 4.1   Diagram of the Classical Orders. Courtesy of Ricochet Productions.

Figure 4.2   Temple of Hera II, Paestum, Italy, ca. 460 BCE. Moemrik / Dreamstime. com.

Athens (see Figure 4.9). The entablature of Doric-style temples is characterized by alternating forms known as *triglyphs* (blocks with vertical bands) and *metopes* (often enriched with small relief sculptures).

The Ionic order is characterized by fluted columns standing on rounded bases and with distinctive scroll-like forms (*volutes*) enriching the capitals. Ionic-style temple entablatures generally consist of continuous sculptural bands (or *friezes*), such as can be seen on the Temple of Athena Nike in Athens from the late fifth century BCE (see Figure 4.3).

The distinctive Corinthian order is recognizable due to its use of foliate capitals—with elegant leafy forms based on the acanthus plant—and tall fluted columns otherwise resembling the Ionic style. Corinthian style capitals are seen on the facade of the Roman Pantheon, ca. 125 CE (see Figure 4.10). The Corinthian and Composite orders (combining Ionic and Corinthian features) were especially employed by the Romans.

Apart from the traditional rectangular (or longitudinal) format, several Greek and Roman temples are also of the circular (or *tholos*) form. The centralized plan was employed both in Greece and Rome primarily for smaller sanctuaries, such as the Roman temple of the Sibyl at Tivoli, ca. 25 BCE (see Figure 4.4). The traditional trabeated (post and lintel) system was augmented significantly by the Roman use of arches as well as concrete construction. Although the true arch form is of some antiquity and disputed origins (corbeled arches were employed in Mycenaean architecture and true arches—based on shaped blocks or *voussoirs*—held in place by a keystone, were employed by the Etruscans)

Figure 4.3   Temple of Athena Nike, Athens, Greece, ca. 427–424 BCE. Scala / Art Resource, NY.

Figure 4.4   Temple of the Sibyl, Tivoli, Italy, early first century BCE. Alinari / Art Resource, NY.

the use of arches on a significant scale is generally credited to the Romans, as well as the use of poured concrete to create impressive structures such as the Pantheon.

The identification of and complex terminology used to describe all the details and decorations of these styles of ancient religious architecture (many of which naturally appear in nonreligious construction too) can be credited largely to the Roman scholar and architect Vitruvius (first century BCE), whose writings were avidly studied in later periods and continue to be so today. Many of the features and forms developed in ancient Greek, Etruscan, and Roman architecture have remained consistently employed or consistently revived in later periods—notably during the 15th- and 16th-century Renaissance period, the 17th-century Baroque, and 18th- and 19th-century neoclassical periods—up to the present day, when even much postmodern architecture references many of the forms and features of ancient classical structures.

Many later architects have made use of the designs and details employed by ancient Greek, Etruscan, and Roman builders for both secular and religious, private and public architecture. The classical architectural vocabulary of forms and designs is still current today. However, the banks, museums, government buildings, libraries, churches, and opera houses that continue to employ this classical vocabulary differ in some significant ways from the ancient, especially religious, precedents on which they are based.

The temples of ancient Greece and Rome were not primarily designed to be public buildings. Similar to the religious structures of ancient Egypt and Mesopotamia, Greek and Roman temples did not function as communal gathering places in the same sense that later Christian churches or Jewish synagogues or Islamic mosques do. The interiors of Greek, Etruscan, and Roman temples were more or less off limits to the general populace, akin also to the ancient Jewish temple. The interior enclosures of ancient temples were regularly visited only by a select few—priests and designated officiants who enacted rituals designed to honor and please the deities and who tended and cared for the cult statues within the temples. The designated sacred space of the temple interior was not used for general worship assemblies but was rather intended to serve as a home for the cult statue, the embodiment of sacred power. Many ancient Greek and Roman temples, although architecturally impressive indeed, were not designed to house many worshipers. Nor does it appear that worshipers were often or regularly invited to ever visit temple interiors even individually or in small groups (such as Hindu practice entails). On particular festivals and during specific periods in an individual's life (rituals associated with marriage, for example) worshipers might be invited to enter a temple briefly or view the interior and cult statue from the doorway. However, the general understanding is that public religious rites in ancient Greece and Rome used the temples as focal points for rituals that did not require or provide large interior gathering spaces for congregations, and that altars for rituals were largely located outside the temples.

Figure 4.5 Apollo, detail, from the west pediment of the Temple of Zeus at Olympia, Greece, ca. 480 BCE. Olympia: Archaeological Museum. Erich Lessing / Art Resource, NY.

Images of Deities

For the most part, the Greeks and Romans visualized and represented the divinities in anthropomorphic form—with human attributes. Numerous freestanding and relief sculptures, often attached to or associated with temples, depict the major deities in various guises and roles. Temple exteriors—especially metopes, friezes, and facade pediments (triangular sections under the sloping roof line of temples)—were frequently enriched with painted sculptures depicting the classical deities and mythological events in which they played prominent roles. For example, both the eastern and western pediments of the early Classical temple of Zeus at Olympia (ca. 480 BCE) contained numerous images of the deities presiding over, or involved with, significant episodes from ancient mythology, such as the famous figure of Apollo, so often lauded as an exemplar of ideal human beauty in divine form (see Figure 4.5).

Freestanding sculptures, in the form of cult statues, were placed in the interiors of temples. Relief sculptures on temple exteriors and interiors (or on other structures within temple precincts) depict images of deities with symbolic attributes emphasizing their cultic importance and traditions, such as the mid-fifth-century BCE relief of Demeter and Persephone from Eleusis (see Figure 4.6). During the Classical period especially, many deities may be identified by specific body types (youthful, more mature), which reflect the development of naturalism in Greek art as well as specific aspects of the personalities or functions of these deities.[29]

Because of the close association with and placement of these images on the interiors and exteriors of temples, these images of the gods and goddesses may be correctly deemed to be examples of religious art. However, it is crucial to note that images of the deities and scenes from mythology also feature frequently in Greek and Roman art in secular contexts as well. Innumerable examples exist of painted clay vessels especially from ancient Greece (of a great variety of shapes, styles, and secular as well as religious functions) that include images of various divinities and mythological and ritual scenes. The image of the grape-bearing god Dionysus on his ocean voyage provides the central motif for the interior of an often-reproduced Attic *kylix* (wine drinking cup) created by the famous artist Exekias, ca. 540–430 BCE (see Figure 4.7). Dionysus had been captured by pirates but turned the crew into dolphins while the mast of the ship sprouted grape vines.

Much visual material for the study of Greek and Roman religion and mythology exists in contexts that are not exclusively religious or directly associated with sacred sites, thus, it is wise to remember that "in ancient Greece . . . religion was totally embedded in society—no sphere of

Figure 4.6 Demeter and Persephone, relief from Eleusis, mid fifth century BCE. Eleusis: Archaeological Museum. Erich Lessing / Art Resource, NY.

Figure 4.7   Dionysus kylix by Exekias, ca. 540–530 BCE. Munich: Staatliche Antikensammlung. Foto Marburg / Art Resource, NY.

life lacked a religious aspect."[30] Many public monuments in ancient Rome were also enriched with representations of deities or religious rites that reinforce the significance of community participation and the priestly duties of the emperors, such as the late second-century CE relief of Marcus Aurelius making a sacrifice in Rome (see Figure 4.8).

EXAMPLES

The Parthenon in Athens, Greece (447–438 BCE) and the Pantheon in Rome, Italy (ca. 125 CE)

The Parthenon in Athens and the Pantheon in Rome are, without doubt, the two architectural monuments most often discussed as exemplars of Greek and Roman religious structures (see Figures 4.9, 4.10, and Plate 7). These two structures are consistently included in general surveys of art history, and the specialized scholarship on these two buildings is more than copious.[31] The Parthenon is often seen as the ultimate representative of Greek aesthetics, with its clear and carefully pleasing proportion systems, and the Pantheon is often seen to represent the heights of Roman ingenuity and innovation in construction and engineering techniques. Both well-studied buildings this have "larger-than-life, iconlike status," and are traditionally regarded as masterpieces of Western civilization.[32] Nevertheless, there are many aspects of their design, construction, and symbolic meanings that continue to provide lively vehicles for scholarly interpretation.

The Parthenon was constructed during the middle of the fifth century BCE, a time period which is often considered to be a Golden Age in Greece, the height of the Classical period. It was erected on the acropolis—the promontory: *acro* (above) the *polis* (city)—of Athens, under the direction of the Athenian ruler Pericles (490–429 BCE) in 447–438 BCE. It is a temple dedicated to the goddess Athena, the patroness and protector of Athens, whose large cult statue—now lost—was originally housed within the building. The Parthenon is often seen to represent a powerful political symbol of Athenian greatness, prestige, and triumph in the recently won Persian War. The Pantheon in Rome is a temple dedicated to the seven major planetary deities of the classical pantheon (hence its name) and was constructed under the direction of the ambitious Roman emperor Hadrian (r. 117–138 CE) during a period of time when the Roman Empire was at a great height of power, prestige, and territorial expansion.

Figure 4.8 Marcus Aurelius making a sacrifice; relief from the Arch of Marcus Aurelius, ca. 176–180 CE. Rome: Palazzo dei Conservatori. Nimatallah / Art Resource, NY.

Both of these structures still stand today—the Pantheon in a much better state of preservation than the Parthenon—although both buildings have undergone losses, renovations, and re-usages through the centuries. The Pantheon was converted into a Christian church in the early seventh century CE and was renamed Sancta Maria ad Martyres (or, more popularly, Santa Maria Rotunda). Although sections of the building were slightly altered in subsequent centuries and bronze roof tiles and other elements were removed and reused during the 7th and the 17th centuries, for the most part the building has survived remarkably intact through several periods of repair and restoration. The "building has on the whole been properly and respectfully maintained."[33]

The much older Parthenon, in contrast, has fared far less well and exists today in relatively fragmentary form. Although the majority of columns are still standing (or have been re-erected), much of the original sculptural decoration was removed in the late 18th century under the direction of Lord Elgin (the British ambassador to the Ottoman Empire from 1799 to 1803) when the structure had already fallen into a state of disrepair. During the medieval period it had been remodeled for use as a Christian church, was later converted into an Islamic

Figure 4.9   Parthenon, Athens, Greece, 447–438 BCE. Valeria73 / Dreamstime. com.

Figure 4.10   Pantheon, Rome, Italy, exterior, ca. 125 CE. Toddtaulman / Dreamstime.com.

mosque, and in the late 17th century, when a section of the building was being used as a storehouse for ammunition, the central area was blown apart after being hit by a Venetian rocket in their siege of the city (then under Ottoman Turkish control). Many of the sculptures were destroyed then or shortly thereafter removed by the Venetians; the remainder were later removed and shipped to England under the direction of Lord Elgin and are displayed today in the British Museum in London, a fact that continues to provide much controversy.[34]

Both the Parthenon and the Pantheon have inspired numerous later monuments that imitate or reference their overall forms or design elements.[35] The Pantheon has been described as "one of the grand architectural creations of all time: original, utterly bold, many-layered in associations and meaning, the container of a kind of immanent universality. It speaks of an even wider world than that of imperial Rome, and has left its stamp upon architecture more than any other building."[36] The Parthenon, similarly, has been described as "a total form whose parts are perfectly realized."[37]

The Pantheon was built on the site of an earlier rectangular temple that had been constructed in about 25 BCE under the direction of Agrippa (63–12 BCE), the chief minister of Augustus (r. 27 BCE–14 CE). The large inscription on the front of the present building constructed in the second century CE still names Agrippa as the founder of the building. "Considerable confusion has resulted from this inscription," but it appears clear that this represents a restoration of the inscription on the original building.[38] The structure consists of a large entrance porch or portico with 20 Corinthian-style columns (several rows deep) topped by a triangular pediment. From the front, the Pantheon appears to be of traditionally rectangular temple format, akin to many other examples. However, the interior of the structure—which has rarely ever failed to inspire awe—consists of a vast and circular domed space (nearly equal in height and in diameter of 142 feet), which was created by a complex and ingenious system of internally hidden arches supporting and supported by a concrete foundation and framework of progressively lighter load toward the top of the dome.[39] At the apex of the coffered round dome is a 27-foot-wide opening (*oculus*), which admits light to the interior of the building. The sphere of illumination moves daily and seasonally across the niches on the walls below, which, several scholars believe, originally held statues of the deities to whom the temple was dedicated (see Plate 7).

The Pantheon is, for all intents and purposes, a perfectly circular building, while the Parthenon is a perfectly rectangular structure based on a harmonious proportion system of lengths, widths, and heights in related ratios. The Parthenon demonstrates many other subtleties as well: the slight mid-height bulge (*entasis*) of the supporting columns and the slight upward rise of the base and entablature mid-span are not immediately obvious to viewers but contribute greatly to the overall optically grounded and stable effect of the structure.

Although these emblematic structures have provided the materials for massive amounts of scholarship and architectural emulation for many ages, a number of issues still remain topics of lively debate. While the names of the architects of the Parthenon are known (Iktinos and Kallikrates), as well as the name of the creator and overseer of the Parthenon's sculptural program (Phidias), the names of the architect(s) of the Pantheon are unknown, and, although this is not at all atypical of ancient monuments, the architectural predecessors of this unique building are not entirely clear either. While circular and domed structures had been constructed previously, and the Roman use, if not invention, of poured concrete construction is well demonstrated in numerous other civic and religious structures before the Pantheon, no other building constructed by the ancient Romans truly resembles the Pantheon in size and scale of the undertaking. Indeed, until the middle of the 20th century, the dome of the Pantheon was purportedly the largest concrete span ever built. Although this remarkable structure, "the most grand, innovative, difficult, and complex"[40] monument of ancient Rome, has inspired scholarly study for many eras, the meaning, significance, and symbolism of the building continue to be freshly discussed and interpreted today.[41]

Similarly, a great deal of scholarship has also been devoted to the Parthenon, not only its architectural form but also to the meaning and iconography of its (largely removed) sculptures (metopes, frieze, and pediments), which depict, in the epitome of high Classical style, scenes from mythology and religious celebrations in honor of the goddess Athena. Although the Parthenon and its sculptures have been extremely well studied, new interpretations of the iconography continue to arise as additional documentary, literary, and archaeological evidence comes to light—and as old sources are reconsidered anew by fresh eyes.[42]

Frescoes from the Villa of the Mysteries, Pompeii, Italy, ca. 60–50 BCE

The wall paintings located in two interior rooms of the Villa of the Mysteries near Pompeii have intrigued scholars of ancient art and religion for many years[43] (see Plate 8). Many believe that the full-length figural scenes found in these chambers reflect or illustrate practices associated with the cult of Dionysus (Bacchus), an extremely popular (and often suppressed) mystery cult of the ancient world. Indeed, the villa derives its modern name from these paintings, which were created in the middle of the first century BCE.

The villa itself was constructed in the late third and early second century BCE and underwent a series of renovations and refurbishment under successive owners up until the devastation of Pompeii and environs caused by the eruption of Mount Vesuvius in 79 CE. Although the villa was covered over by ash and volcanic material, most of the structure and interior paintings were relatively undamaged when unearthed in 1909. The villa is an excellent example of the type of country residence that was very popular among well-to-do Roman citizens who often owned farmland or engaged in agricultural production. As a wine press was discovered in the excavations, it is assumed that the owners of the villa were

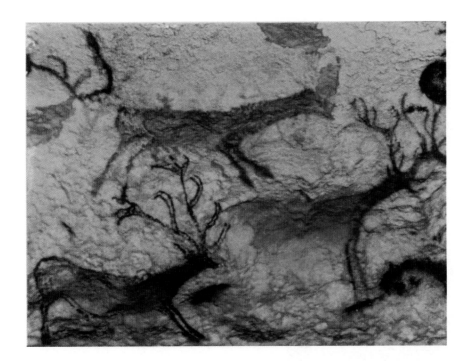

Plate 1 Cave painting, Lascaux, France ca. 15,000–13,000 BCE. Art Resource, NY.

Plate 2 Stonehenge, Wiltshire, England, ca. 3000–1500 BCE. 2009 Jupiterimages Corporation.

Plate 3 Statues of Worshipers from Eshnunna, ca. 2700 BCE. Baghdad: Iraq Museum. Erich Lessing / Art Resource, NY.

Plate 4 The Warka Vase, ca. 3500–3000 BCE. Baghdad: Iraq Museum. Scala / Art Resource, NY.

Plate 5 Pectoral of Tutankhamun, ca. 1336–1327 BCE. Cairo: Egyptian Museum. Scala / Art Resource, NY.

Plate 6 The *Papyrus of Ani* (*Book of the Dead*), ca. 1275–1250 BCE. London: British Museum. Werner Forman / Art Resource, NY.

Plate 7   Pantheon, Rome, Italy, interior, ca. 125 CE. 2009
Jupiterimages Corporation.

Plate 8   Frescoes from the Villa
of the Mysteries, Pompeii, Italy,
ca. 60–50 BCE. Erich Lessing / Art
Resource, NY.

Plate 9 Lintel 24 from Structure 23, Yaxchilán, Mexico, ca. 725 CE, Lady Xoc and Shield Jaguar II. London: The Trustees of The British Museum / Art Resource, NY.

Plate 10 The Codex Fejérváry-Mayer, 15th century CE. Liverpool, England: World Museum M 12014. Werner Forman / Art Resource, NY.

Plate 11 Kwakiutl Crooked-Beak-of-Heaven Mask. Victoria, Canada: Provincial Museum. Werner Forman / Art Resource, NY.

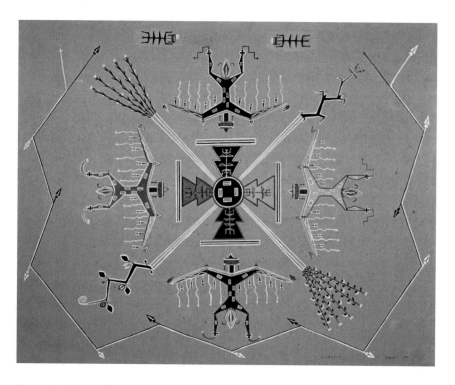

Plate 12 Navajo Shooting Way Chant, sandpainting textile, 20th century. The Art Archive / Wheelwright Museum of the American Indian, Santa Fe, New Mexico.

Plate 13 Spirit Board (*hohao*), late 19th to early 20th century, Papua New Guinea. London: The Trustees of The British Museum / Art Resource, NY.

Plate 14 Te Hau-Ki-Turanga, Maori meeting house, 1842. Wellington, New Zealand: National Museum of New Zealand. Werner Forman / Art Resource, NY.

Plate 15 Suku helmet mask, wood, Democratic Republic of Congo. The Art Archive / Paris: Musée des Arts Africains et Océaniens / Gianni Dagli Orti.

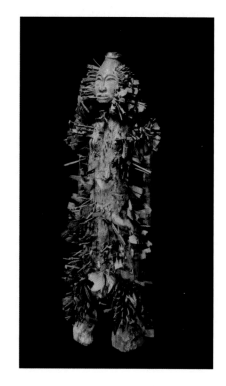

Plate 16 Kongo *Nkisi Nkondi* figure, wood and metal, late 19th century, Democratic Republic of Congo. London: The Trustees of The British Museum / Art Resource, NY.

involved with grape cultivation and wine making. Originally a much smaller residence, the villa, by the first century CE, had been enlarged into a complex of close to 30 rooms, with surrounding gardens, porticos, and terraces, plus the enclosed interior courtyards typical of Roman domestic architecture. Interior wall painting in the fresco technique (painting into wet plaster) was also a well developed and popular form of art of ancient Rome that scholars have categorized into distinct styles and phases. The creation of spatial illusion on a large scale via figural scenes, landscape, or painted architectural elements is typical of the first-century style when the famous mystery frescoes were created.

These are located primarily on all four walls of one large room, which has often been identified as a dining or entertainment hall. The paintings depict numerous, primarily female, figures, seated, standing, interacting with each other, and in the presence of male deities (traditionally identified as Silenus and Dionysus—who is shown reclining on the lap of a female figure often identified as his wife, Ariadne, or his mother, Semele). A naked young boy appears to be reading from a scroll; one woman carries a tray; one seated woman appears to be washing her hands (or participating in a libation ceremony); satyrs, goats, and *erotes* (winged cupidlike figures) are present; several females kneel, while others are shown dancing or running; one kneeling woman lifts a cover from a model of an erect phallus stored in a *liknon* (a winnowing tool traditionally used in Dionysian rites); a winged figure wields a rod or whip; and an older woman sits pensively.

However, because "no text has been discovered to give the true key to interpretation [and] no direct antecedents for the Villa pictures have come to light so far," the exact meaning of the scenes remains a matter of some lively scholarly debate.[44] While it seems that the "women participate in a continuous narrative that begins with ritual purification and preparatory offerings and culminates in a dance of initiation," whether this reflects actual Dionysian ceremonies held in the room (as some have believed), initiation rites associated with female sexual maturity and marriage preparations, or whether the paintings symbolize more enigmatic and mystical concepts remain open to interpretation.[45] The subjects "may, in fact, be eclectic to some degree. It is not likely that the painter of this frieze would have revealed the secret details of a particular mystery cult in a domestic room that seems not to have been a closed shrine."[46] On the other hand, less detailed "representations of the Dionysiac cult are among the most popular scenes of private worship" found in ancient Roman art, providing visual evidence which is simultaneously intriguing but also rather frustratingly unclear, serving to point out yet again how very much is really still unknown and remains to be discovered about religious and cultic practices in the ancient world.[47]

NOTES

1. See the many helpful maps in Peter Levi, *Atlas of the Greek World* (New York: Facts on File, 1991).

2. Although Indo-European influence on the development of Greek, and hence Western, culture has been traditionally postulated, other views have reasserted the potentially greater significance of Afroasiatic cultures in the formation of ancient Greek civilization, especially connections with Egypt. See Martin Bernal, *Black Athena: The Afroasiatic Roots of Classical Civilization* (New Brunswick, NJ: Rutgers University Press, vol. 1, 1987 and vol. 2, 1991); Mary Lefkowitz and Guy Rogers, eds., *Black Athena Revisited* (Chapel Hill: University of North Carolina Press, 1996), and Martin Bernal, *Black Athena Writes Back: Martin Bernal Responds to His Critics* (Durham, NC: Duke University Press, 2001).

3. Jeremy Tanner, "Nature, Culture and the Body in Classical Greek Religious Art," *World Archaeology* 33, no. 2 (2001), 261.

4. Hugh Lloyd-Jones, "Ancient Greek Religion," *Proceedings of the American Philosophical Society* 145, no. 4 (2001), 457.

5. Karl Kerényi, *The Religion of the Greeks and Romans* (Westport, CT: Greenwood Press, 1973), 21.

6. John Scheid, *An Introduction to Roman Religion* (Bloomington: Indiana University Press, 2003), 178–79.

7. Richard Geldard, *The Traveler's Key to Ancient Greece: A Guide to the Sacred Places of Ancient Greece* (New York: Alfred A. Knopf, 1989), 37.

8. Geldard, 41.

9. The 12 Olympian deities of ancient Greece and their Roman counterparts are: Zeus/Jupiter, Hera/Juno, Poseidon/Neptune, Demeter/Ceres, Apollo/Apollo, Artemis/Diana, Ares/Mars, Aphrodite/Venus, Hermes/Mercury, Athena/Minerva, Hephaistos/Vulcan, Hestia/Vesta—or Dionysius/Bacchus.

10. Scheid, 154.

11. Robin Fox, *Pagans and Christians* (New York: Alfred A. Knopf, 1987), especially chapter 9, "Persecution and Martyrdom," 419–92.

12. Geldard, 57.

13. Scheid, 22.

14. Scheid, 57.

15. See the beautifully illustrated volume by Panos Valavanis, *Games and Sanctuaries in Ancient Greece* (Los Angeles: Getty Publications, 2004).

16. Jenifer Neils, ed., *Goddess and Polis: The Panathenaic Festival in Ancient Athens* (Hanover, NH: Hood Museum of Art, 1992).

17. Jan Bremmer, *Greek Religion* (Oxford: Oxford University Press, 1994), 7.

18. Walter Burkert, *Greek Religion* (Cambridge, MA: Harvard University Press, 1985), 95.

19. Susan Blundell and Margaret Williamson, *The Sacred and the Feminine in Ancient Greece* (London: Routledge, 1998), 1.

20. See especially Joan Connelly, *Portrait of a Priestess: Women and Ritual in Ancient Greece* (Princeton, NJ: Princeton University Press, 2007).

21. Many studies have been devoted to all aspects of the worship of the goddess Vesta and the obligations of her priestesses; see, for example, Mary Beard, "The Sexual Status of the Vestal Virgins," *The Journal of Roman Studies* 70 (1980): 12–27.

22. Kerényi, *The Religion of the Greeks and Romans*, 261.

23. Alan Bernstein, *The Formation of Hell: Death and Retribution in the Ancient and Early Christian Worlds* (Ithaca, NY: Cornell University Press, 1993), 91.

24. Jan Bremmer, *The Early Greek Concept of the Soul* (Princeton, NJ: Princeton University Press, 1993).

25. Walter Burkert, *Ancient Mystery Cults* (Cambridge, MA: Harvard University Press, 1987).

26. Karl Kerényi, *Eleusis: Archetypal Image of Mother and Daughter* (New York: Pantheon Books, 1967).

27. Geldard, 61.

28. Much scholarship has been devoted to the sacred landscape of ancient Greece; see especially Vincent Scully, *The Earth, the Temple, and the Gods: Greek Sacred Architecture* (New Haven, CT: Yale University Press, 1979) and the several excellent essays in Susan Alcock and Robin Osborne, eds., *Placing the Gods: Sanctuaries and Sacred Space in Ancient Greece* (Oxford: Clarendon Press, 1994).

29. Tanner, 257–76, and Nikolaus Himmelmann, *Reading Greek Art* (Princeton, NJ: Princeton University Press, 1998), especially 103–38, "Some Characteristics of the Representation of Gods in Classical Art."

30. Bremmer, *Greek Religion*, 2.

31. Innumerable volumes and scholarly articles have been devoted to each building as a whole as well as to specialized and detailed aspects of their construction, history, and meaning. For the Pantheon, an excellent source remains William MacDonald, *The Pantheon: Design, Meaning, and Progeny* (Cambridge, MA: Harvard University Press, 1976).

32. Joan Connelly, "Parthenon and *Parthenoi*: A Mythological Interpretation of the Parthenon Frieze," *American Journal of Archaeology* 100, no. 1 (1996): 55.

33. MacDonald, 19.

34. Theodore Vrettos, *The Elgin Affair: The Abduction of Antiquity's Greatest Treasures and the Passions It Aroused* (New York: Arcade, 1997).

35. Jenifer Neils, ed., *The Parthenon from Antiquity to the Present* (Cambridge: Cambridge University Press, 2005) and Panayotis Tournikiotis, *The Parthenon and Its Impact in Modern Times* (Athens: Melissa, 1996).

36. MacDonald, 11.

37. Richard Brilliant, *Arts of the Ancient Greeks* (New York: McGraw-Hill, 1973), 195.

38. MacDonald, 13.

39. See MacDonald, 44–47, for construction details.

40. Christiane Joost-Gaugier, "The Iconography of Sacred Space: A Suggested Reading of the Meaning of the Roman Pantheon," *Artibus et Historiae* 19, no. 38 (1998): 21.

41. Joost-Gaugier, 21–42.

42. Connelly, "Parthenon and *Parthenoi*," and Robin Osborne, "The Viewing and Obscuring of the Parthenon Frieze," *Journal of Hellenic Studies* 107 (1987): 98–105.

43. See, for example, Otto Brendel, *The Visible Idea: Interpretations of Classical Art* (Washington, DC: Decatur House, 1980), especially 90–138, "The Great Frieze in the Villa of the Mysteries"; Linda Fierz-David and Nor Hall, *Dreaming in Red: The Women's Dionysian Initiation Chamber in Pompeii* (Putnam, CT: Spring Publications, 2005); and Elaine Gazda, ed., *The Villa of the Mysteries in Pompeii: Ancient Ritual, Modern Muse* (Ann Arbor, MI: Kelsey Museum of Archaeology and the University of Michigan Museum of Art, 2000).

44. Burkert, *Ancient Mystery Cults*, 96.

45. Susan Silberberg-Peirce, "The Muse Restored: Images of Women in Roman Painting," *Woman's Art Journal* 14, no. 2 (1993–94): 30.

46. J. J. Pollitt, "Rome: The Republic and Early Empire," In *The Oxford History of Classical Art*, ed. Richard Boardman (Oxford: Oxford University Press, 1993), 283.

47. Silberberg-Peirce, 36, n.26.

BIBLIOGRAPHY AND FURTHER READING

Alcock, Susan, and Robin Osborne, eds. *Placing the Gods: Sanctuaries and Sacred Space in Ancient Greece*. Oxford: Clarendon Press, 1994.

Alles, Gregory. "Surface, Space, and Intention: The Parthenon and the Kandariya Mahadeva." *History of Religions* 28, no. 1 (1988): 1–36.

Beard, Mary. "The Sexual Status of the Vestal Virgins." *The Journal of Roman Studies* 70 (1980): 12–27.

Bérard, Claude. *A City of Images: Iconography and Society in Ancient Greece*. Princeton, NJ: Princeton University Press, 1989.

Bernal, Martin. *Black Athena: The Afroasiatic Roots of Classical Civilization*. New Brunswick, NJ: Rutgers University Press, 1987 (vol. 1), 1991 (vol. 2).

Bernal, Martin. *Black Athena Writes Back: Martin Bernal Responds to His Critics*. Durham, NC: Duke University Press, 2001.

Bernstein, Alan. *The Formation of Hell: Death and Retribution in the Ancient and Early Christian Worlds*. Ithaca, NY: Cornell University Press, 1993.

Blundell, Susan, and Margaret Williamson. *The Sacred and the Feminine in Ancient Greece*. London: Routledge, 1998.

Boardman, John. *Greek Sculpture: The Archaic Period: A Handbook*. New York: Oxford University Press, 1978.

Boardman, John. *Greek Sculpture: The Classical Period: A Handbook*. New York: Thames and Hudson, 1985.

Boardman, John, ed. *The Oxford History of Classical Art*. Oxford: Oxford University Press, 1993.

Boardman, John. *The Parthenon and Its Sculptures*. Austin: University of Texas Press, 1985.

Bremmer, Jan. *The Early Greek Concept of the Soul*. Princeton, NJ: Princeton University Press, 1993.

Bremmer, Jan. *Greek Religion*. Oxford: Oxford University Press, 1994.

Brendel, Otto. *The Visible Idea: Interpretations of Classical Art*. Washington, DC: Decatur House, 1980.

Brilliant, Richard. *Arts of the Ancient Greeks*. New York: McGraw-Hill, 1973.

Burkert, Walter. *Ancient Mystery Cults*. Cambridge, MA: Harvard University Press, 1987.

Burkert, Walter. *Greek Religion*. Cambridge, MA: Harvard University Press, 1985.

Burkert, Walter. *Structure and History in Greek Mythology and Ritual*. Berkeley: University of California Press, 1979.

Cole, Susan. *Landscapes, Gender, and Ritual Space: The Ancient Greek Experience*. Berkeley: University of California Press, 2004.

Connelly, Joan. "Parthenon and *Parthenoi*: A Mythological Interpretation of the Parthenon Frieze." *American Journal of Archaeology* 100, no. 1 (1996): 53–80.

Connelly, Joan. *Portrait of a Priestess: Women and Ritual in Ancient Greece*. Princeton, NJ: Princeton University Press, 2007.

Cotterell, Arthur, and Rachel Storm. *The Ultimate Encyclopedia of Mythology*. London: Hermes House, 1999.

Coulton, J.J. *Ancient Greek Architects at Work: Problems of Structure and Design*. Ithaca, NY: Cornell University Press, 1977.

Ferguson, John. *Among the Gods: An Archaeological Explanation of Ancient Greek Religion*. London: Routledge, 1989.

Fierz-David, Linda, and Nor Hall. *Dreaming in Red: The Women's Dionysian Initiation Chamber in Pompeii*. Putnam, CT: Spring Publications, 2005.

Fox, Robin. *Pagans and Christians*. New York: Alfred A. Knopf, 1987.

Gazda, Elaine, ed. *The Villa of the Mysteries in Pompeii: Ancient Ritual, Modern Muse*. Ann Arbor, MI: Kelsey Museum of Archaeology and the University of Michigan Museum of Art, 2000.

Geldard, Richard. *The Traveler's Key to Ancient Greece: A Guide to the Sacred Places of Ancient Greece*. New York: Alfred A. Knopf, 1989.

Graves, Robert. *Greek Myths*. Garden City, NY: Doubleday, 1961.

Henig, Martin, ed. *A Handbook of Roman Art*. Ithaca, NY: Cornell University Press, 1983.

Himmelmann, Nikolaus. *Reading Greek Art*. Princeton, NJ: Princeton University Press, 1998.

Jenkins, Ian. *The Parthenon Frieze*. London: British Museum Press, 1994.

Johnston, Sarah, ed. *Religions of the Ancient World: A Guide*. Cambridge, MA: Belknap Press of Harvard University Press, 2004.

Joost-Gaugier, Christiane. "The Iconography of Sacred Space: A Suggested Reading of the Meaning of the Roman Pantheon." *Artibus et Historiae* 19, no. 38 (1998): 21–42.

Kerényi, Karl. *Eleusis: Archetypal Image of Mother and Daughter*. New York: Pantheon Books, 1967.

Kerényi, Karl. *The Religion of the Greeks and Romans*. Westport, CT: Greenwood Press, 1973.

Kraemer, Ross, ed. *Maenads, Martyrs, Matrons, Monastics: A Sourcebook on Women's Religions in the Greco-Roman World*. Philadelphia: Fortress Press, 1988.

Lefkowitz, Mary, and Guy Rogers, eds. *Black Athena Revisited*. Chapel Hill: University of North Carolina Press, 1996.

Levi, Peter. *Atlas of the Greek World*. New York: Facts on File, 1991.

Lloyd-Jones, Hugh. "Ancient Greek Religion." *Proceedings of the American Philosophical Society* 145, no. 4 (2001): 456–64.

MacDonald, William. *The Pantheon: Design, Meaning, and Progeny*. Cambridge, MA: Harvard University Press, 1976.

Mellor, Richard, and Marni McGee. *The Ancient Roman World*. Oxford: Oxford University Press, 2004.

Neils, Jenifer, ed. *Goddess and Polis: The Panathenaic Festival in Ancient Athens*. Hanover, NH: Hood Museum of Art, 1992.

Neils, Jenifer, ed. *The Parthenon from Antiquity to the Present*. Cambridge: Cambridge University Press, 2005.

Osborne, Robin. "The Viewing and Obscuring of the Parthenon Frieze." *Journal of Hellenic Studies* 107 (1987): 98–105.

Osborne, Robin. "Women and Sacrifice in Classical Greece." *Classical Quarterly* 43, no. 2 (1993): 392–405.

Perowne, Stewart. *Roman Mythology*. New York: Peter Bedrick, 1984.

Pollitt, J. J. "Rome: The Republic and Early Empire." In *The Oxford History of Classical Art*, ed. Richard Boardman, 217–96. Oxford: Oxford University Press, 1993.

Richter, Gisela. *A Handbook of Greek Art*. Oxford: Phaidon, 1987.

Ridgway, Brunilde. *Fifth Century Styles in Greek Sculpture*. Princeton, NJ: Princeton University Press, 1981.

Rives, James. *Religion in the Roman Empire*. Malden, MA: Blackwell, 2007.

Scheid, John. *An Introduction to Roman Religion*. Bloomington: Indiana University Press, 2003.

Scully, Vincent. *The Earth, the Temple, and the Gods: Greek Sacred Architecture*. New Haven, CT: Yale University Press, 1979.

Silberberg-Peirce, Susan. "The Muse Restored: Images of Women in Roman Painting." *Woman's Art Journal* 14, no. 2 (1993–94): 28–36.

Tanner, Jeremy. "Nature, Culture and the Body in Classical Greek Religious Art." *World Archaeology* 33, no. 2 (2001): 257–76.

Tournikiotis, Panayotis. *The Parthenon and Its Impact in Modern Times*. Athens: Melissa, 1996.

Valavanis, Panos. *Games and Sanctuaries in Ancient Greece*. Los Angeles: Getty Publications, 2004.

Vrettos, Theodore. *The Elgin Affair: The Abduction of Antiquity's Greatest Treasures and the Passions It Aroused*. New York: Arcade, 1997.

—5—

Mesoamerican and Andean Religions

The regions of Central and South America provide the primary focus of this chapter. *Mesoamerica* is a geographic term that refers largely to present-day Mexico, Honduras, Belize, El Salvador, and Guatemala. This chapter also includes discussion of some of the ancient cultures of the South American Andean regions between Ecuador and northern Chile—primarily centered in present-day Peru. For purposes of this study, the focus is on the precolonial period when the art and architectural forms reflected the religious practices of the several successive cultures in these regions largely before contact with western Europeans in the late 15th and early 16th centuries.

ORIGINS AND DEVELOPMENT

The history of ancient Mesoamerica and the Andean regions is traditionally divided up into a series of successive and often overlapping phases associated with the rise and fall of several different but related cultural groups. Evidence of human habitation in these regions dates back to the prehistoric Stone Age. Although it remains unclear when and how humans first arrived in or migrated to these regions, it is generally thought that "the inhabitants of Mesoamerica arrived by crossing the Bering Strait between Siberia and Alaska near the end of the Ice Age."[1] Archaeological evidence appears to demonstrate that Stone Age people were present in the regions from as early as ca. 30,000–10,000 BCE. Agricultural practices developed around 8000–2000 BCE, and it is from this early period that some of the very first cultural groups have been named and identified.

In ancient Mesoamerica, the Pre-Classic period (ca. 2000 BCE–250 CE) is primarily associated with the Olmec civilization (often called the mother culture of ancient Mesoamerica), centered in central Mexico and the lowlands of the southern Gulf Coast. The Classic period (ca. 250–900 CE) is largely associated with the Teotihuacán culture (based on the great metropolis of Teotihuacán near present-day Mexico City), the Maya culture (and significant sites such as Copán, Tikal, and Bonampak), and the Zapotec culture of Monte Albán.[2] The Mayan civilization of Chichén Itzá came to prominence in the Post-Classic period (ca. 900–1521 CE). During this period as well, the Toltecs (ca. 900–1200 CE), with their major center at Tula, and the Aztecs (from the late 12th century), whose capital of Tenochtitlán lies under present-day Mexico City, were extremely important cultural groups.

In the Andean regions, yet other groups have been identified—from the very early Chavín culture (ca. 3000–800 BCE), the Paracas (400–200 BCE), the Nazca (200 BCE–600 CE), the Moche (1–700 CE), the Tiwanaku (100–1000 CE), the Wari (500–800 CE), and, ultimately, the Inca civilization (ca. 1000–1540 CE) with remarkable sites such as Machu Picchu.[3]

The Maya and Aztecs of Mesoamerica and the Incas of South America were, primarily, the last civilizations to have flourished in these regions before the early 16th century, when European explorers, settlers, and Christian missionaries arrived. The dramatic, and ultimately very destructive, consequences of European colonizing interests in these regions simply cannot be underestimated. The initial and subsequent decades of contact between Europeans and the indigenous peoples of Mesoamerica and South America were characterized by aggressive warfare, active resistance, huge losses of lives (due not only to war but also to diseases brought by Europeans), and a great loss of cultural material. Many works of art and ancient cultural heritage were destroyed by the European conquerors, and this fact remains a signal tragedy. The historical context of European colonizing efforts in the 16th and subsequent centuries, the ensuing cultural clashes and conflicts, and the perceptions of indigenous cultures demonstrated by these cultural conflicts are all extremely important factors to consider in any study of Mesoamerican and South American art and religion.

An analysis of the different manners in which history is constructed, and how lost cultures are reconstructed, is also extremely relevant for the materials under consideration in this chapter. Western Europeans only became aware of the peoples residing in Central and South America in the 16th century. Later and modern scholarship into the 20th century often reflects this by the use of the term pre-Columbian for studies of Mesoamerican and Andean cultures. The several voyages of the explorer Christopher Columbus (1451–1506) from Spain to the New World are not without relevance here, but the term *pre-Columbian* has tended to be replaced in current scholarship by other designations such as *precolonial*, or simply *Mesoamerican* and *Andean*.

Although traditionally scholarly work on the history, art, and archaeology of Mesoamerica and the Andean regions continues to be undertaken by both nonnative as well as native experts and researchers now, these evolving studies have also been supplemented by a great deal of more popular literature focusing on the mysterious aspects of these ancient civilizations. The earthworks/drawings in the landscape of Peru (well visible from an aerial perspective), attributed to the Nazca culture, have gripped popular imagination a great deal in recent years as potentially representing communications with extraterrestrials. The countdown to the end of time (or at least, this current era)—based on the apparent preoccupation of several Mesoamerican cultures with keeping time and recording dates—has also spawned a great deal of popular as well as scholarly literature.[4] And, because the cultures and belief systems of Mesoamerican and Andean peoples still survive today in new transformations, any discussion needs to take these complex factors into account as well.[5]

PRINCIPAL BELIEFS AND KEY PRACTICES

The successive and often overlapping cultures in Mesoamerica and the Andean regions all developed distinctive religious beliefs and imagery; however, some fundamental shared characteristics can also be seen. One pervasive theme is the belief that the existence of the world and universe is characterized by a series of cosmogonic eras or ages, all terminating in catastrophic destruction before the commencement of new eras. The number of eras varies somewhat in different cultural traditions; however, the idea that measurable periods of time commence and conclude with cataclysmic events is a concept shared across many Mesoamerican, as well as other world, cultures. The remarkable, complex, and highly sophisticated calendar systems developed by the Maya and Aztec cultures, for example, more than demonstrate the importance of timekeeping within the larger cosmic scheme.

"In Mesoamerican thought, the calendar concerned the definition and ordering of space as well as time."[6] Spatial directions, cosmic cycles, and natural forces were also associated with an extensive range of deities. Similar types of deities were developed by different Mesoamerican and Andean cultures as well as rich traditions of mythology and iconography for depicting the numerous deities.[7] Many deities were visualized in anthropomorphic form—with fundamentally human features—but may also exhibit distinctive markings or nonhuman, animal features as well. Jaguars, serpents and snakes, birds, and monsters of several configurations appear in various combinations and forms. Many deities appear as zoomorphs, combining features of several different animals, and some deities appear in several different guises that emphasize their different aspects and attributes. For example, in Maya imagery

> The sun can appear as a young male, an aged male, an anthromorph with jaguar features or a half-skeletal zoomorph with a sun bowl on its forehead. These contrasting and superficially unrelated forms appear to express different aspects of the same entity—in this case, the newly risen sun, the sun near sunset, the sun in the Underworld and the sun as cosmic object.[8]

The deities often have similar or shared attributes as well, so several scholars believe it is likely that they were seen less as a series of individual and distinct entities but rather as aspects "of a more generalized force, or array of powers and qualities, with a subset relevant to any particular occasion or ceremony . . . as personified representations of the commonest combinations of supernatural elements."[9] On the other hand, scholars have identified a number of principal and distinct deities distinguished by their associations with the sun and the moon, various stars and constellations, the earth, water, rain, and lightening, warfare, death, and bloodletting, knowledge, creation, magic, and sorcery, agriculture, and critical crops such as maize or corn. Maize deities are often represented in the arts of many Mesoamerican and Andean cultures (see Figure 5.1). There were also patron deities of specific occupations and particular cities. Prominent among the many different deities is the well-studied Feathered-Serpent God (Quetzalcoatl or Kukulcan), who was widely venerated by various Mesoamerican cultures in different forms, and was frequently represented in art[10] (see Figures 5.2 and 5.3).

The role and function of the deities and the role of humans in relationship to the deities were intimately connected. The deities were associated with earthly events as well as cosmic eras. They played major roles in the succession of time sequences and were believed to require and reward actions on the part of humans, especially sacrificial blood offerings. Many Mesoamerican cultures employed various methods of human sacrifice and ritual bloodletting as means to honor and appease the deities and to signal the cycles of death and rebirth with which the deities were intimately connected. For the Maya, "it is clear that bloodletting was basic to the institution of rulership, to the mythology of world order, and to public rituals of all sorts."[11]

Many works of art depict ritual bloodletting ceremonies, such as the well-studied relief carvings from the Late Classic Maya site of Yaxchilán in Mexico, ca. 725 CE (see Plate 9). Several carved limestone panels illustrate members of the royal family performing these rites. In the example illustrated, Lady Xoc, the principal wife of the ruler Shield Jaguar II, is shown pulling a rope studded with obsidian shards through her perforated tongue. Her lips and cheeks are covered with scroll-patterns symbolizing

Figure 5.1 Ceramic vessel with anthropomorphic Maize deities, Moche culture, Peru, 1–700 CE. London: British Museum. Werner Forman / Art Resource, NY.

Figure 5.2 The Feathered Serpent God, detail from the Temple of the Feathered Serpent, ca. 200 CE, Teotihaucán, Mexico. Ggordon / Dreamstime.com.

her sacrificial blood. The blood-smeared rope collects on pieces of paper in a ritual basket placed next to her kneeling and elaborately garbed figure. Shield Jaguar II, holding a flaming torch, stands on the left side of the composition, clothed in garments and headdress that also indicate his participation in the sacrificial ceremonies. Rituals such as these indicate "the concept of a reciprocal relationship between humans and the gods. The earth and its creatures were created through a sacrificial act of the gods, and human beings, in turn, were required to strengthen and nourish the gods. . . . blood drawn from all parts of the body—especially from the tongue, earlobes, and genitals—was sustenance for the gods."[12]

Ritual bloodletting and human sacrifice were practiced to a greater or lesser degree in many ancient Mesoamerican and Andean cultures, including the Moche and Inca in South America and the Toltec, Maya, and especially Aztec cultures of Mesoamerica. Much attention has been devoted to this aspect of Aztec civilization in particular.[13] These violent practices were certainly among the aspects of these ancient cultures that most appalled the Spanish settlers and Christian missionaries and that have continued to intrigue and challenge modern sensibilities.

Human sacrifice was often, although not always, associated also with the ritual sport of the ballgame, variations of which appear in several Mesoamerica

Figure 5.3 Stone bust of Quetzalcoatl, Aztec, ca. 1325–1521 CE. London: British Museum. Erich Lessing / Art Resource, NY.

cultures, over many centuries.[14] The game appears not to have been practiced among Andean and South America cultures. The sport was played with a hard, solid rubber ball, and, although the rules of the game are not clearly known (and doubtless varied over the centuries), the aim appears to have been for the individuals or teams of players to keep the ball in motion without touching it with the hands. Stone rings or markers set into the enclosing walls of ball courts are found primarily in the Post-Classic period. It appears that points could be scored by directing the ball through the ring (an achievement requiring enormous skill) or by contacting the ring with the ball. "Ball courts, consisting of two parallel structures (with either straight or sloping sides) flanking an earthen or paved stone alleyway that is the court, appear at almost every site from Olmec times to the Conquest."[15] Although ballgames could be played purely for sport, their close association with religious rituals and human sacrifice is made more than clear by numerous examples of painting and sculpture depicting the sacrifice of players (presumably the losing players). The ballgame featured prominently in the ancient Maya creation myth known as the *Popol Vuh* (Council Book), which recounts the adventures of the Hero Twins who "confronted the Lords of Death in the ballgame. . . . The ballgame was the metaphor for life and death. . . . The ballcourt . . . was a crevice leading into the Otherworld. When the Maya played their game, they remade Creation again and again."[16] The regenerative power and importance of blood sacrifice is more than amply demonstrated here.

Much evidence exists for the use of psychotropic substances in ancient Mesoamerican and South American religious rituals.[17] Altered states of consciousness, visions, hallucinations, and contacts with the spirit world were achieved through the use of various natural chemical hallucinogens derived from plants and animals. Ecstatic and hallucinatory experiences were often also associated with the fasting and bloodletting rituals performed by priests and the nobility. Contacts with the supernatural and attempts to discern the will of the deities are also represented by various divination rituals performed by both male and female practitioners. "Among the diviners were specialists such as astrologers, oracles, illusionists, and interpreters of omens. . . . Some types of practitioners survived, albeit covertly, into the postconquest period, and a few continue to be active even to the present day."[18]

TRADITIONAL ART AND ARCHITECTURAL FORMS

The arts associated with or reflective of religious beliefs and practices in ancient Mesoamerica and the Andes encompass all media from large-scale architecture to small-scale pottery. The availability of specific materials (such as gold and jade) in particular regions, and the traditions of wall painting or relief carving especially developed by particular cultures may stand out as special features of different groups and time periods. Because religion was such an integral aspect of life in these ancient cultures, the impression that a majority of the art that survives was designed for religious purposes is surely correct.

Pyramid-Temple Complexes

The architectural form most characteristic of ancient Mesoamerican religious centers is the *pyramid-temple complex*, a term used by many scholars to describe the numerous examples of elevated structures in pyramidal form associated with smaller related buildings. Numerous examples of these complexes exist, representing a range of dates and differing cultural styles. The fundamental format consists of a raised pyramid (of earth and stone) serving as an axial focal point for a ceremonial plaza, which is often defined by platforms, other enclosures, walls, or columns. The general layout of the Mesoamerican pyramid-temple complex bears some resemblance to the earlier structures of ancient Mesopotamia and Egypt (see chapters 2 and 3) with carefully sited, heavenward-reaching monuments of impressive scale, viewable from some distance.

The earliest example of such a pyramid-temple complex in Mesoamerica is traditionally said to be that of the Olmec site at La Venta, Mexico, dating ca. 1110–400 BCE. The ritual center of the great city of Teotihuacán in Mexico contains two large multiplatformed (or stepped) pyramids made of stone-veneered mounds of earth, probably constructed between the first century BCE and the second century CE (see Figure 5.4). The Pyramid of the Moon is located at the north end of a long causeway, and the larger Pyramid of the Sun is located on the southeastern side of the causeway. The later Mayan site of Tikal in Guatemala contains several exceptionally steep and tall pyramids, largely dating to the seventh and eighth centuries CE (see Figure 5.5). There are excellent examples of pyramid-temples at many other Maya sites such as Palenque, from the 7th century CE , and Chichén Itzá, from the 10th century CE (see Figure 5.6). The pyramid-temple form was employed by the Zapotec, Toltec, and Aztec cultures, as well as several Andean cultures.

Many of the stepped pyramids as well as terraces and other structures in temple complexes make use of *talud* and *tablero* forms—with combinations of

Figure 5.4   Teotihaucán, Mexico, general view. Tompozzo / Dreamstime.com.

horizontal friezes (*tableros*) alternating with sloped planes of masonry (*taluds*). Wall surfaces were often painted and enriched with carved relief sculptures. The temple structures on top of pyramids may have one or more entrances; many temples have elaborate roof combs or *talud*-like elements at their tops.

The function of these structures was often multifaceted as were the rituals and ceremonies enacted. Many pyramids served as burial places for prominent rulers and thus functioned to immortalize their deeds and enhance the prestige of their descendants as well. The tomb of the seventh-century Mayan ruler, Lord Pacal, discovered in the early 1950s within the Temple of the Inscriptions at Palenque is an excellent and well-studied example. Many of the pyramids at other Mesoamerican sites, however, do not seem to have functioned primarily as royal burial sites but rather as locales for the enactment of religious rituals involving sacrificial offerings to the deities and festivals celebrating or commemorating the passage of time and cosmic cycles. In no cases do the interiors of pyramid-temples offer any architectural space for congregational or community gatherings even of a limited number of participants. Like the temples of ancient Greece, these structures primarily served as focal points for religious ceremonies performed outside—rather than inside—the buildings.

Figure 5.5   Temple 1 (Temple of the Great Jaguar), late seventh/early eighth century CE, Tikal, Guatemala. Nhtg / Dreamstime.com.

Figure 5.6 Temple of the Inscriptions, late seventh century, Palenque, Mexico. Koubatian / Dreamstime.com.

Symbols and Glyphs

Much of the degree of confidence with which current scholars discuss ancient Mesoamerican art and culture is due to the painstaking and remarkable decipherment of the picture-writing systems developed by the Maya culture, especially. Like the breakthrough in decipherment of the ancient Egyptian hieroglyphs, this work has added enormously to the field of study.[19] Most of this work is relatively recent and continues to be avidly pursued today. Although some early archaeologists had assumed that the symbols and signs found carved and painted on ancient monuments represented some form of picture-writing system (rather than simply decorative devices), and several early Spanish settlers and missionaries had earlier taken some interest in recording the glyphs and picture-symbols of the Aztec culture, it was not really until the middle of the 20th century that major advances were made in the understanding of ancient Maya writing.[20] "Though still not fully deciphered, Mayan writing is the best understood of all pre-Columbian Mesoamerican scripts. Its characteristic features, found in monumental reliefs, on wood and painted pottery, and in paper codices, can be thought of as the quintessence of the American tradition."[21]

Previously thought to be primarily based on pictograms and other visual symbols (which largely recorded dates and calendar counts), it is now understood as a highly complex system involving both phonetic signs (which denote words and syllabic sounds) interspersed with pictograms. Maya glyphs are generally arranged into blocks in horizontal and vertical rows and are read from left to right in pairs and from top to bottom in columns. The "rapid progress in deciphering the glyphs now permits epigraphers, linguists, archaeologists, and art historians to use Maya inscriptions and pictorial records as a primary source of information on the identity of the Maya, their world view and social system. Maya history can now be understood from records describing the events of their lives, written from their own point of view."[22] Although scholars do not assume that a generally high level of literacy existed in ancient Maya society, it is clear that the glyphic (and often repetitious) inscriptions on public monuments were meant to be read and understood in some form by the general populace, whereas the creation and reading of the more complex glyphic sequences was doubtless the purview of the educated elite classes, priests, scribes, and royalty.

Writing systems were developed in several other Mesoamerican cultures (Olmec, Zapotec, Mixtec, and Aztec), some of which have been partially deciphered and several of which appear to have relied much more on pictography than the Maya system did. The repeated signs and symbols, found in various media from several Peruvian cultures, may also represent examples of written communication systems. Although the Inca never developed a writing system, they kept masterful records of economic transactions as well as events in the form of *quipus*, color-coded and knotted fiber cords.[23]

EXAMPLES

Las Limas Monument 1: "The Lord of Las Limas," ca. 800–300 BCE

The Olmec culture flourished in Mesoamerica from approximately the 15th to 1st century BCE and is often called the Mesoamerican mother culture, or America's first civilization.[24] Although "much has been written about Olmec religion in recent years, most of it is speculative and almost none can be proven beyond a reasonable shadow of doubt."[25] The monuments and mysterious imagery of the Olmecs continue to provide a very rich field for scholarship.

A number of Olmec monuments depict enigmatic creatures that combine human and feline features—traditionally termed "were-jaguars"—such as the reclining figure held in the lap of the seated male figure in this example (see Figure 5.7). Popularly known as the "Lord of Las Limas," this carved greenstone statue (approximately 22 inches tall) was discovered accidentally by two children in 1965 in the village of Las Limas, Mexico, once a major Olmec center. "The modern history of the Lord of Las Limas is as fascinating as the sculpture itself."[26] When first discovered, and because of the sculpture's general resemblance to traditional Christian imagery of the Madonna and Child, it was initially venerated by the villagers as the Matron of Las Limas—a miraculous materialization of the Virgin Mary. Eventually it was moved to the anthropological museum in Veracruz, from which it was stolen a few years later. Ultimately, the sculpture was rediscovered (in a motel room in San Antonio, Texas) and returned to the museum.

Much scholarly attention has been devoted to this object, to the prominent imagery of were-jaguars in Olmec art, as well as to feline motifs generally in Mesoamerican art.[27] Were-jaguars typically show the down-turned mouth and almond-shaped eyes characteristic of Olmec figural representation in general plus varying degrees of feline features, such as a flattened wrinkled nose, protruding fangs, a cleft forehead, and flamelike forms rising from the eyebrows. The were-jaguar, however, "as a typological unit is at best a convenient rather than a precise classification," because it is clear that the specifically feline characteristics do not appear to the same degree in all examples identified as were-jaguars.[28] Such is the case with the Las Limas monument, where the were-jaguar baby held in the lap of the seated figure shows notably few feline features.

Figure 5.7 Las Limas Monument 1: "The Lord of Las Limas," Olmec, ca. 800–300 BCE. The Art Archive / Xalapa Museum Veracruz Mexico / Gianni Dagli Orti.

Several scholars of Mesoamerican mythology have stated that the Olmec believed their ancestors came from a union of humans and the powerful jungle predator, the jaguar. Depictions of human-jaguar copulation scenes have been identified (and disputed) in Olmec art.[29] Other scholars have suggested that the figural and facial deformities shown by the were-jaguars in Olmec art actually represent congenital defects in children born to some early members of the ruling classes, and that the association with jaguars was the result of rulers' concerns with validating their political power. It would be a "definite advantage to identify the child's deformities with the characteristics of the supernatural jaguar and to offer the births to the populace as evidence that jaguar blood ran in the family, producing were-jaguar offspring."[30] Other scholars have described the figure traditionally shown holding the were-jaguar babies as a shaman "or priest, in an attitude of offering, presenting an inanimate being that confers upon him supernatural powers."[31]

Shamans, the actual religious practicers, were men and women whose special powers allowed them to establish contact with the supernaturals. . . . While in trances, often induced by fasting and psychotropic substances, shamans traveled the cosmos accompanied by their animal familiars as they attempted to heal the sick, establish contact with the ancestors, and propitiate forces beyond human control.[32]

The priest/shaman/official of the Las Limas sculpture has incised tattoolike designs on his face, shoulders, and legs, the identification of which has also intrigued scholars. These images have been identified as specific Olmec deities, forerunners of later widely venerated Mesoamerican deities: the god of spring, the fire serpent, the plumed serpent, and the god of death. In this case, the were-jaguar would be associated with the water deity, thus forming an "Olmec Pentateuch, with each figure displaying the oldest known representations of later Mesoamerican supernaturals."[33] It is clear that this work of art, as well as many other remarkable Olmec works, will continue to provide material for much further study.

Drawing of the Lid of the Sarcophagus of Lord Pacal of Palenque, ca. 684 CE

This intriguing and celebrated monument was discovered in the mid-20th century during excavations at the Mayan site of Palenque in Mexico. It pro-

vides an excellent introduction to the many complexities of Mesoamerican religious iconography, beliefs about death and the afterlife, and the important position of royal rulers in the earthly and cosmic scheme. The relief carved limestone cover of Lord Pacal's sarcophagus illustrates his death and descent into the underworld. It is replete with complex symbolism and is reproduced here as a line drawing for greater legibility (see Figure 5.8).

Pacal (or Hanab Pakal, 603–684 CE) ruled for 68 years (ascending to the throne at the age of 12) and is credited with many accomplishments. "The most revered king in Palenque's history and one of the best-known Maya kings to the modern world," during his reign Palenque became an especially important, wealthy, and powerful Maya center and was enriched with numerous monuments including the Temple of the Inscriptions within which his tomb was located.[34] The tomb and the multitiered stepped pyramid-temple were constructed contemporaneously. Pacal was interred in a massive sarcophagus placed in a burial chamber within the heart of the pyramid. After his entombment, the vaulted stairway leading from the temple down to the burial chamber was filled in with earth and stones. This hidden staircase was uncovered

Figure 5.8 Drawing: Lid of the Sarcophagus of Lord Pacal from Palenque, ca. 684 CE. Courtesy of Ricochet Productions.

in the early 1950s by archaeologists who were thrilled and astonished to find the burial chamber, ritual offerings, grave goods, and the elaborately carved sarcophagus of Lord Pacal intact and undisturbed after so many centuries.

The huge stone lid of the sarcophagus measures over 12 by 7 feet, and the complex imagery carved on its surface has been much studied and interpreted. The central figure is Lord Pacal himself, poised, in a half-seated, half-reclining position, at the moment of his death. He appears to be falling backward onto the shape of a monstrous creature, which scholars have identified as the Quadripartite Sun Monster, representing sunset—or the death of the sun. "The sun, poised at the horizon, is ready for the plunge into the Underworld. It will carry the dead king with it."[35] The shapes and patterns at the very bottom of the scene have been identified as the Mouth of the Underworld, consisting of two skeletal dragons forming a U-shape into which Pacal and the Sun Monster will plummet. Rising up from the underworld and partially overlapped by Pacal's body is a shape traditionally identified as the World Tree. A double-headed serpent bar and other branches with square-nosed dragons are found partway up the World Tree, while a Celestial Bird perches atop the tree. Numerous other symbols in the densely packed composition have been identified as references to blood and the bloodletting rituals traditionally performed by the Maya rulers to please and honor the deities. The upward sprouting World Tree and the backward fall of Pacal into the jaws of the Underworld provide a sense of both ascending and descending movement in the composition. Although the sun sets on the horizon at nightfall, it rises again at daybreak. The symbolism thus involves not only death but also rebirth.

> In his eighties at the time of his death, Hanab Pakal may have indeed seemed immortal to his subjects, and the complex burial program he probably helped design conspired to promote the notion. On the surface of the sarcophagus . . . Hanab Pakal dressed as the Maize God. . . . falls into the open maws of death. . . . From his body arises the World Tree, the central axis of the earth that every king was responsible for sustaining in position. On the sides of the sarcophagus, ancestors sprout from the earth that has cracked to let them grow, vivid evidence that Hanab Pakal's death has brought renewal for the entire earth.[36]

Although "Pakal falls in death . . . his very position also signaled birth—his birth into the Otherworld and his eventual rebirth as the Maize God and revered ancestor."[37]

The Codex Fejérváry-Mayer, 15th Century CE

Written and illustrated books were produced in great numbers in preconquest Mesoamerica. However, the majority of these materials were destroyed by European conquerors and missionaries eager to eradicate native traditions and pagan religious practices. Although some copies of old books were made in the postconquest period under the direction of Europeans interested in the history and customs of the conquered Mesoamerican peoples, there are only slightly more than a dozen books of preconquest date that survive today "because the conquerors sent them to Europe as curiosities or because they were secretly kept in native hands as heirlooms."[38]

The Codex Fejérváry-Mayer, housed today in the World Museum in Liverpool, England, is one of the very few surviving preconquest books (see Plate 10). The early history of the manuscript is not known—how and when it arrived in Europe is unclear; it is named after the English collector (Mayer) who purchased the book from its Hungarian owner (Fejérváry) in the 19th century. It is made of deerskin parchment folded accordion or screen-fold style (typical of the format of several other preconquest books) and is painted on both sides of each of the slightly over 20 pages. It is traditionally described as a product of the later Mixtec culture of central Mexico and bears some significant resemblances to several other religious manuscripts known as the Borgia group (named after an especially significant example in the Vatican Library in Rome).

The Codex Fejérváry-Mayer is an excellent example of a *tonalamatl* (an Aztec book of days), a type of divinatory and ritual calendar used by Aztec priests to foretell events in given periods of time.

> The *tonalamatl* was a specialist's tool, consulted by a priest called a *tonalpouhqui* who was esteemed as a wise man and owner of books. This "reader of day signs" was skilled in interpreting its various sets of images, the fates they embodied, and the resulting augural combinations. Weighing these factors, he determined whether a day was auspicious or not for a given action. A day might be judged lucky, unlucky, or a bit of both.[39]

The painted pages are enriched with colorful images of various deities, signs for different days and directions, representations of sacred trees, birds, and other symbolic devices indicating forces believed to influence different days and time periods. Traditionally arranged into a 260-day (yearly cycle) of 20 periods of 13 days (each period under the auspices of a particular deity), the calendar "expressed a specifically religious structuring of time. . . . The *tonalamatl* thus served as a guide for synchronizing the activities of an individual with what was believed to be the will of the gods."[40] Scholars have identified several of the deities depicted in this codex as merchant gods, whose influence would have been especially important for those involved with long-distance trading journeys and other forms of commerce. The influence of the deities on earthly endeavors, the interconnectedness of the sacred and worldly realms, and the critical importance of timekeeping in the Mesoamerican world are factors well demonstrated in this example as well as in the next.[41]

The Aztec Calendar Stone, Early 16th Century

"No single image of ancient Mesoamerica is better known than the Great Calendar Stone: it is reproduced on ashtrays, keychains, liquor labels, and is popular both in and outside of Mexico."[42] The subject of innumerable studies—both scholarly and popular—it is included here as an example of the ancient Mesoamerican beliefs in the cyclic nature of time and the continuing fascination these beliefs hold in today's world. Housed in the National Museum of Anthropology in Mexico City, the calendar stone was discovered in the late 18th century, lying face down in Mexico City's Plaza Mayor, the site of the ancient Aztec city of Tenochtitlán. It is traditionally dated to the reign of Motecuhzoma II (Montezuma), ca. 1502–20, the last ruler of the Aztecs before the dramatic fall of the Aztec empire under the Spanish conquistadors led by Hernando Cortés (1485–1547). The circular basalt stone measures 13½ feet in diameter and exhibits a dense and complex diagram carved in relief, which was originally brightly painted (see Figure 5.9).

Although "the exact orientation and function of the monument have never been ascertained . . . [it] has been used to illustrate Postclassic Mexican cosmological concepts . . . more often than any other single image of the period."[43] Most scholars agree that the object was designed and used in Aztec religious rituals, and "despite its name, the Calendar Stone does not function as any sort of a useful calendar but works rather as a record of calendrical cataclysm."[44]

The complex imagery is arranged, in mandalalike fashion, into a series of concentric rings enclosed on the rim by two snakes, which symbolize the 24-hour daily passage of the sun through day and night. A large solar disk, with pointed projections, forms the core of the carving, while the face of a deity—with gaping mouth—appears at the very center. Scholars have identified the glyphs and symbols ranged in the several rings as referring to specific dates in the Aztec calendar as well as to the four cyclical eras through which the universe had already passed. When the relief was carved, the Aztecs believed the universe had entered into the fifth and final era and that it was only a matter of time before cataclysmic destruction would occur unless proper rituals were regularly undertaken to prevent or at least forestall this.

Figure 5.9 Aztec Calendar Stone, ca. 150–220 CE. Mexico City: National Anthropological Museum. Furzyk73 / Dreamstime.com.

Although early scholars identified the deity at the center of the disk as the Aztec sun god, Tonatiuh, more recent scholarship has identified this fearsome figure as the Lord of the Night, Yohualtecuhtli—with traits and features of the female earth monster, Tlatecuhlti. "The image thus created is of the sun fallen on earth, the cataclysm complete, the Aztec world ended. . . . The Calendar Stone is exhibited and reproduced as a wall panel today, but it was probably set on the ground, with blood offerings anointed on the earth monster to keep the apocalypse at bay."[45]

Within just a few years of the creation of this stone monument, the world as known by the Aztecs did effectively come to an end. Thus, the calendar stone has "come to symbolize for the Mexican people the beauty and complexity of their Pre-Columbian heritage."[46] The image has thus taken on many connotations, primarily reflective of postcolonial social and political concerns up to the present day, when fascinations with Mesoamerican calendar systems have also inspired a great deal of literature concerning the apocalyptic end of time.

Much attention has been devoted to the year 2012, which marks the end of an over 5,000-year cycle in the Maya calendar, according to their long count system. The significance and meaning of this date remain hotly debated and may continue to provide additional topics of investigation (both scholarly and popular) well into the 21st century. Predictions of the end of time and resulting apocalyptic events have traditionally, in many religious systems, engaged and provided a source of concern for humankind. The current wave of popular interest in the calendar systems of ancient Mesoamerica continues to reflect this very well.

Nazca Lines, Peru, ca. 200–600 CE

The Nazca culture flourished in the coastal areas of southern Peru especially between about 100 BCE and 800 CE, although archaeological remains in the region are of much earlier and later dates as well. Among the many arts associated with Nazca culture (such as sculpture, woven textiles, and painted pottery vessels), the lines in the desert have gripped the attention of researchers since they were first rediscovered and began to be studied in the early 20th century (see Figure 5.10). Indeed, "few of the world's most famous artifacts have been more over-dramatized or less well understood" than the Nazca lines, doubtless because "these enormous odd shapes carved on an inhospitable desert remain virtually unique in the world."[47] Many believe that they must have had a religious or ritual function, and—although this is by no means absolutely certain—they serve as an excellent example of the stimulating challenges posed by any study of ancient cultures and belief systems.

The lines are found in an area of close to 200 square miles of the southwestern Peruvian coastal desert and consist of very long straight lines, geometric and curvilinear patterns, and several animal, insect, and humanoid figures. Subjects include several species of birds (hummingbird, condor, and

Figure 5.10   Nazca Lines, ca. 200–600 CE, Peru. Jarnogz / Dreamstime.com.

cormorant), fish, flower, monkey, and spider shapes. Most of the subjects also appear on Nazca painted pottery. The lines were created by removing or scraping away dark (iron-oxide coated or desert-glazed) stones, revealing the lighter and pinkish-colored earth underneath. The dark stones were carefully piled next to the lines, creating black borderlines next to the exposed areas of lighter sand. The date, purpose, and function of the lines remain topics of much scholarly debate and popular speculation. A number of different theories about their meaning have been advanced, ranging from mystico-religious to purely aesthetic. Although the lines were well known to the local populace, their aerial rediscovery by outsiders in the 1930s led many to believe that because the lines seemed to be best viewed from the air, the markings may have been actually meant to be seen from above, for example by the Nazca deities (or even ancient astronauts from outer space, a theory that was especially popular in the 1970s). The early 20th-century aviators who first saw the markings from the air used the term "lines" to describe them—as they may have appeared to look like airplane landing strips from an aerial perspective. It has often been pointed out, however, that the lines are also quite well viewed and experienced from ground level perspective or from the low flanking foothills and high dunes in the area.

Some have claimed that the lines functioned as astronomical markers, pointing to places on the horizon where the sun or particular constellations of stars rose and set at specific times of year. A great deal of painstaking astro-archaeological work has been undertaken attempting to correlate the directions of the lines and patterns, as well as the avian and animal imagery, to cyclic celestial events. Although adherents of these theories have produced much work demonstrating their convictions, not all agree that these theories are accurate. Some have seen the lines as expressions of highly esoteric and advanced geometric knowledge on the part of the ancient Nazca people; others have described the lines as requiring remarkable feats of precise engineering and mapping abilities; yet others have described the lines as examples of early earthwork art forms.

Several scholars most recently have hypothesized that the lines functioned in ancient religious ceremonies related to agriculture and irrigation, a constant and logical concern of inhabitants in these arid regions. Perhaps the lines (or in this case more correctly paths) served as ritual sites on which walking or dancing ceremonies were held to induce rain from the gods, or, to indicate the above- and below-ground courses or channels where water seasonally collects and from which it directionally flows. Some support for these theories is also provided by ethnographic studies of the contemporary practices of native peoples in the regions, where pilgrimages and walking ceremonies along set paths occur seasonally and are linked with the rainfall and drought cycles of the agricultural year.

Although the vast majority of the paths are straight lines that often intersect, or that show various geometric configurations, the bird, animal, and humanoid figures are certainly among the most well-known and popularly reproduced. These particular designs are mostly concentrated in one area of the vast network, and many efforts have been made to explain their meaning and purpose in conjunction with the various theories advanced about the overall line system. For example, the large condor, shown in the figure, has been said to symbolize the advent and cessation of rain in the desert region. The condor was also associated with the mountains—if not also seen as a manifestation of a mountain or rain deity.[48] "Modern Nazca farmers interpret sightings of herons, pelicans or condors as signals of rain, while the mountain spirits usually take the shape of birds in order to 'speak' to priests and sorcerers."[49] The lines and designs may thus indicate messages to the deities and may have been intended to invoke and ensure the necessary seasonal rains.

Whenever evidence exists of human endeavors on such a grand scale as the Nazca lines demonstrate, it is often assumed that religious motivations will offer an explanation—or at least a partial explanation. This may seem a reasonable assumption, but the fact remains that the exact purpose and function of the Nazca lines is yet unclear, and additional theories will doubtless continue to be proposed as further research is undertaken in this exciting and field. "The variety of markings . . . challenges our imagination, and means there will always be room for alternative theories. It seems unlikely that the mystery will ever be fully exhausted, and it would surely be a pity if it was."[50]

NOTES

1. Karl Taube, *Aztec and Maya Myths* (Austin: University of Texas Press, 1993), 8.

2. Joseph Whitecotton, *The Zapotecs: Princes, Priests, and Peasants* (Norman: University of Oklahoma Press, 1977).

3. Richard Burger and Lucy Salazar, eds. *Machu Picchu: Unveiling the Mystery of the Incas* (New Haven, CT: Yale University Press, 2004).

4. See, for example, Barbara Clow, *The Mayan Code: Time Acceleration and Awakening the World Mind* (Rochester, VT: Bear and Company, 2007) and Daniel Pinchbeck, *2012: The Return of Quetzalcoatl* (New York: Jeremy P. Tarcher/Penguin, 2006).

5. William Fash, "Changing Perspectives on Maya Civilization," *Annual Review of Anthropology* 23 (1994): 181–208.

6. Taube, 13.

7. Mary Ellen Miller and Karl Taube, *The Gods and Symbols of Ancient Mexico and the Maya: An Illustrated Dictionary of Mesoamerican Religion* (New York: Thames and Hudson, 1993).

8. Linda Schele and Mary Ellen Miller, *The Blood of Kings: Dynasty and Ritual in Maya Art* (New York: George Braziller, 1986), 44.

9. John Henderson, *The World of the Ancient Maya* (Ithaca, NY: Cornell University Press, 1981), 52. See also Joyce Marcus, "Archaeology and Religion: A Comparison of the Zapotec and Maya," *World Archaeology* 10, no. 2 (1978): 172–91.

10. Neil Baldwin, *Legends of the Plumed Serpent: Biography of a Mexican God* (New York: Public Affairs, 1998).

11. Schele and Miller, 175.

12. Schele and Miller, 176.

13. David Carrasco, *City of Sacrifice: The Aztec Empire and the Role of Violence in Civilization* (Boston: Beacon Press, 1999) and Michael Harnes, "The Enigma of Aztec Sacrifice," *Natural History* 84, no. 4 (1977): 46–51.

14. E. Michael Whittington, ed., *The Sport of Life and Death: The Mesoamerican Ballgame* (New York: Thames and Hudson, 2001).

15. Schele and Miller, 243.

16. Linda Schele and Peter Mathews, *The Code of Kings: The Language of Seven Sacred Maya Temples and Tombs* (New York: Scribner, 1998), 213.

17. Marlene Dobkin de Rios, *Hallucinogens: Cross-Cultural Perspectives* (Prospect Heights, IL: Waveland Press, 1990).

18. Eloise Quiñones Keber, *Codex Telleriano-Remensis: Ritual, Divination, and History in a Pictorial Aztec Manuscript* (Austin: University of Texas Press, 1995), 155. See also James Brady and Keith Prufer, "Caves and Crystalmancy: Evidence for the Use of Crystals in Ancient Maya Religion," *Journal of Anthropological Research* 55, no. 1 (1999): 129–44.

19. See especially Michael Coe, *Breaking the Maya Code* (New York: Thames and Hudson, 1992) and Michael Coe and Justin Kerr, *The Art of the Maya Scribe* (New York: Harry N. Abrams, 1998).

20. Keber, *Codex Telleriano-Remensis*.

21. Steven Fischer, *A History of Writing* (London: Reaktion Books, 2001), 221.

22. Schele and Miller, 325.

23. Marcia Ascher and Robert Ascher, *Code of the Quipu: A Study in Media, Mathematics, and Culture* (Ann Arbor: University of Michigan Press, 1981).

24. Román Piña Chan, *The Olmec: Mother Culture of Mesoamerica* (New York: Rizzoli, 1989).

25. Richard Diehl, *The Olmecs: America's First Civilization* (London: Thames and Hudson, 2004), 98.

26. Diehl, 57.

27. Elizabeth Benson, ed., *The Cult of the Feline* (Washington, DC: Dumbarton Oaks, 1972) and Nicholas Saunders, ed., *Icons of Power: Feline Symbolism in the Americas* (London: Routledge, 1998).

28. Whitney Davis, "So-called Jaguar-Human Copulation Scenes in Olmec Art," *American Antiquity* 43, no. 3 (1978): 455.

29. Davis, 453–57.

30. Carson Murdy, "Congenital Deformities and the Olmec Were-Jaguar Motif," *American Antiquity* 46, no. 4 (1981): 869.

31. Elizabeth Benson and Beatriz de la Fuente, *Olmec Art of Ancient Mexico* (Washington, DC: National Gallery of Art, 1996), 170.

32. Diehl, 100.

33. Diehl, 101.

34. Schele and Mathews, 97.

35. Schele and Miller, 285.

36. Mary Ellen Miller, *Maya Art and Architecture* (London: Thames and Hudson, 1999), 112.

37. Schele and Mathews, 132.

38. Esther Pasztory, *Aztec Art* (New York: Harry N. Abrams, 1983), 179.

39. Keber, 154.

40. Keber, 151.

41. Elizabeth Boone, *Cycles of Time and Meaning in the Mexican Books of Fate* (Austin: University of Texas Press, 2007).

42. Mary Ellen Miller, *The Art of Mesoamerica from Olmec to Aztec* (London: Thames and Hudson, 2001), 211.

43. Cecelia Klein, "The Identity of the Central Deity on the Aztec Calendar Stone," *The Art Bulletin* 58, no. 1 (1976): 1.

44. Miller, *The Art of Mesoamerica*, 213.

45. Miller, *The Art of Mesoamerica*, 213.

46. Klein, 1.

47. Anthony Aveni, "The Nazca Lines: Patterns in the Desert," *Archaeology* 39, no. 4 (1986): 33, 34.

48. Anthony Aveni, *Between the Lines: The Mystery of the Giant Ground Drawings of Ancient Nasca, Peru* (Austin: University of Texas Press, 2000), 198.

49. Evan Hadingham, *Lines to the Mountain Gods: Nazca and the Mysteries of Peru* (New York: Random House, 1987), 256.

50. Hadingham, 260.

BIBLIOGRAPHY AND FURTHER READING

Ascher, Marcia, and Robert Ascher. *Code of the Quipu: A Study in Media, Mathematics, and Culture*. Ann Arbor: University of Michigan Press, 1981.

Aveni, Anthony. *Between the Lines: The Mystery of the Giant Ground Drawings of Ancient Nasca, Peru.* Austin: University of Texas Press, 2000.

Aveni, Anthony, ed. *The Lines of Nazca.* Philadelphia: American Philosophical Society, 1990.

Aveni, Anthony. "The Nazca Lines: Patterns in the Desert." *Archaeology* 39, no. 4 (1986): 32–40.

Baldwin, Neil. *Legends of the Plumed Serpent: Biography of a Mexican God.* New York: Public Affairs, 1998.

Benson, Elizabeth, ed. *The Cult of the Feline.* Washington, DC: Dumbarton Oaks, 1972.

Benson, Elizabeth, and Beatriz de la Fuente. *Olmec Art of Ancient Mexico.* Washington, DC: National Gallery of Art, 1996.

Bierhorst, John. *The Mythology of Mexico and Central America.* New York: W. Morrow, 1990.

Boone, Elizabeth. *Cycles of Time and Meaning in the Mexican Books of Fate.* Austin: University of Texas Press, 2007.

Brady, James, and Keith Prufer. "Caves and Crystalmancy: Evidence for the Use of Crystals in Ancient Maya Religion." *Journal of Anthropological Research* 55, no. 1 (1999): 129–44.

Brennan, Martin. *The Hidden Maya.* Santa Fe, NM: Bear and Company, 1998.

Burger, Richard, and Lucy Salazar, eds. *Machu Picchu: Unveiling the Mystery of the Incas.* New Haven, CT: Yale University Press, 2004.

Carrasco, David. *City of Sacrifice: The Aztec Empire and the Role of Violence in Civilization.* Boston: Beacon Press, 1999.

Carrasco, David, ed. *The Oxford Encyclopedia of Mesoamerican Cultures: The Civilizations of Mexico and Central America.* 3 volumes. New York: Oxford University Press, 2001.

Clow, Barbara. *The Mayan Code: Time Acceleration and Awakening the World Mind.* Rochester, VT: Bear and Company, 2007.

Coe, Michael. *Breaking the Maya Code.* New York: Thames and Hudson, 1992.

Coe, Michael. *The Maya.* New York: Thames and Hudson, 1987.

Coe, Michael, and Justin Kerr. *The Art of the Maya Scribe.* New York: Harry N. Abrams, 1998.

Davis, Whitney. "So-called Jaguar-Human Copulation Scenes in Olmec Art." *American Antiquity* 43, no. 3 (1978): 453–57.

Diehl, Richard. *The Olmecs: America's First Civilization.* London: Thames and Hudson, 2004.

Dobkin de Rios, Marlene. *Hallucinogens: Cross-Cultural Perspectives.* Prospect Heights, IL: Waveland Press, 1990.

Fash, William. "Changing Perspectives on Maya Civilization." *Annual Review of Anthropology* 23 (1994): 181–208.

Fischer, Steven. *A History of Writing.* London: Reaktion Books, 2001.

Gallenkamp, Charles, and Regina Johnson. *Maya: Treasures of an Ancient Civilization.* New York: Harry N. Abrams, 1985.

Hadingham, Evan. *Lines to the Mountain Gods: Nazca and the Mysteries of Peru.* New York: Random House, 1987.

Harnes, Michael. "The Enigma of Aztec Sacrifice." *Natural History* 84, no. 4 (1977): 46–51.

Henderson, John. *The World of the Ancient Maya*. Ithaca, NY: Cornell University Press, 1981.

Keber, Eloise Quiñones. *Codex Telleriano-Remensis: Ritual, Divination, and History in a Pictorial Aztec Manuscript*. Austin: University of Texas Press, 1995.

Klein, Cecelia. "The Identity of the Central Deity on the Aztec Calendar Stone." *The Art Bulletin* 58, no. 1 (1976): 1–12.

Marcus, Joyce. "Archaeology and Religion: A Comparison of the Zapotec and Maya." *World Archaeology* 10, no. 2 (1978): 172–91.

McEwan, Colin. *Ancient Mexico in the British Museum*. London: British Museum Press, 1994.

Miller, Mary Ellen. *The Art of Mesoamerica from Olmec to Aztec*. London: Thames and Hudson, 2001.

Miller, Mary Ellen. *Maya Art and Architecture*. London: Thames and Hudson, 1999.

Miller, Mary Ellen. "A Re-examination of the Mesoamerican Chacmool." *The Art Bulletin* 67, no. 1 (1985): 7–17.

Miller, Mary Ellen, and Simon Martin. *Courtly Art of the Ancient Maya*. San Francisco: Fine Arts Museums of San Francisco, 2004.

Miller, Mary Ellen, and Karl Taube. *The Gods and Symbols of Ancient Mexico and the Maya: An Illustrated Dictionary of Mesoamerican Religion*. New York: Thames and Hudson, 1993.

Morrison, Tony. *Pathways to the Gods: The Mystery of the Andes Lines*. New York: Harper and Row, 1978.

Murdy, Carson. "Congenital Deformities and the Olmec Were-Jaguar Motif." *American Antiquity* 46, no. 4 (1981): 861–71.

Pasztory, Esther. *Aztec Art*. New York: Harry N. Abrams, 1983.

Pasztory, Esther. *Pre-Columbian Art*. London: Weidenfeld and Nicolson, 1998.

Piña Chan, Román. *The Olmec: Mother Culture of Mesoamerica*. New York: Rizzoli, 1989.

Pinchbeck, Daniel. *2012: The Return of Quetzalcoatl*. New York: Jeremy P. Tarcher/ Penguin, 2006.

Ranney, Edward. *Stonework of the Maya*. Albuquerque: University of New Mexico Press, 1974.

Reinhard, Johan. *The Nazca Lines: A New Perspective on Their Origin and Meaning*. Lima, Peru: Los Pinos, 1988.

Saunders, Nicholas, ed. *Icons of Power: Feline Symbolism in the Americas*. London: Routledge, 1998.

Schele, Linda, and Peter Mathews. *The Code of Kings: The Language of Seven Sacred Maya Temples and Tombs*. New York: Scribner, 1998.

Schele, Linda, and Mary Ellen Miller. *The Blood of Kings: Dynasty and Ritual in Maya Art*. New York: George Braziller, 1986.

Solis, Felipe. *The Aztec Empire*. New York: Solomon R. Guggenheim Museum, 2004.

Stierlen, Henri. *Art of the Aztecs and Its Origins*. New York: Rizzoli, 1982.

Stierlen, Henri. *Art of the Incas*. New York: Rizzoli, 1984.

Stierlen, Henri. *The Art of Maya*. New York: Rizzoli, 1981.

Taube, Karl. *Aztec and Maya Myths*. Austin: University of Texas Press, 1993.

Taube, Karl. *The Major Gods of Ancient Yucatan*. Washington, DC: Dumbarton Oaks, 1992.

Whitecotton, Joseph. *The Zapotecs: Princes, Priests, and Peasants*. Norman: University of Oklahoma Press, 1977.

Whittington, E. Michael, ed. *The Sport of Life and Death: The Mesoamerican Ballgame*. New York: Thames and Hudson, 2001.

–6–

Native American Religions

The focus of this chapter is on the indigenous religions of North America—including the continental United States, Alaska, and Canada. Information regarding the indigenous religions of South and Central America can be found in chapter 5, "Mesoamerica and Andean Religions," and discussion of native Hawaiian religious practices can be found in chapter 7, "Indigenous Religions of Oceania."

ORIGINS AND DEVELOPMENT

When Europeans first reached North America in significant numbers in the 16th and 17th centuries, they encountered numerous groups of people already resident in the land. The Italian-born explorer Christopher Columbus (1451–1506) is often credited with the discovery of America in the late 15th century, as well as the use of the term "Indians" to describe the inhabitants he encountered when he landed on the island of San Salvador in the Bahamas in 1492. Columbus was searching for a sea route from Europe to the East Indies in order to advance trade in goods and spices from that region of the world, and believed that he had achieved this goal. The term "Indian" reflects this, as "it was entirely logical for him to call the lands he claimed for Spain 'the Indies,' and its people *Indios.*"[1] However, within a few years after this, because of the additional explorations of figures such as Vasco Nuñez de Balboa (1475–1519) who traveled across Central America to reach the Pacific Ocean in the early 16th century, it became clear that the land was not actually India at all, but rather a whole new region of the world. Nevertheless, the term "Indian" has often continued to be applied to the native peoples of North America up to the present day. The acceptance of this term has varied, however, as it ultimately reflects European usage and misconceptions. Many scholars now prefer to use the term "Native American" as a general descriptor for the great variety of cultural groups represented by the original inhabitants of these world regions, although acceptance of this term has varied widely as well.[2] It is wise to note that any terms (such as "Native American," "Indian," "Native American Indian," or "indigenous peoples") represent attempts to characterize a great diversity of cultures under a single overarching designation—and as such will always be problematic.

Equally, if not even more, problematic are the various theories that have been advanced regarding the dates and origins of human habitation in North America. A majority of scholars, however, believe that many of the original inhabitants of North America arrived from Asia sometime between 20,000 and 10,000 BCE via crossing the now submerged land bridge of Beringia (between Siberia and North America) as well as by boat.[3] These early Paleolithic peoples were hunter-gatherers and eventually spread widely through the regions of North and South America, developing a variety of modes of existence via adaptation to diverse geographic areas and changing climate conditions. Through subsequent millennia, and additional migrations, the patterns of life developed by these ancient ancestral people ultimately resulted in the enormous variety of lifestyles represented among native groups at the time of first contact with Europeans. "By the time Europeans came, millions of Native Americans occupied every conceivable form of landscape, from tropical rainforest to high desert, from grassland plain to boreal forest."[4] Some peoples maintained nomadic lifestyles based on hunting; others developed agricultural farming and aquacultural cultivation methods; in some regions people lived in small family or related groups; in other regions substantial groups of people lived in permanently settled communities characterized by large-scale architectural construction.

The extreme variations in geography and climate within the vast areas occupied by the original inhabitants of North America cannot be overemphasized. Ranging from the Arctic coasts of Alaska and Canada to the hot, dry climate of the Southwest, from the Woodlands areas of the east, to the Great Plains of central Canada and the United States, the native inhabitants of these regions all developed distinctive cultures and traditions. Most studies of Native American peoples thus tend to approach this diversity by adopting a regional method—in other words, identifying large cultural areas into which many different peoples may be grouped and situated: the east, west, north, southeast, and northwest, for example. Or, regions may be defined as: the Arctic (northern coasts of Alaska and Canada plus sections of Siberia and Greenland); the Subarctic (northern Canada); the Northwest Coast (southern coast of Alaska plus western regions of Canada to Washington and Oregon); the Plateau (sections of the northwest United States and southwest Canada); the Great Basin (largely parts of Idaho, Oregon, Nevada, Utah, Arizona, and California); California;

the Southwest (sections of Arizona, New Mexico, Colorado, Utah, Texas, and Nevada); the Plains (central United States and Canada); and the Woodlands (eastern Canada and the United States from the Atlantic Ocean to the Mississippi River). Although this traditional regional approach is useful, the creation of any large, generalized categories runs the risk of treating a wide range of cultures as if they were homogenous. It is estimated that when Europeans arrived in North America, there were close to a thousand different groups of native peoples, speaking several hundred different languages. Although it is wise to be attentive to the regional similarities, it is critical to acknowledge their unique identities and traditions as well.

The disastrous consequences of European colonization and contact with Native American peoples are well known. European settlers brought previously unknown epidemic diseases, resulting in dramatic population declines among Native Americans. The territorial expansion policies of many settlers ultimately led to the removal of many indigenous peoples from their homelands and their resettlement on reservations. Although many Native American groups profited initially from contact with Europeans, by engaging in trade and via their introduction to European commodities such as iron tools, firearms, and horses, and many Native American groups adopted aspects of European life and religion, by and large the coming of the Europeans was a violent and calamitous event in the history of native peoples, with far-reaching consequences to the present day.

PRINCIPAL BELIEFS AND KEY PRACTICES

It is clear that a great many different—as well as related—cultural groups need to be included in any discussion of Native American religion. The religious beliefs and practices of these diverse groups are all unique in many important ways and also reflect the vastly divergent climatic and geographical characteristics of their regions—from the dry and arid climates of the Southwest, the forested areas of the Atlantic Woodlands and Pacific Northwest, the Great Plains regions of central North America, to the cold, rainy, and frozen climates of the Subarctic and Arctic regions.

Nevertheless, it is the response to climate and geography that is one of the overall shared features of Native American religion. Regardless of the vastly varied geography and climates in which native peoples developed their religious beliefs, a sense of closeness to the land and a connection with nature and natural forces may be seen as a shared characteristic of Native American beliefs. Indeed, it might be said that this shared impulse—a sense of reverence for the natural environment—provides the unifying feature among the diverse traditions developed by indigenous peoples in North America. Terms such as "polytheism," "animism," or "nature worship" are really rather awkward designations (or scholarly constructs) that attempt to describe religious belief systems that do not seem to follow or adhere to the Western monotheistic traditions largely represented by Christianity, Judaism, and Islam. Monotheistic belief systems tend to be those that attribute the creation of the universe to a sole divine being, an original generating force, whose guidance was, or is continually, revealed to humans through direct communication or via intermediaries such as prophets or seers. The term "polytheism" is generally used for belief systems in which a variety of different deities are acknowledged and worshiped. Many Native American religious traditions attribute the creation of the universe to an initiating vital force (such as the Great Mother or the Great Father—or their union—or to other spirit beings, such as the Raven) while at the same time paying respect to the various manifestations of this divine force in diverse spirit deities, entities, or powers that may have special influence on certain aspects of human, animal, and vegetable life forms.[5] Efforts to propitiate, celebrate, thank, and acknowledge these forces are a shared motif among the many belief systems of the Native Americans, which also have a greatly popular appeal in today's environmentally sensitive world.

> The importance of land in traditional Amerindian beliefs is rooted in its inherent potential to inscribe an earth-centered hierophany that is itself part of a unitary cosmos. Although there are many themes in traditional Amerindian myth, one attitude appears pervasive: any part of the world may unfold the whole—upperworld, lowerworld, and the ground we stand upon. Any part of the world may unfold the whole more or less according to the strength of individual vision and the cogency of the tribal metaphorical tradition for interpreting that vision.[6]

Works of art produced by Native American peoples demonstrate this sense of connection to the sacred landscape in a diversity of ways—from the materials used to the symbolism involved. Ancient effigy earthworks, such as the Great Serpent Mound in Ohio, represent living creatures of profound symbolic significance in Native American belief systems. The complex designs of the ephemeral Navajo sand paintings are designed to call on the powers of spirit beings to assist in healing ceremonies, serving as temporary sites to connect to powerful and all-pervasive forces. The annual appearance of the masked kachinas among the Hopi and other peoples of the Southwest represents the acknowledgment of humankind's fundamental reliance on the favor of natural forces in order to survive. The spirit beings and clan symbols carved on wooden objects created by many Northwest Coast native groups represent related concerns—of propitiating natural forces and seeking alignment with these forces. In all Native American traditions, the importance of creating and ensuring a harmonious balance between humans and the natural world—a world in which humans and their endeavors are simply one facet—is paramount. It often said that

> to Native Americans, religion, art, and daily life are all the same thing. In fact, art is not a strictly accurate term. Many Indian languages lack a distinct word for art, since there is no distinction between art and life. Art is life. The two are inseparable. A life lived in balance is a work of art, and any object made by a balanced person is an object of art. Or to put it another way, an artfully crafted object reflects the true path of life being walked by its maker.[7]

Communication with the spirit world via intermediaries known as shamans is also a shared aspect of many Native American belief systems and practices. Shamans are special individuals who, via dreams, trance states, visions, or inherent sensitivity, may contact the dead, communicate with the spirits, and receive supernatural instructions by interpreting dreams, omens, and via various forms of divination. Shamans may perform healing, foretell the future, and influence events. Their roles and powers are conceived somewhat differently among various peoples; in some societies both men and women may be called or train extensively to be shamans; in other groups, shamans may be exclusively men or women. The English word *shaman* is generally not used by native peoples, who all have their own language terms for these gifted, revered, and often feared individuals. Many works of art are associated with shamanic practices—ranging from masks, drums, rattles, amulets, and special garments. Shamanism is not unique to North American native peoples, by any means, but has many manifestations in wide-ranging world cultures from prehistory to the present day.[8]

TRADITIONAL ART AND ARCHITECTURAL FORMS

The traditional art and architectural forms developed by Native Americans and those forms specifically associated with their religious beliefs and practices are as diverse as the landscapes inhabited by these different cultural groups. The forms and materials used in art production vary greatly depending on the natural or imported resources available. The use of adobe or mud bricks for architectural construction is characteristic of the indigenous peoples of the Southwest for example, whereas the use of wood for creating architectural enclosures and sculptural monuments is, logically, most characteristic of peoples for whom these resources were more available. The nomadic lifestyle of many of the cultural groups in the central or Plains region of North America resulted in the creation of portable religious objects as well as practices emphasizing the creation and veneration of sacred space in appropriately changing locales.

Architectural structures designed for sacred purposes take on a variety of forms. For example, the spectacular cliff dwellings of Mesa Verde, Colorado (notably the Cliff Palace), constructed by the Anasazi people in the mid-13th century, include numerous kivas—sacred enclosures typical of many ancient as well as contemporary Pueblo people[9] (see Figure 6.1). Kivas may be round or rectangular, built of stone or adobe, often have wooden roofs, and are traditionally entered via ladder through the roof. They customarily include a central cavity or floor shrine known as a *sipapu*, which is understood to symbolize the place from which humans originally emerged from Mother Earth. Of varying sizes, some kivas include benches, wall paintings, and hearths. They represent "the oldest type of religious building in continuous use in the Western hemisphere," and are used for social-ceremonial meetings, dances, and for a variety of sacred and secret rituals.[10]

Figure 6.1 Cliff Palace, Mesa Verde, Colorado, ca. 1250. Kropewnicki / Dreamstime.com.

Other Native American people created structures specifically for religious ceremonies, such as the wooden big houses used by the Delaware peoples for annual harvest and New Year rituals, the rain houses used for agricultural rites in the Southwest, and the Plains Indians sun dance lodges. Other structures, such as sweat lodges, were used for ritual purification.

Many structures, such as the impressive wooden longhouses characteristic of the Northwest Coast, served both domestic and religious purposes, being "ritually transformed from secular to sacred structures for . . . ceremonies"[11] (see Figure 6.2). Indeed, Native American domestic dwellings often symbolize key religious beliefs. The Haida longhouse, for example, was understood to stand at the center of the universe, representing the intersection of the three zones: sky, earth, and underworld. A central pole extending through the house was used during religious ceremonies to connect to the spirits and powers of the sky world. The design of Navajo hogans was believed to have been based on instructions originally given by the supernatural being known as Talking God. These wooden structures with earthen floors are carefully oriented with their entrances facing east to the rising sun, and are symbolically divided on the interior into zones symbolizing the other cardinal directions and spheres of sacred influence. While some hogans may be constructed and used only for ritual purposes, it is more often the case that rituals (such as those associated with healing and the creation of sand paintings) are carried out in domestic hogans.

Figure 6.2 Haida Longhouse, Vancouver, Canada. Werner Forman / Art Resource, NY.

The idea that houses served as models of the universe is suggested by the folklore and architectural terms of native groups as distant from one another as the Eskimo, the Mohave, the Navajo, the Hopi, the Delaware, and the Blackfeet. To the Navajo, mountains were models for the first house, its four principal posts symbolically equated with the four cardinal directions, and its floor space divided into day and night domains. The Hidatsa of North Dakota believed the universe was a massive earthlodge, its sky dome held up by four enormous pillars just like those of their own four-post lodges.[12]

Many different types of objects may be used in religious ceremonies. The creation and offering of prayer sticks is an important tradition among many Pueblo peoples of the Southwest (see Figure 6.3). Prayer sticks or praying sticks (known as *telikinanne* among the Zuni, and *paho* among the Hopi) are carved, peeled, and painted wooden sticks to which bird feathers, shells, and other objects may be attached. The creation of prayer sticks involves important preparations, cleansing, and purification practices. They may be made as offerings to the dead, and used especially in winter and summer solstice ceremonies. After the creation and ritual consecration of prayer sticks, they are planted in fields, springs, river beds, under trees or shrubs, or put in caves, under floors, or on special communal or private altars. The different colors of the prayer sticks

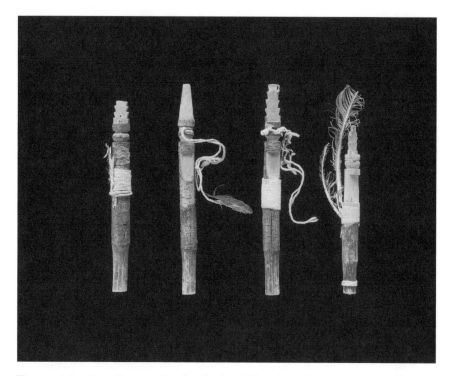

Figure 6.3   Zuni Praying Sticks. Berlin: Ethnologisches Museum. Bildarchiv Preussischer Kulturbesitz / Art Resource, NY.

and objects attached to them vary greatly according to their purposes and the spirits to whom they are dedicated. Among the Zuni, "men plant their turquoise prayer sticks for the Sun Father . . . and women plant their yellow prayer sticks for the Sun Father's younger sister, the Moonlight-Giving Mother."[13] The feathers (of eagles, ducks, and other birds) are believed to send breath prayers to the spirits. Prayer sticks are extremely significant components in rituals that also involve drumming, dancing, singing, feasting, and masked performances.

Ceremonial costumes, masks, and special garments are traditionally employed in many Native American religious rituals. Dances in which animal masks or costumes may be donned could serve to honor and propitiate animal spirits or ensure their continued availability as a food source for humans. For example, the Okipa or Buffalo Dance of the Plains Mandan people was held annually to pray for plentiful buffalo and other blessings. The bull dancers dressed in identical costumes and masks (see Figure 6.4).

Masks and ritual costumes feature prominently among many native peoples of the Southwest. The ceremonies associated with the return and propitiation of the spirit beings known as kachinas involve use of elaborate headdresses, special costumes, and masks such as the painted, feathered, buffalo hide example illustrated in Figure 6.5. This mask represents the sun, and was probably worn like a shield on the back of a dancer.

Figure 6.4 Mandan Buffalo Head Mask, ca. 1860. The Art Archive / Chandler-Pohrt Collection, Gift of Mr. William D Weiss / Buffalo Bill Historical Center, Cody, Wyoming / NA.203.359.

Figure 6.5 Hopi Kachina Mask. Private collection. Werner Forman / Art Resource, NY.

The materials used and symbolism involved varies widely from region to region. The masks produced by native peoples of the Northwest are generally carved of wood (especially cedar) and are often boldly painted with curvilinear designs. Many represent mythological creatures, such as the monster bird known as the Crooked-Beak-of-Heaven, who plays a prominent role in Kwakiutl lore and ceremonies[14] (see Plate 11). This monster is one of several fearsome man-eating creatures believed to live in the far north who return in the winter to prey on humans and cause them to become cannibals. This mask features especially during the Kwakiutl winter ceremonies of Tseyka (or Tsetseka). These complex rituals often span several days with the dance of the Hamatsa being the most dramatic.

> The Hamatsa, protegé and personification of the Man-eater, returns from the monster's house and is captured and tamed by the tribesmen. His gradual return to human sense in a series of dances is disrupted when he loses his self-control and runs wildly around the firelit floor and out behind a painted curtain . . . From behind that screen the snapping of a great beak sounds, the singers begin the song of the masks, and a figure . . . appears. First stepping high from side to side, then

circling in crouching jumps, and finally sitting on the floor, the dancer moves the great mask, sweeping and cocking the beak from side to side and finally snapping the voracious jaws. At each new verse another dancer appears . . . Then they leave one by one and the Hamatsa returns for his final series of dances by which his wildness is removed and he is brought back to a tame, human state.[15]

As the preceding quote well indicates, it is always critical to remember that any ceremonial objects were originally designed and intended to function as aspects of multifaceted, vibrant, and often dramatic performances. When displayed in galleries and museum collections, they have been removed from their context. In addition, many pieces of Native American art housed in museums today were acquired via extremely unethical means and in that way also have been deprived of their original sanctity and power.[16]

Powerful life-prolonging and health-promoting ceremonies connected with the Midewiwin Society (associated with several Plains Indian groups) involved use of special objects, spirit figures, and headdresses, in initiation rituals signaling a member's acceptance into the society after lengthy instructions in healing rites and moral codes of conduct. Various levels of achievement within the society brought different responsibilities, knowledge, and the privilege to handle and use sacred objects. The objects used in these ceremonies were carefully stored and guarded as containers of sacred powers (see Figure 6.6).

Special garments, such as men's shirts and women's dresses, were created during the mid- to late 19th century especially among several Plains Indians groups for use in Ghost Dance rituals (see Figure 6.7). The Ghost Dance was a movement that arose from the visions and teachings of several prophetic figures who foresaw renewal of life, power, and prosperity for Native Americans. During this period, when many native groups were enduring severe hardships and deprivations, the hope of reunion with deceased ancestors on a reborn and harmonious earth was extremely appealing, as well as serving, among some groups, as a vehicle for resistance against the European oppressors.[17]

Figure 6.6 Midewiwin Society Spirit Figure and Headdress. Washington, DC: Museum of the American Indian. Werner Forman / Art Resource, NY.

Many variations of chants and ritual associated with Ghost Dance practices developed. The cloth or buckskin garments created for use in the dances often include painted designs of traditional religious and cosmological symbols: sun, moon, and solar eclipse—during which visions had been received by the prophet Wovaka (ca. 1856–1932)—images of birds (such as crows and white-tailed magpies: messengers from the ancestors and guardian spirits), cedar trees, turtles, and buffalo. The garments are often fringed and include attached feathers. Several groups of practitioners among the Ghost Dancers believed that these sacred garments had protective powers and were able to stop bullets. This belief was dramatically disproved, especially at Wounded Knee in 1890, when scores of Lakota men, women, and children were massacred by military troops.

Figure 6.7 Arapaho Ghost Dance Dress, ca. 1890. The Art Archive / Chandler-Pohrt Collection, Gift of Mary J. and James R. Jundt / Buffalo Bill Historical Center, Cody, Wyoming / NA.204.4.

EXAMPLES

Great Serpent Mound

The Great Serpent Mound, located in Adams County, southern Ohio, is one of the most impressive and well preserved of ancient earthworks in North America (see Figure 6.8). It has long fascinated and puzzled researchers since its discovery in the mid-19th century. Although a series of archaeological excavations have been undertaken at the site in the 19th and 20th centuries, and much scholarship continues to be devoted to the Great Serpent Mound, its exact purpose and date remain uncertain.

It is classified as an effigy mound, meaning that it represents the giant shape of a creature—in this case, a long snake undulating for a total length of over 1,300 feet atop a bluff overlooking a creek. It terminates in a tightly coiled tail, and its head is represented by a hollow, oval-shaped mound (variously interpreted as depicting the eye of the serpent or as the serpent's open mouth clasping an egg, the sun, or a body of a frog). The average width of the mounded body varies from 20 to 25 feet, and the height varies between 4 to 5 feet. "The ancient builders of Serpent Mound carefully planned this oversized effigy by first outlining a monstrous snake nearly one-quarter of a mile long with small stones and lumps of clay. They then piled up countless basket loads of yellow clay over the outline, burying their markers. The result is a flawlessly modeled serpent, forever slithering northward."[18]

Figure 6.8 Great Serpent Mound, Ohio. The Art Archive / Global Book Publishing.

Similar, smaller effigy mounds exist elsewhere (notably in parts of Iowa, Minnesota, and Wisconsin) that represent the shapes of various birds, lizards, turtles, and other animals such as deer, bears, bison, and panthers. Effigy mounds are distinguished by their shapes from the hundreds of other conical or platform temple mounds also widely distributed in the eastern and Midwestern United States. Excavations have revealed that the temple mounds generally served as burial places, and were also often topped with (no longer extant) wooden structures.[19] Effigy mounds, in contrast, generally contain no evidence of having been used as burial sites or as locales for temples or other architectural structures.

For many years, scholars attributed the construction of the Great Serpent Mound to the Adena or Hopewell cultures, which flourished in the region during the first millennium BCE up to about 500 CE. The Adena and Hopewell peoples were ambitious mound builders and constructed many impressive burial mounds, which were often filled with lavish and ornamental objects as well as more utilitarian grave goods.[20]

More recent study of the Great Serpent Mound, however, has placed its date much later into the early second millennium CE, ca. 1000–1100 CE. Archaeologists working at the site in the 1990s discovered several charcoal fragments that (via radiocarbon dating analysis) revealed a date of ca. 1070 CE, thus perhaps associating the mound with the Fort Ancient peoples, one of numerous Mississippian cultures that flourished between about 750 and 1500 CE. Nevertheless, the date of the Great Serpent Mound, as well as the purpose and function of the monument, remains a topic of much scholarly debate.

Typical of many other effigy mounds, the Great Serpent Mound was not used for burial purposes. "This suggests to some that the effigies defined sacred, ceremonial ground rather than mortuary areas."[21] Some scholars believe that the effigy mounds served as markers of territory, as representations of totemic creatures associated with specific clans or groups, as gathering places for religious ceremonies, as ritual devices to connect with animal spirits, or as evidence of ancient astronomical study. Indeed, the late 11th-century date proposed for the Great Serpent Mound

> corresponds almost exactly to two amazing astronomical events. In AD 1054, light from the supernova that produced the Crab nebula first reached the earth, remaining visible during daytime for at least two weeks. Then, in AD 1066, Halley's Comet appeared in its brightest manifestation ever, visible around the world. Could it be that some Native American observers in the Ohio River valley set out to create a permanent memorial to these remarkable celestial events? Maybe the wriggling earthwork is not a serpent at all; could the oval (the "egg") actually represent the head of Halley's Comet, with the "serpent's body" actually representing its fiery tail?[22]

Many other theories have been proposed about the meaning and symbolism of the Great Serpent Mound. Snakes play a prominent and powerful role in the religious beliefs of many Native American groups, sometimes as embodiments of evil and danger, other times as protective and benevolent spirits, or as symbols of eternity, renewal, growth, and transformation (via shedding skin). Perhaps the Great Serpent Mound was used for ceremonies celebrating renewal and the cycles of the year. It has been suggested that groups of people might have walked the outlines of the mound, moving "in solemn procession from the serpent's tail until arriving at the head. There the celebrants 'reversed' direction—perhaps during a solstice or equinox, when the seasons likewise turned around—and headed downward again, to be symbolically reborn and renewed for another annual cycle."[23]

"Have we heard the final word about the Great Serpent Mound? Probably not. But one thing is certain. Serpent Mound . . . still bewilders. It still has magnetism. And if we continue to protect its fragile profiles, it always will."[24]

Navajo Sand Painting Textile

The Navajo, who today represent the largest group of Native American people, are the descendants of nomadic hunters who originally migrated from Alaska and Canada to arrive in the Southwest sometime between 1200 and 1500 CE. "These newcomers to the Southwest were adaptable and innovative, transforming aspects of Pueblo religion and art into a distinctly Navajo . . . configuration."[25] Among the most distinctive forms of art associated with the Navajo, the creation and use of temporary images in the form of sand paintings (or dry paintings) is perhaps the most well known and, in some ways, also the most puzzling to Western-trained scholars whose idea of art involves values of longevity and endurance (see Plate 12). Sand paintings are ephemeral forms of religious expression, created for specific purposes, charged with powerful symbolism, created by trained specialists, and always destroyed after use. Although some of the designs and symbols of sand paintings have been captured in more permanent forms (such as the woven rug example illustrated in Plate 12), and the production of permanent sand paintings for commercial/secular purposes became a major aspect of Navajo economy in the 20th century, these permanent examples are to be firmly distinguished from the traditional use of sand paintings in religious rituals.[26]

> The Navajo word for sandpainting ('iikááh) means "place where the gods come and go." Sandpaintings serve as impermanent altars where ritual actions can take place. But they are much more than that. In their proper setting, if ritual rules are followed, they are the exact pictorial representation of supernaturals. These stylized designs are full of sacred symbols and through consecration are impregnated with supernatural power, thereby becoming the temporary resting place of holiness. They are essential parts of curing ceremonies whose purpose is to attract the Holy People so that they will help with the complex curing process. The supernatural power sandpaintings contain is considered dangerous, and they can be safely used only in the proper controlled context, at the right time, under the direction of highly trained specialists.[27]

The specialists who create sand paintings and who conduct the ceremonies associated with their use are known as hataalí (singers, chanters, or medicine men.) The ceremonies are elaborate, multistaged events that can involve the creation of numerous sand paintings of particular designs in specifically ordered sequences, over a period of several days. Sand paintings are created to promote healing or a restoration of harmony and balance (either physical or psychological) in the individuals for whom they are created. Careful preparations are involved on the part of the trained singer who creates and chants the sacred blessings, traditional myths, and songs associated with the specific needs of individuals in need of healing. Sand paintings serve as an integral part of this process, as the individuals for whom the ceremonies are performed are asked to sit on or within the paintings during important moments of the ceremonies while the singer performs sacred chants to evoke the healing powers of the spirits.

Sand paintings are created from crushed, colored minerals carefully sprinkled either onto a bed of sand laid out on the earthen floor of hogan, or onto a buckskin base. Crushed flowers, pollen, corn meal, powdered bark, and roots may also be employed in sand paintings or as coloring agents. Paintings can vary greatly in size; some may be created in an area of a foot or less while the diameters of larger paintings can be up to 20 feet or more. These larger examples may require that several men work for many hours on their creation, while the smaller examples may be completed in a few hours by one or more artists. There are two basic compositional patterns traditionally employed: rows of figures enclosed with boundary lines on three sides or centralized designs radiating from a focal point, also enclosed by boundary lines on three sides. In all cases, the symbolic elements and colors are carefully chosen to accord with the traditional sacred designs appropriate for each ceremony or chant.

There are hundreds of different chants and related images created in sand paintings. Although scholars and researchers of Navajo culture and religion have been extremely active in defining and categorizing these different chants and their related pictorial imagery, the symbols and images are really not meant to be accessible to outsiders but, rather, form a critical aspect of the highly sacred and guarded lore of the Navajo people. The power of the images and the efficacy of the rituals depend on their sacred status. That is why commercial works of art produced for collectors and tourists may replicate some aspects of these sacred designs in decorative form but are not used, or intended to be used, for actual ritual purposes.

The woven rug example illustrated here includes designs associated with the Shooting Way Chant, one of many ceremonial healing rituals of the Navajo.[28] The Shooting Way Chant and related sand paintings are primarily intended to recreate balance in an individual who is suffering from various illnesses including colds and fevers, or to prevent infection caused by lightning strikes, snakes, and arrows. The composition is typically clear, symmetric, and carefully organized to show the four directions (north, south, east, and west) with east at the top. Unlike many Western style maps (especially of the Renaissance and post-Renaissance periods), the east as the direction of the rising sun is often indicated at the top of Navajo sand paintings. Unlike the other three cardinal directions, the east is often represented as unbounded and unenclosed by boundary lines. This is the direction that the patient faces when sitting in the painting, and the direction from which the properly evoked healing powers will arrive.

This design is bounded by zigzagging arrow/lightning forms. Images of the Four Thunders (of the four cardinal directions) and Four Sacred Plants (corn, tobacco, squash, and beans) radiate from the central element. The central circle represents the home of the Thunder People; it is shown as a lake with four rectangular rainbow forms. The east (top of the painting) is protected by two guardian figures. The Thunders are represented as birdlike forms with outstretched wings from which hang waterspouts and lightning rays. Triangular arrows project from the tops and tips of their wings. Their lozenge-shaped tails contain symbols representing rain. Curving forms indicating thunder sounds also project from their tails. Their bodies are enriched with short rectangular forms symbolizing rainbows.

There are hundreds of different designs and compositions associated with the Shooting Way Chant, and singers select those patterns that will best suit the healing needs of the individual patient.

According to Navajo belief, a sandpainting heals because the ritual image attracts and exalts the Holy People; serves as a pathway for the mutual exchange of illness and the healing power of the Holy People; identifies the patient with the Holy People it depicts; and creates a ritual reality in which the patient and the supernatural dramatically interact, reestablishing the patient's correct relationship with the world of the Holy People.[29]

Hopi Kachina

Kachinas (or *katsinam*) are spirit beings who feature prominently in the religious beliefs and social customs of several Native American groups of the Southwest, notably the Hopi, Zuni, and Tewa peoples.[30] Kachina dolls (or *tithu*) are small, carved, painted, and decorated wooden images representing the spirit beings who otherwise appears as masked performers in elaborate and extensive yearly ceremonies (see Figure 6.9). *Tithu* are not dolls in the conventional sense but, rather, function as powerful symbols and reminders of the important role of the kachinas. Although these objects are often given to small infants of both sexes, and thereafter only to young girls, they are not designed as toys or playthings but are displayed (often hung on walls or rafters in homes) and are "treated respectfully, as blessings."[31]

The kachinas have distinct but interdependent manifestations—first, as spirit beings; second, as the physical counterparts of the spirit when they are given substance and personality through masks, costumes, paint, symbols, and actions by human impersonators, who thereby cease being ordinary people and are transformed into spirits; and third, by the small wooden effigies called *kachin-tihus* by the Hopi and kachina dolls by outsiders.[32]

The ultimate origins of the kachinas and the practices associated with them are matters of some speculation. Spanish explorers and settlers of the Southwest in the 16th century noted the customs and rituals of the Pueblo peoples, including the dances and ceremonies associated with the kachinas. Many scholars believe that these practices have very ancient roots in the region and see evidence in rock art and pottery depictions of masked figures and spirit beings from perhaps as early as the 11th through 14th centuries CE.[33] Some scholars have speculated that the carved wooden *tithu*

Figure 6.9 Hopi Kachina, 20th century. Private collection. Werner Forman / Art Resource, NY.

were partially inspired by the painted, sculptural depictions of saints and holy figures brought to the region by European settlers and Christian missionaries. Very few surviving kachina images predate the 19th century, however, and from that time to the present day, the production of carved *tithu* (especially among the Hopi) has also increased in response to the interests of collectors and tourists with many examples—in an evolving variety of styles—being produced purely for commercial rather than religious purposes.[34]

In religious contexts, "Katsina rituals are directly linked to the seasonal demands of agriculture."[35] Among the Hopi, the kachina season lasts from the winter solstice to the summer solstice, whereas among other groups (for example, Zuni) the kachina rituals take place throughout the year. The kachina are regarded as bringers of life, spirit beings whose benevolence ensures growth, fertility, and success in agriculture—especially in their ability to bring rain to these hot and arid regions. In some versions of Hopi mythology regarding the kachina, it is told that ancestral peoples, suffering through a great drought, heard singing and dancing in the nearby mountains. They traveled to the mountains and met the spirit beings (kachina), who returned with them to their villages and assisted them with a successful farming season. This annual return of the kachina spirits is celebrated by their appearance in the form of costumed figures who, for six months "live with the Hopi people, performing ceremonies for them in the kivas during the cold winter months and dancing in the plazas in spring and early summer for the enjoyment of all."[36] They are "welcomed and treasured as powerful friends and guardians who bring gifts of rain, crops, bird songs, flowers, summer greenery, happiness, health, and long life."[37]

The number and appearance of the kachinas varies widely between regions, villages, and clans. Kachinas represent a living tradition, with the knowledge of the meaning and power of specific kachinas closely guarded by elders and revealed via initiation rites held at important stages in the lives of community members. "A veil of secrecy surrounds each kachina society and clan, privileged information and responsibilities are passed down through generations to each exclusive group."[38] The forms of the kachinas have evolved and transformed over the centuries. It is estimated that between two to three hundred spirit beings are (or have been) recognized, many of which appear only during specific ceremonies such as Soyal (the winter solstice ceremony, which marks the return of the kachinas), Powamu (the Bean Dance), the Water Serpent ceremony, and Niman (the Home Dance, or summer solstice ceremony, which thanks and celebrates the kachinas before their seasonal departure). The attributes of the kachinas are varied, bespeaking their different natures and spirit essences, with the costumes, masks, and *tithu* often showing characteristics of flowers and plants (cactus, corn), birds (eagles and owls), snakes, animals (such as deer, bears, and mountain lions), or symbols of clouds, rain, the sun, morning, and symbols representing powerful warrior and leader figures. Kachinas are both male and female, although only men perform in the rituals and dances. Some kachinas are playful, others are frightening and severe. Specific color symbolism is also used, relating to "the six different sacred directions. North is represented by blue or green, west by yellow, south by red, east by white, zenith by multicolors, and nadir by black."[39]

The 20th-century Hopi *tihu* illustrated represents a *katsinmana*, a maiden or female spirit, wearing an elaborate stepped headdress (or *tablita*) representing the impressive headgear worn by costumed dancers in ceremonies. *Tithu* are traditionally carved from the dense, dry roots of dead cottonwood trees; many are painted in vibrant colors and often have attachments of feathers and plant materials. Zuni *tithu* are often clothed in costumes of animal skin or woven cloth. *Tithu* are carved by artists versed in the craft and ancient traditions, who are familiar with the traditional forms and symbolism. Before the modern period, *tithu* (such as the example illustrated) largely appear as static standing figures, without bases. Modern *tithu* often show more active stances, may have moveable limbs, and are placed on carved bases.

Northwest Coast Totem Poles

The creation of carved wooden totem poles is characteristic of several native peoples of the Pacific Northwest (see Figure 6.10). Totem poles represent the largest freestanding sculptures created by native peoples of North America, as well as some of the largest wooden sculptures ever created worldwide. They have "become the very symbol of Northwest Coast native people and their art."[40]

Due to the wet climate and perishable nature of the material, few totem poles presently exist that predate the mid- to late 19th century; however, the art form continues to be vibrantly practiced today. The first Europeans to reach the Pacific Northwest Coast in the late 18th century described seeing impressive and intriguing carved posts on the interiors and exteriors of native dwellings; even so, it remains unclear when the art form originated and for how long it had developed before European contact. The evolu-

Figure 6.10 Totem Poles, Vancouver, Canada. The Art Archive / Stephanie Colasanti.

tion of the large, freestanding totem pole can be traced primarily in the late 19th and 20th century.

While it has been argued that these carved monuments are nonreligious in nature, and served primarily secular purposes in displaying symbols, objects, and animals associated with specific families or clans (as "the equivalent of a European crest or coat of arms"), many of the images carved on totem poles are not simply decorative designs but many have their origins in ancient myths of supernatural beings, animals, and their encounters with ancestral figures.[41] Although totem poles are not themselves objects of worship, they often include important religious symbolism.

> The people's understanding of the interconnectedness of all living things and their dependence on certain animal and plant species fostered belief in the supernatural and spirit world . . . To show these spirits respect ensured their continued return or regrowth in the years ahead. . . . The people's spirituality ran deep, and their sense of identity was strong. Through costumed spiritual transformation and re-enactments, they brought past histories and adventures into the present. Thus, the carved beings of crests and legend portrayed on the totem poles, often recreated in masks worn by dancers, sprang to life. When the dances and ceremonies ended, the sculptured poles in front of the houses continued to confirm the identity and rank of those who dwelt there.[42]

Totem poles are traditionally carved of red cedar trees from which the bark has been stripped. Carving is done by a team—often a master carver with several assistants. Appendages such as beaks, wings, and fins are added by pegging or mortise and tenon joints. Once painted, poles are raised in stages by teams of people using ropes and wooden supports or scaffolds. Although heights of totem poles vary widely, many are as much as 80 feet or more tall.

The completion of the undertaking could be integrated into the ceremonial event known as a "potlatch" ("to give away").[43] Potlatches were elaborate events regularly orchestrated by many Northwest Coast peoples. These were times of gift-giving, feasting, dancing, religious rituals, and affirmation of the wealth and prestige of the hosting family or clan. Often held in conjunction with a major event, such as a marriage or a death, potlatches involved the host's distribution of gifts to all attendees.

The designs of totem poles often include images or crests associated with specific clans.

> The central feature of the ceremonial art of the Northwest Coast is the concept of the "crest"—family, clan, or lineage-owned badges—representing natural phenomena, mythical creatures and ancestors. Many of these are likely to have originated as spirit helpers of individuals, handed down from one generation to another, so that symbols of religious origins may have in time become transformed into symbols of family or political significance.[44]

Traditional designs include the powerful thunderbird spirit (always shown with great wings outstretched—as in the examples illustrated), raven (revered by many Pacific Northwest groups as the creator of the world), wolf (symbol of strength and prowess in hunting), eagle (symbol of prestige and strength), bear (symbol of power), symbols of the sun and moon, and numerous other animals, zoomorphs, and human figures. Northwest Coast art represents a series of distinctive styles based on "a general system of design principles. Depending on how these are used, the crest or motif being portrayed can vary from realistic and easily recognizable to involved and somewhat difficult to figure out—or the identity of the figure can become totally abstracted through the rearrangement of its anatomical parts."[45]

Many totem poles created today still follow the traditional imagery and design structure, though they may be created for nontraditional purposes (commissioned by corporations, government agencies, museums, and educational centers) and they may also be created of more durable modern materials (such as fiberglass). Even so, they preserve the traditional forms, "proclaiming the people's pride in their past and the strength of their culture, now and in the future."[46]

NOTES

1. Brian Fagan, *The Great Journey: The Peopling of Ancient America* (London: Thames and Hudson, 1987), 15.

2. Opinions on this diverge widely. Some cultural groups dislike the term "Native American" because for them it represents a misguided and politically correct academic attempt at whitewashing the historical facts—including the original European misnaming of the peoples of America. Having been mislabeled as Indians, and perceived and treated for so many years as foreign peoples inferior to whites, some peoples prefer to retain the term "Indian" as it continues to symbolize the history of their perception and mistreatment by Europeans. Thus, after years of being called Indians, many groups still prefer this term and now dislike being called Native Americans. Ideally, all Indian/Native American groups should be referred to by their actual names: Zuni, Hopi, Cherokee, and so forth. See the useful and provocative discussion by Christina Berry, "What's in a Name? Indians and Political Correctness," *All Things Cherokee*, http://www.allthingscherokee.com/articles_culture_events_070101.html.

3. For a detailed discussion see Fagan, *The Great Journey*, especially 101–44.

4. Fagan, *The Great Journey*, 239.

5. Regarding the Great Mother figure, see Kathleen Dugan, "At the Beginning Was Woman: Women in Native American Religious Traditions," in *Religion and Women*, ed. Arvind Sharma (Albany: State University of New York Press, 1994), 39–60.

6. Maureen Korp, *Sacred Art of the Earth: Ancient and Contemporary Earthworks* (New York: Continuum, 1997), 52.

7. Jeremy Schmidt, *In the Spirit of Mother Earth: Nature in Native American Art* (San Francisco: Chronicle Books, 1994), 27.

8. The literature on shamanism is extensive. Useful sources include: Miranda Aldhouse-Green and Stephen Aldhouse-Green, *The Quest for the Shaman: Shape-Shifters, Sorcerers, and Spirit-Healers of Ancient Europe* (London: Thames and Hudson,

2005); John Halifax, *Shaman: The Wounded Healer* (London: Thames and Hudson, 1982); Norman Hunt, *Shamanism in North America* (Buffalo, NY: Firefly Books, 2003); and Allen Wardwell, *Tangible Visions: Northwest Coast Indian Shamanism and Its Art* (New York: Monacelli Press, 1996).

9. J.J. Brody, *The Anasazi: Ancient Indian People of the American Southwest* (New York: Rizzoli, 1990).

10. Peter Nabokov and Robert Easton, *Native American Architecture* (New York: Oxford University Press, 1989), 376.

11. Nabokov and Easton, 11.

12. Nabokov and Easton, 38.

13. Barbara Tedlock, "Zuni Sacred Theater," *American Indian Quarterly* 7, no. 3 (1983): 94.

14. Bill Holm, *Crooked Beak of Heaven: Masks and Other Ceremonial Art of the Northwest Coast* (Seattle: University of Washington Press, 1972).

15. Bill Holm, *Spirit and Ancestor: A Century of Northwest Coast Art at the Burke Museum* (Seattle: University of Washington Press, 1987), 100.

16. Janet Berlo and Ruth Phillips, "Our (Museum) World Turned Upside-Down: Re-Presenting Native American Arts," *The Art Bulletin* 77, no. 1 (1995): 6–10.

17. Gregory Smoak, *Ghost Dances and Identity: Prophetic Religion and American Indian Ethnogenesis in the Nineteenth Century* (Berkeley: University of California Press, 2006).

18. David Thomas, *Exploring Ancient Native America: An Archaeological Guide* (New York: Macmillan, 1994), 130.

19. Maureen Korp, *The Sacred Geography of the American Mound Builders* (Lewisten, NY: E. Mellen, 1990).

20. See Brian Fagan, *From Black Land to Fifth Sun: The Science of Sacred Sites* (Reading, MA: Addison-Wesley, 1998), especially chapter 9, "The Moundbuilders of Eastern North America," 184–219.

21. Thomas, 144.

22. Thomas, 133.

23. Peter Nabokov, *Where the Lightning Strikes: The Lives of American Indian Sacred Places* (New York: Viking, 2006), 38.

24. Thomas, 133.

25. Janet Berlo and Ruth Phillips, *Native North American Art* (Oxford: Oxford University Press, 1998), 61.

26. Nancy Parezo, *Navajo Sandpainting: From Religious Act to Commercial Art* (Albuquerque: University of New Mexico Press, 1983).

27. Parezo, 1.

28. Franc Newcomb, *Sandpaintings of the Navajo Shooting Chant* (New York: Dover, 1975); Gladys Reichard, *Navajo Medicine Man: Sandpaintings* (New York: Dover, 1977); Leland Wyman, *Sandpaintings of the Navaho Shootingway and the Walcott Collection* (Washington, DC: Smithsonian Institution, 1970).

29. Trudy Griffin-Pierce, *Native Peoples of the Southwest* (Albuquerque: University of New Mexico Press, 2000), 337.

30. The use and spelling of terminology varies. Some scholars prefer to use the term *katsina* (plural: *katsinam*) to refer to the spirit beings themselves, as differentiated from their carved representation in the form of dolls (kachina; plural: kachinas). The term *tihu* (plural *tithu*) is also used for kachina dolls. See Helga Teiwes, *Kachina Dolls: The Art of Hopi Carvers* (Tucson: University of Arizona Press,1991), 145.

31. Teiwes, 33.

32. Peter Furst and Jill Furst, *North American Indian Art* (New York: Rizzoli, 1982), 30.

33. Polly Schaafsma and Curtis Schaafsma, "Evidence for the Origins of the Pueblo Katchina Cult as Suggested by Southwestern Rock Art," *American Antiquity* 39, no. 4 (1974): 535–45, and Polly Schaafsma, "The Prehistoric Kachina Cult and Its Origins as Suggested by Southwestern Rock Art," in *Kachinas in the Pueblo World*, ed. Polly Schaafsma (Albuquerque: University of New Mexico Press, 1994), 63–79.

34. J. J. Brody, "Kachina Images in American Art: The Way of the Doll," in *Kachinas in the Pueblo World*, ed. Polly Schaafsma (Albuquerque: University of New Mexico Press, 1994), 147–60.

35. Teiwes, 11.

36. Teiwes, 11.

37. Furst and Furst, 30.

38. Lois Jacka, *Art of the Hopi: Contemporary Journeys on Ancient Pathways* (Flagstaff, AZ: Northland, 1998), 7.

39. Dorothy Washburn, "Kachina: Window to the Hopi World," in *Hopi Kachina: Spirit of Life*, ed. Dorothy Washburn (Seattle: University of Washington Press, 1980), 42.

40. Hilary Stewart, *Looking at Totem Poles* (Seattle: University of Washington Press, 1993), 13.

41. David Campbell, ed., *Native American Art and Folklore: A Cultural Celebration* (Avenel, NJ: Crescent Books, 1993), 155.

42. Stewart, *Looking at Totem Poles*, 17.

43. For information on potlatches, see Aldona Jonaitis, ed., *Chiefly Feasts: The Enduring Kwakliutl Potlatch* (New York: American Museum of Natural History, 1991), and Joseph Masco, "Competitive Displays: Negotiating Genealogical Rights to the Potlatch at the American Museum of Natural History," *American Anthropologist* 88, no. 4 (1996): 837–52.

44. John Mack, ed., *Masks and the Art of Expression* (New York: Harry N. Abrams, 1994), 116–17.

45. Hilary Stewart, *Looking at Indian Art of the Northwest Coast* (Seattle: University of Washington Press, 1979), 16.

46. Stewart, *Looking at Totem Poles*, 23.

BIBLIOGRAPHY AND FURTHER READING

Aldhouse-Green, Miranda, and Stephen Aldhouse-Green. *The Quest for the Shaman: Shape-Shifters, Sorcerers, and Spirit-Healers of Ancient Europe*. London: Thames and Hudson, 2005.

Berlo, Janet, and Ruth Phillips. *Native North American Art*. Oxford: Oxford University Press, 1998.

Berlo, Janet, and Ruth Phillips. "Our (Museum) World Turned Upside-Down: Re-Presenting Native American Arts." *The Art Bulletin* 77, no. 1 (1995): 6–10.

Bernstein, Bruce, and Gerald McMaster, eds. *First American Art: The Charles and Valerie Diker Collection of American Indian Art*. Washington, DC: Smithsonian Institution, 2004.

Berry, Christina. "What's in a Name? Indians and Political Correctness." *All Things Cherokee*, http://www.allthingscherokee.com/articles_culture_events_070101. html.

Branson, Oscar. *Fetishes and Carvings of the Southwest*. Santa Fe, NM: Treasure Chest Publications, 1976.

Brody, J. J. *The Anasazi: Ancient Indian People of the American Southwest*. New York: Rizzoli, 1990.

Brody, J. J. "Kachina Images in American Art: The Way of the Doll." In *Kachinas in the Pueblo World*, ed. Polly Schaafsma, 147–60. Albuquerque: University of New Mexico Press, 1994.

Campbell, David, ed. *Native American Art and Folklore: A Cultural Celebration*. Avenel, NJ: Crescent Books, 1993.

Dugan, Kathleen. "At the Beginning Was Woman: Women in Native American Religious Traditions." In *Religion and Women*, ed. Arvind Sharma, 39–60. Albany: State University of New York Press, 1994.

Fagan, Brian. *From Black Land to Fifth Sun: The Science of Sacred Sites*. Reading, MA: Addison-Wesley, 1998.

Fagan, Brian. *The Great Journey: The Peopling of Ancient America*. London: Thames and Hudson, 1987.

Fane, Diana, Ira Jacknis, and Lisa Breen. *Objects of Myth and Memory: American Indian Art at the Brooklyn Museum*. Seattle: University of Washington Press, 1991.

Feest, Christian. *Native Arts of North America*. New York: Thames and Hudson, 1992.

Fitzhugh, William. *Inua: Spirit World of the Bering Sea Eskimo*. Washington, DC: Smithsonian Institution Press, 1982.

Furst, Peter, and Jill Furst. *North American Indian Art*. New York: Rizzoli, 1982.

Griffin-Pierce, Trudy. *Native Peoples of the Southwest*. Albuquerque: University of New Mexico Press, 2000.

Halifax, John. *Shaman: The Wounded Healer*. London: Thames and Hudson, 1982.

Hessel, Ingo. *Inuit Art: An Introduction*. New York: Harry N. Abrams, 1998.

Hill, Tom, and Richard Hills, eds. *Creation's Journey: Native American Identity and Belief*. Washington, DC: Smithsonian Institution Press, 1994.

Hirschfelder, Arlene, and Paulette Molin. *Encyclopedia of Native American Religions*. New York: Checkmark Books, 2001.

Holm, Bill. *Crooked Beak of Heaven: Masks and Other Ceremonial Art of the Northwest Coast*. Seattle: University of Washington Press, 1972.

Holm, Bill. *Spirit and Ancestor: A Century of Northwest Coast Art at the Burke Museum*. Seattle: University of Washington Press, 1987.

Hunt, Norman. *Shamanism in North America*. Buffalo, NY: Firefly Books, 2003.

Jacka, Lois. *Art of the Hopi: Contemporary Journeys on Ancient Pathways*. Flagstaff, AZ: Northland, 1998.

Jonaitis, Aldona, ed. *Chiefly Feasts: The Enduring Kwakliutl Potlatch*. New York: American Museum of Natural History, 1991.

Joseph, Robert, ed. *Listening to our Ancestors: The Art of Native Life along the North Pacific Coast*. Washington, DC: Smithsonian Institution, 2005.

Korp, Maureen. *Sacred Art of the Earth: Ancient and Contemporary Earthworks*. New York: Continuum, 1997.

Korp, Maureen. *The Sacred Geography of the American Mound Builders*. Lewisten, NY: E. Mellen, 1990.

Mack, John, ed. *Masks and the Art of Expression*. New York: Harry N. Abrams, 1994.

Masco, Joseph. "Competitive Displays: Negotiating Genealogical Rights to the Potlatch at the American Museum of Natural History." *American Anthropologist* 88, no. 4 (1996): 837–52.

Mather, Christine. *Native America: Arts, Traditions, and Celebrations*. New York: Clarkson Potter, 1990.

McCoy, Ronald. "Summoning the Gods: Sandpainting in the Native American Southwest." *Plateau* 59, no. 1 (1988): 1–32.

Nabokov, Peter. *Where the Lightning Strikes: The Lives of American Indian Sacred Places*. New York: Viking, 2006.

Nabokov, Peter, and Robert Easton. *Native American Architecture*. New York: Oxford University Press, 1989.

National Museum of the American Indian, http://www.nmai.si.edu/

Newcomb, Franc. *Sandpaintings of the Navajo Shooting Chant*. New York: Dover, 1975.

Nunley, John, and Cara McCarty. *Masks: Faces of Culture*. New York: Harry N. Abrams, 1999.

Parezo, Nancy. *Navajo Sandpainting: From Religious Act to Commercial Art*. Albuquerque: University of New Mexico Press, 1983.

Penny, David. *Native American Art Masterpieces*. New York: Hugh Lauter Levin Associates, 1996.

Penny, David. *North American Indian Art*. New York: Thames and Hudson, 2004.

Penny, David, and George Longfish. *Native American Art*. New York: Hugh Lauter Levin Associates, 1994.

Phillips, Ruth. "What Is 'Huron Art'?: Native American Art and the New Art History." *Canadian Journal of Native Studies* 9, no. 2 (1989): 161–86.

Portago, Andrea. *Classic Hopi and Zuni Kachina Figures*. Santa Fe: Museum of New Mexico Press, 2006.

Ray, Dorothy. *Aleut and Eskimo Art: Tradition and Innovation in South Alaska*. Seattle: University of Washington Press, 1981.

Reichard, Gladys. *Navajo Medicine Man: Sandpaintings*. New York: Dover, 1977.

Rubin, William, ed. *"Primitivisim" in Twentieth Century Art: Affinity of the Tribal and the Modern*. 2 vols. New York: Museum of Modern Art, 1984.

Schaafsma, Polly. *Indian Rock Art of the Southwest*. Santa Fe, NM: School of American Research, 1980.

Schaafsma, Polly, ed. *Kachinas in the Pueblo World*. Albuquerque: University of New Mexico Press, 1994.

Schaafsma, Polly. "The Prehistoric Kachina Cult and Its Origins as Suggested by Southwestern Rock Art." In *Kachinas in the Pueblo World*, ed. Polly Schaafsma, 63–79. Albuquerque: University of New Mexico Press, 1994

Schaafsma, Polly, and Curtis Schaafsma. "Evidence for the Origins of the Pueblo Katchina Cult as Suggested by Southwestern Rock Art." *American Antiquity* 39, no. 4 (1974): 535–45.

Schmidt, Jeremy. *In the Spirit of Mother Earth: Nature in Native American Art*. San Francisco: Chronicle Books, 1994.

Scully, Vincent. *Pueblo: Mountain, Village, Dance*. Chicago: University of Chicago Press, 1989.

Sharma, Arvind, ed. *Religion and Women*. Albany: State University of New York Press, 1994.

Smoak, Gregory. *Ghost Dances and Identity: Prophetic Religion and American Indian Ethnogenesis in the Nineteenth Century*. Berkeley: University of California Press, 2006.

Sommer, Robin. *Native American Art*. New York: Smithmark, 1994.

Stewart, Hilary. *Looking at Indian Art of the Northwest Coast*. Seattle: University of Washington Press, 1979.

Stewart, Hilary. *Looking at Totem Poles*. Seattle: University of Washington Press, 1993.

Stewart, Hilary. *Totem Poles*. Seattle: University of Washington Press, 1990.

Taylor, Colin. *Buckskin and Buffalo: The Artistry of the Plains Indians*. New York: Rizzoli, 1998.

Tedlock, Barbara. "Zuni Sacred Theater." *American Indian Quarterly* 7, no. 3 (1983): 93–110.

Teiwes, Helga. *Kachina Dolls: The Art of Hopi Carvers*. Tucson: University of Arizona Press, 1991.

Thomas, David. *Exploring Ancient Native America: An Archaeological Guide*. New York: Macmillan, 1994.

Villaseñor, David. *Tapestries in Sand: The Spirit of Indian Sandpainting*. Healdsburg, CA: Naturegraph Company, 1966.

Walters, Anna. *The Spirit of Native America: Beauty and Mysticism in American Indian Art*. San Francisco: Chronicle Books, 1989.

Wardwell, Allen. *Tangible Visions: Northwest Coast Indian Shamanism and Its Art*. New York: Monacelli Press, 1996.

Warner, John. *The Life and Art of the North American Indian*. Secaucus, NJ: Chartwell Books, 1990.

Washburn, Dorothy, ed. *Hopi Kachina: Spirit of Life*. Seattle: University of Washington Press, 1980.

Washburn, Dorothy. "Kachina: Window to the Hopi World." In *Hopi Kachina: Spirit of Life*, ed. Dorothy Washburn, 39–49. Seattle: University of Washington Press, 1980.

Werness, Hope. *The Continuum Encyclopedia of Native Art: Worldview, Symbolism, and Culture in Africa, Oceania, and North America*. New York: Continuum, 2000.

Whitley, David. *The Art of the Shaman: Rock Art of California*. Salt Lake City: University of Utah Press, 2000.

Wyman, Leland. *Sandpaintings of the Navaho Shootingway and the Walcott Collection*. Washington, DC: Smithsonian Institution, 1970.

−7−

Indigenous Religions of Oceania

ORIGINS AND DEVELOPMENT

Oceania refers to a vast region of the world traditionally comprising the continent of Australia and the numerous Pacific Island groups of Polynesia, Micronesia, and Melanesia. The geographic scope of the region is enormous and often is demarcated in different ways. For purposes of this present study, Australia is included as one of the four major Oceanic regions, along with the three large Pacific Island groups—themselves representing thousands of lands of various sizes situated across millions of miles in the Pacific Ocean. From the outset, it is important to note that the terms *Polynesia, Melanesia,* and *Micronesia* all reflect names developed by European explorers in the 18th and 19th centuries and thus "there is a certain artificiality about the demarcation of such regions which have had waves of migration and degrees of cultural overlap."[1]

Polynesia (a term meaning "many islands") comprises a huge expanse of the Pacific Ocean and includes, at its southernmost range, the islands of New Zealand and, at its northernmost range, the Hawaiian Islands. Polynesia stretches to the east as far as Easter Island, an isolated locale 2,000 miles from the Chilean coast of South America, and also includes Tahiti, the Marquesas, Society, and Cook Islands. Fiji is often considered to be part of Polynesia, although it may also be included in Melanesia. *Melanesia* (a term meaning "islands of the blacks") includes the large island of New Guinea, plus numerous islands and island groups including the Solomon Islands, New Caledonia, Vanuatu, New Britain, New Ireland, and the Admiralties. *Micronesia* (a term meaning "small islands") includes thousands of little islands north of New Guinea and east of the Philippines in several major archipelagos: the Marshalls, Carolines, Marianas, and Gilberts.

Evidence of human presence and activity in Oceania is of widely divergent dates. Some areas (such as New Guinea and Australia) were populated extremely early in the prehistoric period by peoples migrating from Asia, when water levels were much lower and land masses now separated were closer or even connected. Some rock paintings and engravings in Australia, for example, have been dated to as early as 30,000–20,000 BCE, and evidence of human activity in New Guinea is similarly ancient. In other regions of Oceania, however, human habitation is relatively more recent. Around 3000 BCE, the Lapita culture (from southeast Asia or the Philippines) became established in Melanesia and, during the second and first millennia BCE, began to expand to various Polynesian islands such as Fiji, Samoa, and Tonga. The Lapitas were accomplished sailors and traders and used "outrigger canoes and highly developed navigational skills involving knowledge of prevailing winds, open water currents, cloud patterns over land areas, bird behavior, and the positions of the stars" to travel impressively vast distances.[2] Many of the Micronesian islands were reached (probably from the Philippines and Indonesia) by non-Lapitan cultures around 2000 BCE. By the first century BCE, descendants of the Lapita culture traveled to the islands of the Marquesas. Over the subsequent centuries, more regions were populated by settlers. The far-flung islands of Hawaii to the north and Easter Island to the southeast were reached by the sixth or fifth century CE. Peoples from the Marquesas reached the Cook, Austral, and Society Islands by ca. 600 CE and from there traveled southwest to New Zealand probably by the 9th or 10th century CE, making New Zealand "the last large habitable area of the world to be populated."[3]

> Other contacts between the various Polynesian peoples occurred after these initial migrations. Voyages from Tahiti to Hawaii and New Zealand in the eleventh century have been surmised, and intermittent connections between the various island groups undoubtedly were made over the centuries before the coming of the Europeans. . . . However, periods of isolation allowed for independent development, which of course accounts in part for the distinctive artistic expressions to be found on each of the island groups.[4]

The vast region of the world represented by Oceania was largely unknown to Europeans until the 16th-century voyages of exploration in the Age of Discovery. The Portuguese explorer Ferdinand Magellan (1481–1521) was one of the first Europeans to sail to the Philippines (where he was killed). Magellan is also credited with naming the Pacific Ocean (Mare Pacificum, "peaceful ocean"). Spanish explorers in the 16th century reached New Guinea and the Solomon Islands. The 17th-century Dutch explorer Abel Janszoon Tasman (1603–1659) discovered New Zealand and the southern Australian island of Tasmania. In the 18th century, French explorers reached many Polynesian islands, and the

English explorer James Cook (1728–1799), in several major voyages, contacted eastern Australia and the Hawaiian Islands (where he was killed).

The term "Polynesia" (originally meaning all the Pacific Islands) was first used by the French writer Charles de Brosses (1709–1777) and later refined by the French explorer Jules Sébastien César Dumont d'Urville (1790–1842), who made several voyages in the Pacific, to Australia, New Zealand, and as far as Antarctica. Dumont d'Urville is credited with devising the term "Oceania" (for the entire region) and the differentiating terms "Micronesia" and "Melanesia," as regions distinct from "Polynesia."

European explorers were interested in trade and colonization, gaining wealth and territory. They were also interested in cartography, geography, geology, natural history, botany, and the customs of the strange and foreign people they encountered in their voyages.

> Another appeal of the Pacific for the European public lay in the idealized expectation of a Pacific paradise. This has ancient roots in the myth of a lost paradise and a nostalgia for recovering it. In the eighteenth century Jean-Jacques Rousseau [1712–1778] voiced the idea of the "noble savage" who was a child of nature, unspoilt by Western civilization. It is not surprising therefore that this expectation could feed on travellers' tales of idyllic ease and freedom from restraints in the Pacific.[5]

This idealized freedom from conventional restraints also resulted in much disastrous European exploitation of the indigenous peoples of Oceania, who were often viewed much less as noble savages but as primitive and backwards peoples in need of Western civilizing influence and corrected religious beliefs. While many ethnographers and Christian missionaries were instrumental in gathering information on indigenous beliefs and religious practices, the tasks of converting peoples to Christianity in many cases resulted in the wholesale destruction of art works and objects deemed pagan. Ultimately, in Oceania, "as a result of the missionary work by Christian churches, the majority of peoples have been converted to some form of Christianity which has now become indigenized in varying degrees."[6] Nevertheless, many ancient traditions still live on, in various degrees of preservation or modification, or can be reconstructed through archaeological and documentary records.

It is important to note also that a number of religious art works from Oceania, now found in world museum collections, were given to missionaries as symbols of the people's conversion to Christianity. Such practices are, of course, not unknown at all in other world regions when new imported religious traditions replace or supplement older traditions. For example, the carved wooden figure of the god A'a (or Tangaroa), among the most celebrated works of Oceanic art in the collection of the British Museum in London, was gifted to the missionary John Williams by people from the island of Rurutu (Austral Islands, Polynesia) in 1821 (see Figure 7.1). A'a was one of several figures presented to the

missionaries, indicating the people's acceptance of Christianity by giving up their old gods and beliefs. This wooden figure, about 44 inches tall, depicts the god A'a in the process of creating other gods and humans, indicated as little figures springing forth from and clinging to his body. The object has a removable back and may have originally served as a container for human bones. The London Missionary Society produced several replicas of this piece in the 19th century, not due to aesthetic appreciation or interest in the cultural context of the object, but "in order to demonstrate as widely as possible to its supporters 'how hideous pagan idols could be.'"[7] The French artist Pablo Picasso (1881–1973) had a bronze cast of this image created, and objects such as this provided a great deal of inspiration for many Western artists of the 20th century.

Figure 7.1   The god A'a, wood, Rurutu, Austral Islands. London: The Trustees of The British Museum / Art Resource, NY.

PRINCIPAL BELIEFS AND KEY PRACTICES

The geographic vastness and cultural diversity of Oceania poses challenges for any discussion of principal beliefs and key religious practices. The peoples of this widespread region all developed distinctive sets of beliefs and customs. Even so, it may be possible to identify several common themes related to views about the creation of the universe, the position and role of humans, death, ancestors, and the world of spirits.

> Most of the art of Oceania is religious by nature. It is made in response to a series of related beliefs that the universe is governed by invisible forces that can determine and influence the events of life. These forces are thought to be everywhere. While they do not actually cause the behavior and nature of inanimate objects and living beings or the inexplicable phenomena of the world, they are expressed by them. Through these forces, a mystical relationship between the people and the elements of their environment is established.[8]

Creation and Dreamtime

Among the many Aboriginal cultures of Australia is a shared belief in the Dreaming or Dreamtime—when the world came into being. During this time, ancestral spirits emerged from beneath the ground or from elsewhere and took on the shape of primeval animals, natural elements, and some human characteristics. These beings (such as the Rainbow Serpents, Lightning Men, Tingari, and Wandjina) shaped the surface of the earth and created the landscape, ultimately withdrawing or transforming themselves into landscape features but also leaving behind a living body of sacred traditions, moral and ritual obligations to be followed by their heirs. It is important to see that the Dreamtime is understood to have "existed before individuals were born and will continue to exist after they have died; people play a role in keeping it alive and as a consequence are part of its change and transformation."[9] In other words, "the Dreaming is not an exercise of the imagination in sleep or fantasy but a spiritual outlook incarnated in traditional rites and in things and places in the world."[10] "The Dreaming is the overarching cosmic order within which Aboriginal people, both as individuals and as communities, are related to the environment as a living landscape. In this the ancestral past is a reality continuous with the present. It is a meaningful universe, filled with symbols."[11]

Images of ancestral and spirit beings are frequently found in Aboriginal art, ranging in date from prehistoric rock paintings (see chapter 1, "Prehistoric Belief Systems") to more contemporary examples in a variety of media, which follow ancient traditions. For example, a 20th-century bark painting from Western Arnheim Land shows a scene of a kangaroo and a hunter (see Figure 7.2). Images of this nature are frequent in Aboriginal art, and paintings on bark are among the more common art forms of modern times.[12] The large kangaroo is depicted in what is known as X-ray style, in which the spine and internal organs of the animal are shown. In this case, the heart and lungs are represented by a three-lobed shape; the liver is shown by a four-lobed shape, and the stomach and intestines are also indicated.[13] The specific cross-hatched patterns (*rarrk*) often found in these paintings may "identify clans and imbue the object on which they are painted with the power of supernatural beings."[14] The small sticklike figure spearing the kangaroo is a *mimi* (or *mimih*) spirit; although not considered among the ancestral or creator beings, many stories of *mimi* and their encounters with humans in the Dreamtime are found in Aboriginal mythology.[15]

Figure 7.2 Bark painting, Mimi hunter and Kangaroo, 20th century, Western Arnheim Land. Private collection. Werner Forman / Art Resource, NY.

Some spirit beings were friendly and helpful, others caused harm and had to be avoided or propitiated. The Mimi of Western Arnheim Land were typical of these spirit people. They lived on the rocky plateau where they had families, hunted, and made love, just as people did. The Mimi were so thin the wind would carry them away, so they travelled only on still days. If humans approached, the Mimi would blow on a large rock causing it to split. After the Mimi passed through, the rock would reseal itself.[16]

Other stories tell that the *mimi* taught humans how to hunt animals, cut them up and cook their meat, and that they also taught humans how to sing and dance and create rock paintings.

Gods, Spirits, and Ancestors

The simultaneous past/present continuity represented by the Dreamtime in Aboriginal thinking, although a unique cultural expression, finds reflections elsewhere in Oceania where beliefs in spirit forces and a sense of human connectedness to the environment are also extremely evident. In some societies, specific named deities were venerated, generally associated with natural forces or elements. For the Maori of New Zealand, for example, the four major deities active in the world were associated with the forests (the god Tane), the sea (the god Ta'aroa), land or agriculture (the god Rongo), and warfare (the god Ku). In Hawaii, the war god was also known as Ku (or Kuka'ilimoku, "the snatcher of land").

In Melanesia generally, specific deities were not worshiped, but a number of spirit forces active in the world were acknowledged, as is well demonstrated in the creation of painted spirit boards (*gope, koi, kwoi,* or *hohao*) typical of the Papuan Gulf region of New Guinea (see Plate 13). Often created from long boards taken from old canoes, these images typically represent specific spirits (or *imunu*) associated with particular land or sea elements whose powers were believed to assist and protect different clans of groups of people. Customarily displayed in shrines within communal dwelling houses, "the spirit boards . . . gazed down upon the living men below, the supernatural powers of the *imunu* ensuring the ongoing fertility and prosperity of the clan and its continuing success in war."[17] The example illustrated in Plate 13 was created in the late 19th or early 20th century by the Elema peoples and depicts a forest spirit wearing a shell necklace. The complete body of the figure is shown in this example, although many other variations exist that consist simply of a face or highly stylized body parts. The figure's navel is a prominent central motif typical of spirit board imagery. "The navel is said to be the element that supernaturally enlivens the board and likely served as the portal through which the spirit entered the board."[18] The prominent kneecaps of the figure are shown, one slightly higher than the other. This is meant to indicate that the spirit is dancing, as if participating in the ceremonial masked performances traditionally and frequently held to honor the spirits and seek their support.[19]

With few exceptions, ancestral spirits (of specific people or as symbols of clan lineages) also play an extremely important role in Oceanic religious beliefs and practices. Elaborate funerary rites, involving dancing, feasting, and the construction of specific shelters and ritual objects are customarily associated with the veneration of ancestral spirits. Although traditions vary from region to region, as well as the distinctive types of art forms produced and used, the veneration of ancestral spirits is another common thread linking the diverse cultural groups of Oceania.

Mana and Tapu

The critical importance of maintaining traditions and customs is also generally evident in Oceanic social and religious practices. Many Oceanic societies share the underlying concepts of *mana* ("supernatural power linked with genealogical rank, fertility, and protocol") and *tapu* (restrictions which protect the maintenance of *mana*).[20] The terms *tapu* and *mana* may also be understood as "spiritual potential" and "realized potential," the powerful forces that govern the material world and the spiritual universe, the forces that affirm social order, earthly, and spiritual obligations.[21] "According to these principles, each society developed distinctive hierarchical traditions tied to sacred rituals in which special objects of art were used."[22] People, as well as objects, places, and natural elements, may be regarded as inherently imbued with, or having the potential to achieve, different degrees of *mana*. *Mana* was a powerful contagious force that could be lost or depleted by improper contacts and actions. The English word "taboo" derives from the terms *tabu, tapu,* and *kapu.*

"Taboo means forbidden, consecrated, placed under a ban or restriction, debarred from ordinary use, touch or treatment. In effect, taboo constituted a collection of laws that protected property, persons, and the life force of mana. . . . Mana and taboo prevailed at all times."[23] These concepts provide the essential underpinnings of many Oceanic societies, influencing customs, social roles, and the creation and use of art objects.

TRADITIONAL ART AND ARCHITECTURAL FORMS

Studies of the traditional art and architectural forms of Oceania and Australia have faced many of the same challenges as in other world regions such as Africa (see chapter 8) and with other cultural groups, such as Native Americans (see chapter 6). Any discussion of native, tribal, or indigenous forms of art is always fraught with terminological controversies, especially when descriptors such as *primitive* are used. Western Europeans and Americans, when they came in contact with the arts of the Pacific Islanders, the Maori of New Zealand, and the Aboriginal peoples of Australia, found their forms of art difficult to understand. These strange and foreign peoples, their cultures, religious practices, lifestyles, and art seemed primitive and undeveloped to Western eyes, certainly not reflective of the types of art and architectural forms traditional in Western European societies and civilizations. Although certain Romanticized views of the noble savage, as well as idealized visions of a paradisiacal lifestyle represented by humans living in harmony with nature in the Pacific Island cultures, characterized much European discourse in the 18th and 19th centuries especially, the persistent and traditional use of the term *primitive* to describe

Oceanic art reflects the challenges faced by outsiders in approaching these different cultures as well as an attempt (well-intentioned or not) to describe the art forms and related religious practices of Oceanic peoples.

Much scholarship has been devoted to analyzing the powerful impressions that Oceanic as well as African art made on Western European artists of the 19th and 20th centuries. The French artist Paul Gauguin (1848–1903), for example, was notably inspired by his visions of the idyllic island lifestyle of the Polynesians to spend several years of his life living in Tahiti productively further developing his unique Post-Impressionist style inspired by the vibrant colors, themes, and motifs of the Polynesian ambiance he experienced or imagined.[24] The reactions of other early 20th-century Western artists, such as Pablo Picasso and his peers, to the displays of ethnographic materials exhibited in Paris in the early years of the 20th century have also inspired much scholarly discussion.[25] The ongoing reception and responses of Western artists to non-Western art forms and the influence of these arts on the development of early modern styles in Western art have been well investigated, as have the parallel if not reciprocal influences that Western art styles and modes of display and presentation have also had on the arts produced in Oceania, after contact with Europeans and to the present day.

Among the most challenging issues for scholars of Oceanic art are the traditional collection and display modes adopted for presentation of cultural artifacts typified by many museum installations in the past and present. Although collecting objects of interest or importance, and preserving and presenting these collections privately or publicly, has an extremely lengthy history in many cultures worldwide, collection and display modes often serve to create major artifices as well as promote knowledge and understanding. When works of art—which were never intended to be preserved, collected, or displayed or perhaps even viewed outside their original context—are extracted from their settings, these objects may be much admired, at best, but only as mute reflections of their original usage and significance.

It may be very useful and elucidating for art historians to study these works out of context, and, indeed, much substantial and very sensitive scholarship of this nature has been undertaken in the past several years. It is clear that certain styles and visual forms are typical of specific cultures of Oceania during particular time periods and that particular forms of religious art are most typical of specific cultures. Large-scale figural sculpture in materials such as stone and wood are common in Polynesia; the creation of masks for ceremonial purposes is most common in Melanesia; the complex elaboration of decorative designs is characteristic of Micronesian art; while the Maori of New Zealand and Aborigines of Australia have distinctive art traditions and styles as well.

These traditions continue—and continue to develop to the present day—often in the form of art produced for tourists and visitors, as well as in new modes that bespeak ancient traditions. This is another fraught and often discussed issue in studies of Oceanic art generally. While art works created by contemporary Australian Aborigines and other Pacific Island peoples may lack the same antique stamp as many objects that were so avidly collected by Europeans in previous centuries, in many ways these more modern works also need to be very seriously considered in the overall picture of Oceanic arts.[26]

Environmental and Ephemeral Art Forms of Oceania

A notable feature of Oceanic art is the diversity of materials employed. "The artists of the Pacific used almost anything from their natural environment to give expression to [their] beliefs . . . It seems that practically everything that existed was at some time skillfully worked into an element of visual expression."[27] For example, a 19th-century mask from the Melanesian island of New Ireland demonstrates the use of fiber, bark, and dried fruit peels (see Figure 7.3); many masks made from fiber, mud, and shells were created in the Sepik River areas of New Guinea (see Figure 7.4); *tapa* (unwoven bark cloth) and basketry frames were employed for many masks of New Guinea and elsewhere (see Figure 7.5); and the colorful and prized feathers of birds were often used in conjunction with other materials (see Figure 7.6). The Hawaiian Feather God illustrated in Figure 7.6 was an important ritual object, carried into battles by the priests of the war god. This particular feather and basketry sculpture also includes plaited human hair and a fearsome wide mouth lined with over a hundred dog teeth. This object was collected on one of Captain Cook's voyages and is presently located in the British Museum in London.

The use of organic and perishable materials (leaves, ferns, shells, nuts, moss, flowers, roots, grasses, and so on) indicates not only the fact that many objects of Oceanic art have long deteriorated or disappeared but also that the objects collected and displayed in museums today are but vague reflections of their original appearance.

Not only have the grasses, leaves, fibers, and fruits that were originally attached to them long since fallen off, but those bits and pieces that remain are now dried out, brown, and lifeless, providing only a hint of the vibrancy and even more spectacular appearance they once had. This is particularly true of Melanesian art, much of

Figure 7.3 Mask from New Ireland, 19th century. Berlin: Ethnologisches Museum. Bildarchiv Preussischer Kulturbesitz / Art Resource, NY.

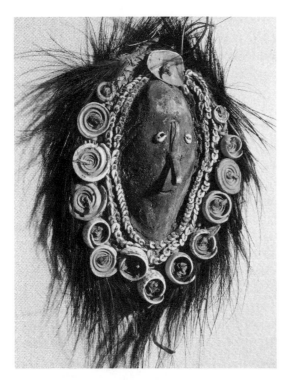

Figure 7.4 Mask from Sepik River area, New Guinea. The Art Archive / Paris: Musée des Arts Africains et Océaniens / Alfredo Dagli Orti.

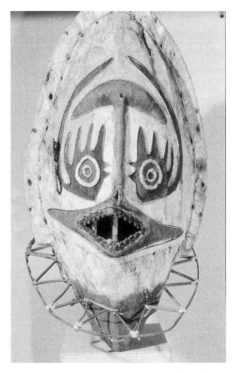

Figure 7.5 Mask from Papua New Guinea. The Art Archive / Paris: Musée des Arts Africains et Océaniens / Gianni Dagli Orti.

which was newly created for each ceremony, or, if old, renewed with fresh materials before each ritual appearance.[28]

The process of preserving objects of this nature—and especially objects that were never intended to last—poses many challenges and issues for museum professionals.[29]

On the other hand, many Oceanic art forms were created with relatively more durable materials, such as wood, and extremely long-lasting materials, such as stone. These objects were certainly "made to last and were carefully kept and preserved so that they could be passed on from one generation to the next."[30] Several cultures in Oceania also developed impressive traditions of stone architectural construction, primarily in the form of ceremonial structures and enclosures used for burials and religious rituals. Such sites in Hawaii are known as *heiau* and often consisted of several large stone platforms with other (stone or wooden) structures built on them designed to house priests and store sacred ritual items and cult images representing various deities. *Heiau* traditionally include altars (*ahu*) on which sacrifices were offered. They were considered to be highly sacred enclosures with access restricted to priests (*kahuna*) and certain high chiefs (*ali'i*). Many of the surviving wood carvings of different Hawaiian deities were originally kept in *heiau*.[31] The term *marae* describes similar types of sacred enclosures found elsewhere in Oceania. Some were private, associated with individual families and used for ceremonies for deceased relatives, whereas larger official *marae* were often associated with specific tribal leaders and served as sites for ritual sacrifices of animals and humans.

EXAMPLES

Uli Figure

Uli (or *nalik*) figures, a characteristic art form of New Ireland, were created for the funerary ceremonies honoring prominent chiefs or head men (see Figure 7.7). Often of imposing size (the example illustrated is 52 inches tall), these carved and painted statues typically depict a specific individual whose spirit was believed to reside within the image. These statues were powerful and trea-

Figure 7.6 Feather God, Hawaii, pre-19th century. London: The Trustees of The British Museum / Art Resource, NY.

sured possessions, created for grand and lengthy ceremonies involving feasting and dances. After their ceremonial use and display, the figures were typically carefully preserved and kept in communal dwellings; they were often repainted for use in further funerary ceremonies.

Uli figures are generally shown in "ceremonial dress in the form of wristlets, anklets, and a crested headpiece similar to those worn by people in times of mourning."[32] An especially striking characteristic of these figures is their hermaphroditic appearance, with female breasts and male genitalia. Although the figures are meant to represent male chiefs, it is believed that the addition of breasts "signified the importance of fertility and the chief's care for the women in the village."[33] Indeed, in some of the rituals associated with *uli* figures, it has been reported that male members of the community donned costumes with false breasts, further reinforcing this male/female symbolism.

Malagan Image

"Spectacular and ephemeral, the brightly painted *malagan* images of northern New Ireland are the most colorful and complex sculptures in the Pacific"[34] (see Figure 7.8). These sculptures were created for use and display in several

Figure 7.7 Uli Figure, 18th to 19th century, New Ireland. The Art Archive / Musée du Quai Branly Paris / Gianni Dagli Orti.

related ritual contexts, primarily for elaborate funerary commemorations marking the initial death of a community member and for the final and often prolonged period of mourning held in honor of, sometimes several, deceased community members. The creation and display of *malagan* images may also serve purposes such as ratifying social contracts, solving disputes, removing certain prohibitions, and validating transactions between clans or groups.[35] They are used in a variety of calendrical rites related to agriculture, and the advent, conclusion, and return of the seasons of the year. The term *malagan* (or *malaggan* or *malanggan*) refers not only to the carved images themselves but also to all the ceremonies and rituals with which they are associated. During funeral rituals and other rites, the images function "as temporary abodes for supernatural beings associated with the clan."[36] They were displayed in specially constructed shelters in enclosed courtyards within which the funerary rituals (dancing, feasting, sacrifices of pigs) were held. At the conclusion of the ceremonies, both the house and the *malagan* carvings were traditionally either "destroyed, allowed to rot, or sold to outsiders."[37] The funerary rites, especially, were designed not only to honor and commemorate the dead but also to ensure that the soul of the deceased would enter the world of the spirits/ancestors and provide continued protection for the living who remain on earth.

The ephemeral nature of *malagan* carvings, created for one-time-only usage, may seem (especially in Western thinking) to be at odds with their signally important role in the Melanesian culture of New Ireland. However, the birth and death of the images represents powerful acknowledgment and affirmation of cyclic forces—both earthly and spiritual.[38] These powerful figures and their specific iconography also represent highly complex symbols and designs signifying the social status and prestige of individuals or family groups. "From early infancy to revered old age, through inheritance, purchase, or occasionally, supernatural revelation, men and women gradually accumulate the rights, similar to Western copyrights, to commission specific named forms of *malagan* images and to perform the songs and rites associated with them."[39] The images are created by special carvers in accordance with the specific forms to which the commissioners are entitled. It is important to note, however, that "the institution of *malagan* is not to be seen as a static complex of repetitive patterns, but as a living complex of changing syntheses that uses a limited but changing stock of motifs."[40]

There are many forms of *malagans*, including carved friezes, single figures, vertical poles with multiple figures, carved heads placed on figures made of other materials, and masks. Human and animal imagery are frequently combined often to represent spirit beings associated with specific clans or to convey particular stories.

> Every *malagan* has a story connected with it. Just as the production of a *malagan* is legitimized by the knowledge of that story, its authentic version can only be told by the owner of the rights to the *malagan* . . . Because most of the *malagans* now in collections around the world were gathered by people whose main interest was their aesthetic aspects . . . those works have lost their stories; that is to say, they have been artificially silenced. A major part of the iconographer's difficulty is this removal of the *malagans* from their context.[41]

Figure 7.8 Malagan Image, 19th century, New Ireland. The Art Archive / Musée du Quai Branly Paris / Gianni Dagli Orti.

The example illustrated here dates to the 19th century and typifies the complex and often mysterious combination of forms typical of these works, the meaning of which is often undisclosed. "*Malanggan* figures command attention without speaking or touching and address without naming . . . each *malanggan* is a visual assemblage of parts that slot together like the pieces of a puzzle. The parts appear in the form of motifs that are strangely opaque, directing attention away from the subtle combinations that entice recognition."[42]

Maori Wood Carvings

The Maori of New Zealand are descended from Polynesian-speaking peoples who probably first arrived in New Zealand from the Marquesas and Society Islands by the 9th or 10th centuries CE. The arts produced by the Maori exhibit several distinctive style features—notably the use of intricate patterns often based on flowing curvilinear forms and a tendency toward decorative elaboration. These characteristic style features developed over several centuries of Maori art production in a variety of media and may be especially well seen in numerous examples of wood carving from the 19th century.

> Maori carving has been praised as the highest achievement of Maori art . . . From our knowledge of classical carving traditions, it was believed to be derived from the gods and to be safeguarded by careful training of the experts (*tohunga*) in carving and the related arts of house and canoe construction. For this reason, carving was surrounded by *tapu* restrictions . . . and preceded by rituals at every stage; for instance, incantations (*karakia*) were offered to the god Tane in the forest before the cutting down of trees for carving. Various stories were told about an ancestor, Rua, who started the art of carving after seeing images in the carved house of the sea god Tangaroa.[43]

Elaborately carved and painted wooden meeting houses (*wharemi* or *whare whakairo*) are of special importance in Maori customs and rituals. Used for events ranging from funeral rites to wedding ceremonies, initiations, and important community gatherings, these structures are generally rectangular with a shallow open entrance porch and an interior space supported by poles and beams. Carvings appear both on the interior and exterior, on pillars, vertical panels, gable boards, doorframes, lintels, thresholds, and roof finials.

The Te Hau Ki Turanga built for the Ngati Kaipoho tribe in the middle of the 19th century, is an excellent and well-preserved example[44] (see Plate 14). It is now located in the National Museum of New Zealand in Wellington. The design of the structure and carving are attributed to a named artist and chief, Raharuhi Rukupo (ca. 1790–1873), whose self-portrait appears in a large carving flanking the entrance on the interior of the structure. Rukupo is renowned as one of the greatest Maori carvers, and the Te Hau Ki Turanga house (completed with the assistance of a team of 18 other carvers) is often regarded as his masterpiece. The name of the house may be translated as "spirit" or "good tidings from Turanga" or "breath" or "vitality of Turanga" (one of the major Maori deities), and the building was constructed as a memorial to Rukupo's elder brother, Tamati Waka Mangere. The elaborate detail and complex iconography of the carvings are typical of Maori ornamented houses, especially as developed by the early to mid-19th century.

The rectangular house has a shallow entrance veranda and is replete with upright carved wooden panels (*poupou*), patterned panels woven from reeds (*tukutuku*), and painted designs on the rafters. It includes an ornamental threshold, carved and painted gable boards, and carved interior posts. Many of the carvings represent *tiki* figures of humanlike appearance (symbolizing ancestors, gods, or spirits), often combined with *manaia* (creatures combining human features with bird or reptilian elements). The painted rafters show the spiral, crescent, and *koru* patterns (bulbed stalklike stems), which abound in Maori decorative vocabulary. The interior represents "a horizontally and vertically ordered space conceptualized as a model of the cosmos and a metaphor of the history and embodiment of the ancestors of the group."[45] The house is visualized not only as a sacred enclosure symbolizing the sky outside and the earth inside, but also as a symbol of the body of the ancestor. The ridgepole represents the spine, the rafters are ribs, while arms, fingers, and head are also symbolized by the carved gables and exterior finial. The overall effect of this richly decorated and colorful structure is extremely powerful, bespeaking its sacred significance.

A carved wooden lintel (or *pare*) from another Maori meeting house, dating to the late 1840s, again demonstrates the sacredness of the enclosed space as well as the open space (or *marae*) used as an assembly area in front of the structure (see Figure 7.9). The transition from exterior to interior space is understood to represent the passage between realms dominated by different deities. The exterior space is sometimes known as the domain of the war god Tumatauenga, whereas Rongo, the god of peace, presides over the interior space. This lintel illustrates the Maori story of the creation of the world, when the earth deity Papa (or Papatuanuku) and the sky deity Rangi (or Ranginui) were pushed apart from their perpetual embrace by their children, thus allowing light to enter the world. "This is not a story of gods creating the world but of the emergence of the world from the primeval parents."[46] The center figure is probably Tane, the god of the forests. The other children of the primeval couple became gods of the sea, the winds, agriculture, and war. Light and knowledge entering the world is symbolized by the spiraling forms surrounding the figures.

Carvings representing ancestors are commonly found in and on Maori meeting houses and on other types of architectural structures such as storehouses (or *patakas*), designed to store items such as food, tools, and weapons. These structures are generally set above ground on sturdy carved supports and may be enriched with carved gable finials (or *tekotekos*) as well (see Figure 7.10). The early 19th-century example illustrated depicts an ancestor of the Tuwharetoa people, placed there to represent the esteemed genealogy of the building's owner as well as to protect the building and its contents. "Ancestors, or *tupuna*, play a central role in Maori art and culture. They include all forebears, from the founding ancestors who arrived in canoes from eastern Polynesia and gave

Figure 7.9   Lintel from a Maori meeting house, wood, late 1840s. London: British Museum. Werner Forman / Art Resource, NY.

Figure 7.10 Gable finial, ancestor figure, wood, Maori, early 19th century. Berlin: Ethnologisches Museum. Werner Forman / Art Resource, NY.

rise to the different Maori groups, or *iwi*, that exist today to individuals who were born and died within living memory."[47] The gaping mouth of the figure indicates his strength and protective powers. The hands of the figure are depicted as "three birdlike claws, a reference to the mystical connections between man and birds that are found in New Zealand and throughout Polynesia."[48]

The elaborate surface ornamentation of much Maori art in general, and in figural sculpture especially, also reflects the importance of bodily embellishment in the form of tattooing in Maori culture.[49] Both men and women underwent this highly ritualized process, acquiring designs, often over a lifetime, representing specific clan symbols or marks indicating the passage of different stages of life or achievements. Maori tattoo (*moko*) is an art form still vibrantly practiced today.[50]

Easter Island Moai Figures

Rapa Nui—or Easter Island, so named by the Dutch explorer Jabob Roggeveen (1659–1729), the first recorded European visitor, who encountered the island on Easter Sunday 1722, is a remote location, representing the far reaches of the watery expanse of Polynesia, thousands of miles off the coast of Chile in South America, and substantially far away from any other island or land mass. Even so, the massive stone figures (or *moai*) of Easter Island are, arguably, among the most well-known and popularly reproduced images of Polynesian art (see Figure 7.11). These rows of figures and heads are found in several areas on the small (63 square mile) island. They have long gripped scholarly as well as popular attention because of their impressive size and mysterious ambiance. Hundreds of them exist, in various states of construction, preservation, and destruction. Clearly, the creation and erection of these huge, heavy, monolithic stone monuments was an activity that consumed the attention and energy of the island's inhabitants—presumably for extremely significant reasons—over a prolonged period of time. Most scholars agree in the assumption that these figures played an important role in the religious beliefs of the islanders and that they represent spirit or ancestral figures associated with different families or family groups among the island's early inhabitants.[51]

Figure 7.11 Easter Island Moai Figures of Ahu Tongariki, ca. 1000 CE. Joetex1 / Dreamstime.com.

With a few exceptions, all of the *moai* were carved from volcanic tufa stone, widely available in several quarries on the island. Unfinished examples still exist in several quarries. This evidence has assisted researchers in determining how the figures were produced and how they might have been moved (often great distances) from the quarries to the stone platforms (or *ahus*) on which they were set up. The statues were carved using stone tools and were probably moved on wooden rollers or sledges (or carefully pulled with ropes in an upright position) from their carving sites. The exact processes for rolling or walking the *moai* remain unclear. Researchers have experimented with replicating both modes—the rolling-on-logs methods being the most successful. In any case, the large scale and massive weight of the figures required supreme efforts on the part of doubtless hundreds of people involved with their creation and transportation.

Some of the tallest *moai* to be erected are between 30 and 40 feet in height. Many weigh between 70 and 80 tons. The largest example (unfinished and left in its quarry location) is estimated to have been intended to be close to 70 feet tall and weigh close to 300 tons. Although the *moai* are often referred to as the Easter Island heads, their general appearance is of enlarged, oversize, angular heads on thick, legless torsos with carved inset arms placed in various positions close to the body. The faces have heavy brows, elongated noses with curling nostrils, thin, protruding lips, and big eye sockets designed to hold large eyes of coral and black obsidian. It is believed that the figures were originally painted with mineral pigments, traces of which remain on some examples. Many of the figures have topknots (or *pukaos*), which look like cylindrical hats. *Pukaos* were often carved separately and added to the figures later. The figures were generally arranged in groups (of upwards of 15) aligned along the *ahu* platform. With few exceptions, the *moai* look inward toward the land rather than outward to the ocean.

When the first Europeans reached Easter Island in the early 18th century, most of the *moai* were still standing. But later 18th-century visitors, such as Captain Cook, reported that many of the *moai* had been neglected or toppled from their ceremonial platforms. Some appeared to have been deliberately decapitated. The unfinished examples in the quarries also indicate that the production of *moai* and the regard in which they were held had long ceased by this time. Many believe that the *moai* were constructed primarily between about 1000 and 1500 CE, although earlier dates have been proposed as well.

Various dates have also been proposed for the first migration of people to Easter Island. Many scholars believe that the first people to reach Easter Island came from the Marquesas Islands of Polynesia sometime in the early centuries CE (perhaps in the fifth or sixth century CE, contemporary with the initial settlement of the Hawaiian Islands). Other researchers, notably the Norwegian explorer Thor Heyerdahl (1914–2002), have speculated and attempted to prove by his famous 1947 expedition on his wooden raft, *Kon-Tiki*, that the early inhabitants of Easter Island arrived from the Peruvian coast.[52] Although varying theories of the origins of the Easter Islanders remain avidly discussed, it does seem clear that this remote volcanic island, once it was populated by humans, had diminishing natural resources to support the growing population. Originally forested with several species of trees (especially palms), it appears that the island was eventually deforested by the inhabitants, who used the trees to build dwellings, boats, and (as is speculated) sledges or rollers for the process of moving and erecting the large *moai* sculptures. Diminishing resources and shortages of food ultimately, as many believe, resulted in fierce competition and internal warfare among the people. The attacks on and toppling of the *moai* may have been a result of this, as the *moai* represented ancestral figures of powerful and battling clans.

Much of the history and culture of Easter Island remains enigmatic. The population was severely decimated in the 19th century by the incursion of Peruvian slave raiders who killed or abducted over half of the remaining people. Diseases were also brought to the island by Westerners in the 19th century, and, by the late 19th century only slightly more than 100 people were living there.

The standing *moai* of Easter Island today largely represent careful restorations by various teams of researchers. The 15 *moai* of Ahu Tongariki, illustrated in Figure 7.11, were just recently re-erected in the 1990s. These figures had previously been toppled, and the *ahu* (platform) had been swept inland by a tsunami earlier in the 20th century.

Although much scholarly attention has been devoted to Easter Island, many questions still remain about the dramatic history of the island and the changing beliefs and religious practices of the people. Ancestral worship, represented by the *moai* figures, appears to have been replaced or supplemented by the 17th or 18th century with other practices revolving around worship of the birdman (*tangata manu*), the cult of which dominated the later history of the island. It is wise also to remember that the *moai*, although perhaps the most visibly impressive examples of Easter Island art, take their position within a complex culture in which other forms of art were also produced. Smaller statuary, abundant petroglyphs, and wooden tablets inscribed with a distinctive and largely undeciphered hieroglyphic script system known as *rongorongo* are all among the important visual survivals from this remote region of the world.[53]

NOTES

1. Albert Moore, *Arts in the Religions of the Pacific* (London: Cassell, 1995), 2–3.

2. Allen Wardwell, *Island Ancestors: Oceanic Art from the Masco Collection* (Seattle: University of Washington Press, 1994), 7.

3. Wardwell, 7.

4. Wardwell, 7.

5. Moore, 5.

6. Moore, 22.

7. William Rubin, *"Primitivism" in Twentieth Century Art: Affinity of the Tribal and the Modern*, vol. 1 (New York: Museum of Modern Art, 1984), 332.

8. Wardwell, 8.

9. Howard Morphy, *Aboriginal Art* (London: Phaidon, 1998), 145, 48.

10. Moore, 34.

11. Moore, 40.

12. Luke Taylor, *Seeing the Inside: Bark Painting in Western Arnheim Land* (Oxford: Clarendon Press, 1996).

13. Luke Taylor, "Seeing the 'Inside:' Kunwinjku Paintings and the Symbol of the Divided Body," in *Animals into Art*, ed. Howard Morphy (London: Unwin Hyman, 1989), 371–98.

14. Wally Caruana, *Aboriginal Art* (New York: Thames and Hudson, 1993), 27.

15. Louis Allen, *Time Before Morning: Art and Myth of the Australian Aborigines* (New York: Thomas Y. Crowell, 1975), especially 140–44, and Peter Carroll, "Mimi from Western Arnheim Land," in *Form in Indigenous Art: Schematisation in the Art of Aboriginal Australia and Prehistoric Europe*, ed. Peter Ucko (Canberra, Australia: Australian Institute of Aboriginal Studies, 1977), 119–30.

16. Louis Allen, *Australian Aboriginal Art: Arnheim Land* (Chicago, IL: Field Museum Press, 1972), 3.

17. Eric Kjellgren, *Oceania: Art of the Pacific Islands in the Metropolitan Museum of Art* (New York: The Metropolitan Museum of Art, 2007), 126.

18. Kjellgren, 126.

19. Robert Welsch, Virginia-Lee Webb, and Sebastian Haraha, *Coaxing the Spirits to Dance: Art and Society in the Papuan Gulf of New Guinea* (Hanover, NH: Dartmouth College, Hood Museum of Art, 2006).

20. Adrianne Kaeppler, *The Pacific Arts of Polynesia and Micronesia* (Oxford: Oxford University Press, 2008), 5.

21. John Elder, *Art of Polynesia* (Honolulu, HI: Hemmeter, 1990), 14.

22. Kaeppler, 5.

23. Elder, 26–27.

24. Many studies have been devoted to Gauguin's interest in Polynesia and the impact of this on his art. See, for example, Ziva Amishai-Maisels, "Gauguin's Early Tahitian Idols," *The Art Bulletin* 60, no. 2 (1978): 331–41, and Charles Harrison, Francis Frascina, and Gill Perry, *Primitivism, Cubism, Abstraction: The Early Twentieth Century* (New Haven, CT: Yale University Press, 1993) for additional bibliography.

25. See Rubin, ed., *"Primitivism" in Twentieth Century Art,* and Marianna Torgovnick, *Gone Primitive: Savage Intellects, Modern Lives* (Chicago, IL: University of Chicago Press, 1990).

26. Peter Sutton, ed., *Dreamings: The Art of Aboriginal Australia* (New York: George Braziller, 1988); Fred Myers, "Representing Culture: The Production of Discourse(s) for Aboriginal Acrylic Painting," *Cultural Anthropology* 6, no. 1 (1991): 26–62; and Fred Myers, "Re/Writing the Primitive: Art Criticism and the Circulation of Aboriginal Painting," in *Meaning in the Visual Arts: Views from the Outside: A Centennial Commemoration of Erwin Panofsky (1892–1968),* ed. Irving Lavin (Princeton, NJ: Princeton University Press, 1995), 65–84.

27. Wardwell, 8.

28. Wardwell, 9.

29. Miriam Clavir, "Reflections on Changes in Museums and the Conversation of Collections from Indigenous Peoples," *Journal of the American Institute for Conservation* 35, no. 2 (1996): 99–107; Michelle Maunder, "The Conservation of Sacred Objects," in *Godly Things: Museums, Objects and Religion,* ed. Crispin Paine (London: Leicester University Press, 2000), 197–208.

30. Wardwell, 9.

31. J. Halley Cox and William Davenport, *Hawaiian Sculpture* (Honolulu: University of Hawaii Press, 1988.)

32. Wardwell, 114.

33. Wardwell, 114.

34. Kjellgren, 159.

35. Michael Gunn, "The Transfer of Malagan Ownership on Tabar," in *Assemblage of Spirits: Idea and Image in New Ireland,* ed. Louise Lincoln (New York: George Braziller, 1987), 74–83.

36. Kjellgren, 161.

37. Kjellgren, 161.

38. Susanne Küchler, *Malanggan: Art, Memory, and Sacrifice* (Oxford: Berg, 2002).

39. Kjellgren, 159.

40. Peter Heintze, "On Trying to Understand Some Malagans," in *Assemblage of Spirits: Idea and Image in New Ireland,* ed. Louise Lincoln (New York: George Braziller, 1987), 42.

41. Heintze, 42.

42. Küchler, 116.

43. Moore, 169–71.

44. Terence Barrow, *A Guide to the Maori Meeting House Te Hau-Ki-Turanga* (Wellington, New Zealand: National Museum, 1976).

45. Kaeppler, 63.

46. Moore, 162.

47. Kjellgren, 309.

48. Wardwell, 202.

49. David Simmons, *Ta Moko: The Art of Maori Tattoo* (Auckland, New Zealand: Reed, 1986).

50. Hans Neleman, *Moko–Maori Tattoo* (Zurich, Switzerland: Edition Stemmle, 1999).

51. An excellent recent study of Easter Island is Jo Anne Van Tilburg, *Easter Island: Archaeology, Ecology, and Culture* (Washington, DC: Smithsonian Institution Press, 1994).

52. Thor Heyerdahl, *Easter Island: The Mystery Solved* (New York: Random House, 1989); Thor Heyerdahl, *The Kon-Tiki Expedition* (Chicago, IL: Rand McNally, 1950); and Thor Heyerdahl and Christopher Ralling, *Kon-Tiki Man: An Illustrated Biography of Thor Heyerdahl* (San Francisco: Chronicle Books, 1991).

53. Steven Fischer, *Rongorongo: The Easter Island Script: History, Traditions, Texts* (Oxford: Clarendon Press, 1997).

BIBLIOGRAPHY AND FURTHER READING

Allen, Louis. *Australian Aboriginal Art: Arnheim Land*. Chicago, IL: Field Museum Press, 1972.

Allen, Louis. *Time Before Morning: Art and Myth of the Australian Aborigines*. New York: Thomas Y. Crowell, 1975.

Amishai-Maisels, Ziva. "Gauguin's Early Tahitian Idols." *The Art Bulletin* 60, no. 2 (1978): 331–41.

Barrow, Terence. *A Guide to the Maori Meeting House Te Hau-Ki-Turanga*. Wellington, New Zealand: National Museum, 1976.

Barrow, Terence. *An Illustrated Guide to Maori Art*. Honolulu: University of Hawaii Press, 1984.

Bell, Diane. *Daughters of the Dreaming*. Melbourne: McPhee Gribble, 1983.

Berndt, Ronald, ed. *Australian Aboriginal Art*. New York: Macmillan, 1964.

Burenhult, Gören, ed. *New World and Pacific Civilizations: Cultures of the Americas, Asia, and the Pacific*. San Francisco: Harper San Francisco, 1994.

Burenhult, Gören, ed. *Traditional Peoples Today: Continuity and Change in the Modern World*. San Francisco: Harper San Francisco, 1994.

Carroll, Peter. "Mimi from Western Arnheim Land." In *Form in Indigenous Art: Schematisation in the Art of Aboriginal Australia and Prehistoric Europe*, ed. Peter Ucko, 119–30. Canberra, Australia: Australian Institute of Aboriginal Studies, 1977.

Caruana, Wally. *Aboriginal Art*. New York: Thames and Hudson, 1993.

Charlesworth, Max, Howard Morphy, Diane Bell, and Ken Maddock, eds. *Religion in Aboriginal Australia: An Anthology*. St. Lucia, Australia): University of Queensland Press, 1984.

Clavir, Miriam. "Reflections on Changes in Museums and the Conversation of Collections from Indigenous Peoples." *Journal of the American Institute for Conservation* 35, no. 2 (1996): 99–107.

Cox, J. Halley, and William Davenport. *Hawaiian Sculpture*. Honolulu: University of Hawaii Press, 1988.

Elder, John. *Art of Polynesia*. Honolulu, HI: Hemmeter, 1990.

Fischer, Steven. *Rongorongo: The Easter Island Script: History, Traditions, Texts*. Oxford: Clarendon Press, 1997.

Flenley, John, and Paul Bahn. *The Enigmas of Easter Island: Island on the Edge*. Oxford: Oxford University Press, 2002.

Flood, Josephine. *Archaeology of the Dreamtime*. Honolulu: University of Hawaii Press, 1983.

Gathercole, Peter, Adrienne Kaeppler, and Douglas Newton. *The Art of the Pacific Islands*. Washington, DC: The National Gallery of Art, 1979.

Guiart, Jean. *The Arts of the South Pacific*. New York: Golden Press, 1963.

Gunn, Michael. "The Transfer of Malagan Ownership on Tabar." In *Assemblage of Spirits: Idea and Image in New Ireland*, ed. Louise Lincoln, 74–83. New York: George Braziller, 1987.

Hanson, Allan, and Louise Hanson, eds. *Art and Identity in Oceania*. Honolulu: University of Hawaii Press, 1990.

Harrison, Charles, Francis Frascina, and Gill Perry. *Primitivism, Cubism, Abstraction: The Early Twentieth Century*. New Haven, CT: Yale University Press, 1993.

Heintze, Peter. "On Trying to Understand Some Malagans." In *Assemblage of Spirits: Idea and Image in New Ireland*, ed. Louise Lincoln, 42–55. New York: George Braziller, 1987.

Heyerdahl, Thor. *Easter Island: The Mystery Solved*. New York: Random House, 1989.

Heyerdahl, Thor. *The Kon-Tiki Expedition*. Chicago, IL: Rand McNally, 1950.

Heyerdahl, Thor, and Christopher Ralling. *Kon-Tiki Man: An Illustrated Biography of Thor Heyerdahl*. San Francisco: Chronicle Books, 1991.

Kaeppler, Adrienne. *The Pacific Arts of Polynesia and Micronesia*. Oxford: Oxford University Press, 2008.

Kjellgren, Eric. *Oceania: Art of the Pacific Islands in the Metropolitan Museum of Art*. New York: The Metropolitan Museum of Art, 2007.

Küchler, Susanne. *Malanggan: Art, Memory, and Sacrifice*. Oxford: Berg, 2002.

Lavin, Irving, ed. *Meaning in the Visual Arts: Views from the Outside: A Centennial Commemoration of Erwin Panofsky (1892–1968)*. Princeton, NJ: Princeton University Press, 1995.

Lincoln, Louise, ed. *Assemblage of Spirits: Idea and Image in New Ireland*. New York: George Braziller, 1987.

Maunder, Michelle. "The Conservation of Sacred Objects." In *Godly Things: Museums, Objects and Religion*, ed. Crispin Paine, 197–209. London: Leicester University Press, 2000.

Mead, Sidney, ed. *Exploring the Visual Art of Oceania*. Honolulu: University of Hawaii Press, 1979.

Mead, Sidney, ed. *Te Maori: Maori Art from New Zealand Collections*. New York: Harry N. Abrams, 1984.

Moore, Albert. *Arts in the Religions of the Pacific*. London: Cassell, 1995.

Morphy, Howard. *Aboriginal Art*. London: Phaidon, 1998.

Morphy, Howard, ed. *Animals into Art*. London: Unwin Hyman, 1989.

Morwood, M. J. *Visions from the Past: The Archaeology of Australian Aboriginal Art*. Washington, DC: Smithsonian Institution Press, 2002.

Myers, Fred. "Representing Culture: The Production of Discourse(s) for Aboriginal Acrylic Painting." *Cultural Anthropology* 6, no. 1 (1991): 26–62.

Myers, Fred. "Re/Writing the Primitive: Art Criticism and the Circulation of Aboriginal Painting." In *Meaning in the Visual Arts: Views from the Outside: A Centennial Commemoration of Erwin Panofsky (1892–1968)*, ed. Irving Lavin, 65–84. Princeton, NJ: Princeton University Press, 1995.

Neleman, Hans. *Moko–Maori Tattoo*. Zurich, Switzerland: Edition Stemmle, 1999.

Newton, Douglas. *The Art of Africa, the Pacific Islands, and the Americas*. New York: The Metropolitan Museum of Art, 1981.

Paine, Crispin, ed. *Godly Things: Museums, Objects and Religion*. London: Leicester University Press, 2000.

Parks, Nancy, and G. Edward Maxedon. "Instructional Resources: Looking into Oceanic Art." *Art Education* 50, no. 3 (1997): 24–40.

Parsons, Lee. *Ritual Arts of the South Seas*. St. Louis, MO: The Saint Louis Art Museum, 1975.

Poignant, Roslyn. *Oceanic Mythology*. London: Paul Hamlyn, 1967.

Quaill, Avril. *Marking Our Times: Selected Works of Art from the Aboriginal and Torres Strait Islander Collection at the National Gallery of Australia*. Canberra, Australia: National Gallery of Australia, 1996.

Rubin, William, ed. *"Primitivism" in Twentieth Century Art: Affinity of the Tribal and the Modern*. 2 volumes. New York: Museum of Modern Art, 1984.

Schmitz, Carl. *Oceanic Sculpture*. Greenwich, CT: New York Graphic Society, 1962.

Simmons, David. *Ta Moko: The Art of Maori Tattoo*, Auckland, New Zealand: Reed, 1986.

Sutton, Peter, ed. *Dreamings: The Art of Aboriginal Australia*. New York: George Braziller, 1988.

Taylor, Luke. *Seeing the Inside: Bark Painting in Western Arnheim Land*. Oxford: Clarendon Press, 1996.

Taylor, Luke. "Seeing the 'Inside:' Kunwinjku Paintings and the Symbol of the Divided Body." In *Animals into Art*, ed. Howard Morphy, 371–98. London: Unwin Hyman, 1989.

Torgovnick, Marianna. *Gone Primitive: Savage Intellects, Modern Lives*. Chicago, IL: University of Chicago Press, 1990.

Trompf, Garry. *Melanesian Religion*. Cambridge, UK: Cambridge University Press, 1991.

Ucko, Peter, ed. *Form in Indigenous Art: Schematisation in the Art of Aboriginal Australia and Prehistoric Europe*. Canberra, Australia: Australian Institute of Aboriginal Studies, 1977.

Van Tilburg, Jo Anne. *Easter Island: Archaeology, Ecology, and Culture*. Washington, DC: Smithsonian Institution Press, 1994.

Waite, Deborah. *Art of the Solomon Islands from the Barbier-Müller Museum*. Geneva, Switzerland: Musée Barbier-Müller, 1983.

Wardwell, Allen. *Island Ancestors: Oceanic Art from the Masco Collection*. Seattle: University of Washington Press, 1994.

Welsch, Robert, Virginia-Lee Webb, and Sebastian Haraha. *Coaxing the Spirits to Dance: Art and Society in the Papuan Gulf of New Guinea*. Hanover, NH: Dartmouth College, Hood Museum of Art, 2006.

−8−

Indigenous Religions
of Africa

ORIGINS AND DEVELOPMENT

As with several other chapters in this study that purport to cover vast world
regions populated, in the past and at present, by many different cultural groups,
similar challenges are more than posed by the materials to be considered here.
The African continent represents an enormous geographic area, second only in
size to Asia, with an extremely lengthy history as well as signally important prehistory. Evidences of some of the very first human activity on earth have been
traced to Africa, and many believe that humans first evolved in Africa millions
of years ago. Some of the world's earliest art—in the form of charcoal drawings
of animals on stone—has been found in Africa, from approximately the same
time as, or even earlier than, some of the most ancient Paleolithic examples
in Europe. From these remote beginnings, the history of human habitation in
Africa can be traced through many subsequent millennia, representing an enormous variety of different cultures spread across the vast geographic expanse.
At present, the African continent is composed of over 50 different countries
(representing modern political boundaries) in which hundreds of different languages are spoken by many distinct cultural and ethnic groups.

Any attempt to discuss the religious arts of Africa is thus very much challenged, if not quite daunted by, the vastness and diversity of the material to
be covered. Scholars have faced these challenges in a number of different
ways. Many specialists in African art and religion have devoted their attention
to highly detailed studies of specific cultural groups or regions or time periods. Some of these scholars have focused on archaeological materials—or on

anthropological studies of the current traditions represented by various cultural groups in Africa—or have combined the archaeological and anthropological approaches to identify and discuss the historical traditions represented in past and present African regions. A vast amount of specialized bibliography of this nature exists.

Other scholars have taken a more comprehensive approach and have produced extremely impressive studies covering the history and religions of the African continent as a whole.[1] This continentally comprehensive approach well serves to point out the extremely complex and lengthy history of Africa from prehistory to the present day and, for example, critically reminds readers that the arts and religious practices of civilizations such as that of ancient Egypt (which flourished in northeastern Africa from approximately the third millennium BCE to first century CE—see chapter 3) may or should appropriately be included in any discussion of the African continent as a whole, in spite of the fact that ancient Egypt is often regarded as a separate field of study—the venue of Egyptologists rather than Africanists.[2]

Comprehensive coverage of the religious arts of the African continent as a whole will also necessarily include and acknowledge the influence and importance, especially, of the religions of Christianity (see chapter 10) and Islam (see chapter 11) in the formation and development of African religious art forms in numerous regions of the continent. While fully acknowledging the importance and influence of these imported religions, other scholars of African religious art have chosen to focus on the native and indigenous traditions, attempting to restrict their discussion to regions, cultures, and peoples in Africa who—in various manners and with varying degrees of success—appear to have maintained ancient traditions and to have avoided, or fended off, influences from nonnative and colonizing peoples.

Many such discussions of the traditional religious arts of Africa thus exclude, for example, not only ancient Egyptian civilization, but also the distinctive Christian art styles of Ethiopia, as well as the important examples of Islamic art and architecture found in many African regions. These studies tend to focus on particular regions or cultures in Africa that appear to have, in spite of both highly disastrous as well as profitable contact with European, American, and Asian traders and colonizers, maintained some degree of cultural autonomy. Many studies of African art and religion thus separate and segment Africa into a series of regions in which traditional religions were and continue to be practiced, relatively unaffected by outside influences, and regions in which outside influences have greatly affected the art and religious forms.

Terminology: Issues and Challenges

The study and discussion of the religions and arts of Africa seems to have always been exceptionally fraught by terminological issues.[3] A great deal of continued contention persists in current scholarship to the present day about the appropriate usage of specific terms to describe African religious art. At every turn, it appears that even terms such as "art" and "religion" when used to describe African religious arts may be problematic, let alone terms such as "primitive," "primal," "tribal," "traditional," "native," and "indigenous."[4] "What passes as African art and the terms employed to describe it whether by museums, scholars, collectors, etc., are as revealing about the latter as they are about the art itself."[5] It is always extremely wise to be highly attentive to any cultural biases implied in the usage of specific descriptive terminology, no matter the field of study.[6] Approaches to the study of African art reveal these challenges extremely well and demonstrate the many pitfalls involved with imposed classification systems, methodologies, and descriptive labels.[7]

In particular, the traditional use of the term "primitive" to describe African art has been hotly debated for many decades now as reflective of Eurocentric implied value judgments about the relative skill, sophistication, intellectual/philosophical content, or overall importance of African arts within the hierarchy of the traditionally Western art forms of large-scale architecture, sculpture, and painting.[8] Indeed, the response to the primitive arts of Africa on the part of Western European artists of the early 20th century and the role of these arts in the formation of major modern Western art styles such as Cubism has long been the topic of much lively discussion as well.[9]

Although many books about primitive art (including African, Oceanic, and American Indian arts) have been published well into the late 20th century, and academic courses, museums, and exhibitions have used the term "primitive" for many years as well, semipreferred terminological alternatives at present include "native," "tribal," "traditional," and "indigenous," in spite of copious objections to these terms as well. The designation "tribal" has been criticized as representing "a hegemonic Western construction rooted in the colonial and neocolonial epoch,"[10] although many studies continue to be published on African tribal arts.[11] Similarly, the use of the term "traditional" has been analytically critiqued also as reflective of socially and politically manipulative Western-created and Western-imposed concepts.[12] Because the term "traditional" can imply static, unchanging, and noninnovative, its use has been seen as representing "an attempt by Europeans and Americans to 'freeze-dry' all that they consider to be 'authentic' and 'ideal' in African culture. [The term] is associated in many Westerners' minds with notions of authenticity and purity, implying that it could only include art forms produced and used by African villagers around the end of the nineteenth century."[13]

Many of the terms used to describe specific types of African art are also highly problematic. Some of these terms reflect, at best, Western attempts to categorize works of art using vocabulary that strives to most accurately capture the (often untranslatable) variety of African language terms used for particular types of art works. At worst, however, some of the terminology used to describe specific types of African art reflects not only grave misunderstandings about the function of these art works but also the deliberate usage of terms that have pejorative or negative connotations. Terms such as "fetish" have, for example, been rather indiscriminately applied to numerous works of African art whose original functions were of widely ranging purposes, and terms such as "dolls" have been used to describe works of art that, far from being mere playthings, have extremely serious cultural significance. Many scholars have made very useful progress during the past several decades in encouraging the use of alternate terminology for describing specific types of African art objects, and this process continues to provide lively debate today.

Similarly, "the study of African religions is no less controversial than the study of African art."[14] Some scholars have used the term "primal" to describe the non-Western-influenced religions of Africa, characterizing these belief systems as representative of ancient and deep-rooted responses of humankind to fundamental questions about life, death, and the supernatural—not in a primitive (unsophisticated, nonintellectual) fashion but in a manner that places these beliefs firmly within the world's oldest and most fundamental religious traditions.[15] Even so, as has been repeatedly pointed out, the use of Western terms such as *holy, sacred, supernatural, mystical,* and so on, "is hampered by the problems of translation from African languages" in which many different words are used to define these concepts in ways that include multiple and nuanced meanings often quite lost or misrepresented in Western translation.[16] Many significant studies have been produced exploring these complex issues.[17]

This chapter is carefully titled "Indigenous Religions of Africa." The hope and intention is to thus avoid *at least some of* the terminological contention by focusing primary attention on the religious arts of Africa that appear to best represent and present the distinctive and unique qualities of traditional African religious arts as viewed and used within the contexts of their original creation and purpose.

PRINCIPAL BELIEFS AND KEY PRACTICES

As is clear from the preceding discussion, any attempt to neatly summarize the fundamental beliefs and key practices associated with the multitude of traditional African cultures (past and present) runs the severe risks of not only over-generalization but serious terminological misrepresentation. For example, the use of terms such as "monotheism," "polytheism," and "animism" may all be seen as inadequate constructions that tend to confuse the issues rather than explicate. The many cultural groups of Africa all have religious beliefs and practices that are unique to their societies, as well as different vocabulary to describe these beliefs and practices. The degree to which traditions have been affected by or modified in response to historical or ongoing and contemporary influences varies greatly, as well as the forms that traditional African religion has taken on in various areas of the world outside the African continent.

Nevertheless, some common themes may be noted. Most traditional African religions ascribe the creation of the world to an all-powerful divinity. This supreme being (male, female, or both) has many different names but is under-stood to be the ultimate agency through which the world and its human and animal inhabitants came into being.

> Although in myths the Supreme Being is spoken of in a personal manner, as if he were a man with a body, and often with a wife and family, yet many African say-ings and proverbs speak of God in an abstract and philosophical fashion. God is the abstract idea, the cause. He is also a personal deity, generally benevolent, who cares for men and does not strike them with terror. Further, he is an indwelling power, which sustains and animates all things. God knows everything, he sees all, he can do whatever he wishes. . . . He is indescribable, the only reality.[18]

A belief in a sole divine force—omnipotent, indescribable, and all powerful—is generally termed *monotheism*. But, in addition to the supreme creator deity, many traditional African religions recognize and venerate numerous other dei-ties or spirits, as facets, aspects, or reflections of divinity. These figures/deities/ spirits "may be called personifications of natural forces and other glorified heroes of the past; some are both."[19]

A belief in multiple deities is generally termed *polytheism*. These spirits or deities (both male and female) may be associated with storms, rain, wind, light-ning, water, the earth, rocks, mountains, human concerns of birth, death, and illness, and activities such as hunting and agriculture. On the other hand, the belief that deities or spirits associated with natural forces, landscape elements, or human activities are present to actively guide these events, or that these forces are manifested in natural phenomena, is generally termed *animism*.

None of these terms seem truly applicable—across the board—to describe the variety of traditional African religious beliefs and practices. Monotheistic faith systems such as Christianity and Islam have been widely adopted by many peoples in Africa who also continue to practice older, or syncretized, traditions with remarkable degrees of flexibility in the maintenance as well as develop-ment of worship forms.

Thus, the veneration of and communication with deities and spirits takes on many different forms in Africa. Offerings of food and drink, animal sacrifices, and libations may be placed in traditional African shrines and sanctuaries. Dances and masking ceremonies are regularly performed, with singing, chant-ing, prayers, and musical accompaniment.

Much knowledge of traditional African beliefs is based on and promulgated via oral traditions. Of course, many oral traditions have been committed to writing, but traditional African religions are not text or scripture-based. Sacred texts, representing divine revelations (akin to the Bible or Qur'an) do not play a part in traditional African religion. Memory, as well as secrecy, are critical elements in African traditional religions.[20] Commemoration of ancestors, the maintenance and development of traditional ceremonies for communication with the spirit world, and the importance of guarding these powerful practices via initiatory rites and memberships achieved in secret societies are all shared customs. Elders and priests with special knowledge or power often manage and control the rituals. Much recent scholarship has been devoted to the important roles of women in these traditions as well.[21] Practices of divination are widespread and varied,[22] as well as various forms of alchemy, spell-casting, and enchantment.[23]

These general features are common to many traditional African religious practices, although details vary widely through different regions and cultural groups. Various forms of art are employed in religious practices, again, with important regional and cultural variations. It is wise to be mindful of the specific practices of diverse cultures in any generalizations about African religion and religious art.

TRADITIONAL ART AND ARCHITECTURAL FORMS

The religious arts of Africa comprise a great many media including painting, sculpture, architecture, textiles, ceramics, metalwork, and so on. It is an unfortunate reality that many of the world's museums house or display their collections of African art in settings that are not wholly conducive to viewing and understanding these arts in their original contexts.[24] In most museum collections, works of African art are often separated from other chronologically or thematically grouped materials and displayed in special galleries devoted to non-Western art. The objects grouped together in the African art galleries are likely to represent a great diversity of materials and original purposes, ranging widely from the religious to the secular. Objects designed for domestic use, such as carved furniture, are displayed alongside works of art of grand courtly regalia. These touch elbows with dramatic and striking works produced for religious and ceremonial usage, such as masks and power figures, never designed to be so displayed and studied. This mixture of collected pieces of African art is often quite mystifying for viewers and may lead to the impression that all African art is somehow religious or mystical in some primal form.

Works of traditional African religious art (such as masks, ancestor figures, and carved or painted images of other spirits) were never intended to be collected or displayed in museums, but rather were designed to be used in vibrant performances and ceremonies involving music and dance and active engagement on the part of multiple participants (see Figure 8.1).

> Most works of art were viewed very differently in their original context from the way they were or are seen in Western museums. In Africa some figures were kept in dark shrines, only visible to a few persons, while others were covered with cloth, accouterments, offerings, and surrounded by music and dancing. Such objects . . . lose meaning by being made accessible to the visual culture of the West.[25]

However, the extraction of any work of art from its original context poses serious challenges to scholars in all fields. The display of any religious objects

Figure 8.1 Dogon *dama* ceremony, Bandiagara Hills, Mali. Werner Forman / Art Resource, NY.

as cultural artifacts or art works divorces them from their original context—whether it be Western medieval reliquaries containing saints' bones, or African masks and spirit figures, or Byzantine icons, or images of the Buddha taken from Asian temples, or ancient Greek sculptures removed from their original settings. Many complex issues are certainly involved with the collection and display of religious art works.[26] One could argue that all religious art is ultimately designed to inspire viewer participation and that one cannot understand a religion without participating in it or without seeing the associated art in its original context. Nevertheless, sincere attempts to understand the religion and art of any culture will understand that "meaning is continually emergent, elusive, and constructed from available evidence, namely oral and written literature, the discourse of local specialists, the close examination of the historical and cultural milieu of the work, its morphology, imagery, uses, and its relationship to other arts in performance contexts."[27]

Masks and Masking Performances

Among the many forms of African religious art, masks are doubtless the most well known and are certainly well familiar to Western audiences because of their long history of collection and display in various sorts of museums. Indeed, it could be said that "masks have come to be emblematic of African culture in general."[28] Thousands of examples of masks exist, representing a great variety of types and functions, created from a multitude of different materials, such as wood, clay, metal, fabric, beads, leaves, feathers, animal skins, horns, shells, and so on. Although many scholars believe that the use of masks in ritual ceremonies can be traced back to prehistoric times in Africa, and travelers' reports from the Western medieval and Renaissance periods include descriptions of masks and masking performances, the majority of African masks found in public and private collections today primarily date to the 18th, 19th, and 20th centuries. This is largely due to the perishable nature of the materials often used for their creation, as well as their active ceremonial use. Masks, of ancient styles as well as innovative and evolving forms, continue to be produced and used in traditional African religious contexts today. The significance of understanding masks within the contexts of their original use and function simply cannot be overemphasized.

> We should recall that the objects that sometimes seem to lie so lifelessly in their museum display cases were conceived for an entirely different setting and atmosphere. . . . Accompanied by music and song, gestures and rhythms were determined by the type and purpose of the masquerade. Some masks were intended to shock or horrify, others to astonish or to make audiences laugh. Even the most mystifying of masks . . . had a meaning or a message to convey.[29]

It is also critical to be aware that "Many masks now in museums and private collections have been, as it were, mutilated, only the aesthetically appealing face or head portion having been saved."[30] Many masks originally included elements that are now missing, such as fabric, fiber, and feathers. Masks must be understood as having functioned as components in entire costumes of varying degrees of elaboration, accompanied by other ritual objects held by the masker, as visual elements in multisensory performances involving music, dance, gesture, and motion.

Many excellent studies of African dances and ceremonies have been produced that well serve to remind viewers of the great challenges involved with seeing inert objects (masks, costumes, and other accessories) that once functioned in vibrant motion-filled events. Bodily attitudes, stances, poses, gestures, movements of standing, sitting, kneeling, crouching, turning, spinning, and stamping, and elements of grace, balance, smoothness, vibration, pace, and tempo all provided the original essential components now lacking in museum display contexts.[31] Additionally, it should be noted that not all African dances and ceremonies involve the use of masks.[32]

In ordinary Western usage, the terms "mask," "masquerade," and "masking" often have primary connotations of playfulness, entertainment, and amusement. Masks are often considered simply as funny faces donned for festive occasions or nonserious events. In African cultures, as well as in the plethora of other world cultures in which masks are used in social and religious rituals, masks often function in ways that far exceed the concepts of entertainment or purely theatrical spectacle.[33] Even so, attempts to draw distinctions between the fun and serious use of masks are doubtless less useful than the recognition that "in reality, any masked performance has a complex of purposes, and even the most 'serious' are not without their humorous, entertaining aspects. . . . Masking performances can without discrepancy be both serious ritual and captivating entertainment."[34] Masks are used in a great variety of social contexts, and "generally speaking, it is doubtful whether the blanket terms 'religious' and 'secular' do justice to the actual meaning of many masquerades."[35] Masks can serve as extremely powerful vehicles for spiritual and psychological transformation, as means to communicate directly with the supernatural—spirits of the ancestors, gods, and nature. Masks are used during rites of passage, such as births, funerals, coming of age, and marriage ceremonies; they feature in rituals associated with initiation and membership in secret societies that represent political and religious power and authority; they are also used as hunting disguises and in rituals to promote the success of hunting and agricultural activities.

African masks represent an enormous variety of forms, but some basic types can be identified.[36] These include face masks (which cover the front of the wearer's face either fully or partially) (see Figure 8.2), helmet masks (which fit over the wearer's entire head) (see Plate 15), helmet crests (worn like caps on the top of heads) (see Figure 8.3), forehead masks or cap crests (perched on the wearer's forehead), headdress masks (worn on the very top of the head) (see Figure 8.7), and shoulder masks (large heavy masks that rest on the shoulders) (see Figure 8.4). Some masks are extremely tall or multistoried; others have long horizontal extensions or appendages; some masks are designed to be worn by several people simultaneously. Some masks are not worn on the face or head but rather as pendants or strapped elsewhere on the body. Other masks are held in the hands and manipulated in various ceremonial

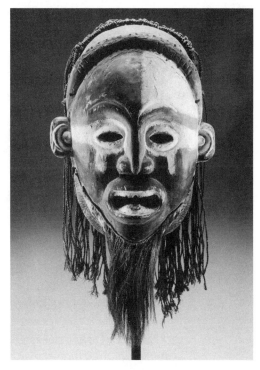

Figure 8.2 Vili face mask, 19th century, wood, fiber, leopard skin, hair, Democratic Republic of Congo. Berlin: Ethnologisches Museum. Bildarchiv Preussischer Kulturbesitz / Art Resource, NY.

Figure 8.3 Edo crest mask, 18th century, metal, Nigeria. Washington, DC: National Museum of African Art. Jerry L. Thompson / Art Resource, NY.

actions, and painted depictions of masks appear in architectural shrine/sanctuary contexts as well. The arts of face and body painting, as well as tattooing and scarification, are closely related to the use and purposes of masks also.[37]

The images and themes of African masks also vary greatly depending on their position, meaning, and function. Some masks have recognizable human features; others have highly abstract designs based on human faces; many show animals (antelopes, leopards, elephants, fish, and birds); other are zoomorphic combinations of animal forms; and others show zooanthropomorphic combinations of human and animal features. Some masks are female and others are male. While masking performances are traditionally dominated by men (with some important exceptions),[38] it is important to note that many "masking societies identify women as, if not always the inventors, then the original familiars of the entities portrayed in masking."[39]

Although masks are among the most familiar and ubiquitous forms of African art, and art historians and collectors have identified many different formats, regional styles, and, in some cases, the names of the artists responsible for creating the masks, awareness of the contextual usage of masks contributes essentially to understanding their significant and complex roles in African society and religious practices.

Shrines, Sanctuaries, and Power Figures

Needless to say, the creation of sacred space is as signally important in traditional African religious practices as in all faith traditions. Space can become sacred by virtue of architectural enclosure or by other means. Dances and rituals can render a space sacred through the power of the actions that take place there. Sacred space does not always require architectural construction of dedicated religious structures within which rituals (either closed to the general public or more widely attended) are enacted. African traditional religious practices reflect this diversity as well.

The creation of dedicated sacred spaces—in the form of shrines and sanctuaries—is common to many traditional African religions. Naturally, these forms of architecture are always influenced by the available building materials, whether it be stone, wood, brick, clay, soil, grass, palm, bamboo, and so on. It might be said that, in general, the enclosed sacred spaces of traditional African religions are designed to house powerful objects that provide a focal point for religious ceremonies of a variety of sorts, as is common in many of the world's religions.

Both religious and domestic buildings in Africa are often of cylindrical hut format (meaning that they are single-celled interior spaces) and have conical roofs (see Figure 8.5). Rectangular and square-planned buildings are also common, often in the form of houses consisting of several structures with related functions arranged around a central courtyard. Buildings, such as temples, shrines, and cult houses, may be dedicated to specific spirits or deities and contain sculptures representing the deity as well as worshiping figures (see Figure 8.6). Shrines for housing the relics of ancestral spirits are common, as well as shrines to deities and spirits whose propitious influence on particular aspects of human life may be sought. Meeting houses set aside for

Figure 8.4 Baga shoulder mask, wood, Guinea. Newark, New Jersey: The Newark Museum / Art Resource, NY.

members of secret societies may contain altars and relics and serve to house ritual objects specifically associated with the group of initiates. Many traditional African religious structures are enriched with carved and painted interior and exterior decoration often in the form of powerful symbols that bespeak the importance of the structure and also serve to guard its contents. Power figures contained within these structures may be masks, sculptures of deities and worshipers, ancestral relics, and objects devoted to specific practices of divination.

EXAMPLES

Bamana Chi Wara Headdress Mask

The Bamana (or Bambara) kingdom was established in Mali during the 17th century, and the Bamana people remain the largest ethnic group in the region. Among the best known and highly collected of their many forms of art, the wooden headdresses of the Chi Wara (Tji Wara or Tyi Wara) society have long been admired for their graceful elegance and stylized forms (see Figure 8.7) Most examples of Chi Wara headdresses represent the curved body

Figure 8.5 Keita Ancestral Shrine, Kaba Kangaba, Mali. Werner Forman / Art Resource, NY.

Figure 8.6 Yoruba Shango Shrine, Nigeria. Werner Forman / Art Resource, NY.

of an antelope with tall horns, large ears, and a protruding notched mane. There are a number of regional variations and formats. Some Chi Wara headdresses are tall and vertical with soaring horns (as in the example illustrated in Figure 8.7) while others are of more horizontal format with the antelope's horns projecting over its back; other examples combine additional animal forms and features. In some examples, the antelope, or other animals, are clearly recognizable; other variations are more abstract. Different degrees of additional elaboration are also seen; carved and incised patterns such as triangles, circles, and zigzags enrich many examples.

Traditionally, the Bamana people have been farmers, challenged by the fact that the dry savanna region in which they live is characterized by low quality soil and a restricted growing season. "To work this land and make it yield has always required tremendous effort. For the Bamana however, farming is not only a necessity, but the noblest of professions in life."[40] The Chi Wara headdresses are connected with Bamana farming

Figure 8.7   Bamana Chi Wara headdress mask, wood, fiber, shell, metal, Mali. Washington, DC: National Museum of African Art. Aldo Tutino / Art Resource, NY.

practices, being used in ritual dances and ceremonies designed to ensure agricultural fertility and to celebrate human prowess with tilling the earth. Members of the Chi Wara society traditionally wear these distinctive headdresses in ceremonies involving displays of skill with tilling the earth under the guidance and encouragement of the watchful spirits. Both male and female Chi Wara masks are paired in these ceremonies, again emphasizing the desire for fertility and sustaining growth.

According to traditional Bamana legends, "the primordial being Tyi Wara was the first farmer, a wild beast who taught mankind how to cultivate the fields."[41] Field research among the Bamana peoples in the mid- to late 20th century has demonstrated, however, that

the number of people who know the details of this legend today are small. . . . Many are aware that the Tyi Wara has something to do with agriculture, but in some areas people no longer even know this. If you go into a Bamana village today and ask if they have a Tyi Wara among them, they will most probably answer in the affirmative. What they have in mind is . . . an *excellent farmer*.[42]

The importance of field research and contextual studies is well demonstrated yet again here. Chi Wara masks continue to be produced and used by many Bamana peoples, as well as understood in new ways. "No doubt the common practice of calling an excellent farmer Tyi Wara had its origins in people being compared to the supernatural personality who was the best farmer the earth had ever seen."[43] Even so, the associations of Chi Wara headdresses, dances, and rituals with a specific primordial agricultural deity need to be seen within the ongoing and vibrantly shifting associations of traditional African religious art forms. Many Bamana peoples have converted to Islam, and, although traditional Chi Wara dances may still be performed today, these practices have taken on different connotations and meanings.

In point of fact, the Chi Wara headdresses, so prized by Western collectors for their "semi-naturalistic or abstract manner with beautiful rhythmic flowing lines, angles and spaces" represent a relatively modern form of mask headdress developed by the Bamana people in the early years of the 20th century.[44] Far from being examples of ancient African art, reflective of long-standing and primal traditions, the Chi Wara headdresses serve to well reflect the vibrancy and ongoing innovations in African art. Their appeal to Western tastes in the early to mid-20th century ("Europeans saw the headdresses and desired to have them") resulted in the purchase, as well as thefts—often orchestrated by middlemen—of these objects, not to mention the production of new examples of these objects for the collecting and tourist trade.[45]

Kongo *Nkisi Nkondi* Figure

Widely produced by the Bakongo peoples of central Africa during the late 19th and early 20th century (and to some extent to the present day at well), figures known as *nkisi* (plural: *minkisi*) are among the most well-known and perhaps also most dramatic examples of African religious arts (see Plate 16). Removed from their original contexts and displayed in museums, these figures may appear extremely startling and difficult to understand. Often described as magical figures or fetishes, the term *nkisi* is fundamentally untranslatable. Perhaps the best equivalent (if the term needs to be translated at all) is "power figure."

Minkisi figures exist in a variety of forms. The late 19th-century example illustrated in Plate 16 is a *nkisi nkondi* or hunter figure, in the form of a standing male. The core wooden figure bristles with metal blades and nails, which have been driven in on all sides, partially obscuring all of the figure apart from the face. "*Minkisi* as found today in numerous museums are no more than parts of the material apparatus necessary for the performance of rituals in pursuit of particular goals."[46] In the case of *nkondi* ("hunter") figures, it is traditionally said that their major purpose "was to identify and hunt down unknown wrongdoers, such as thieves and those who were believed to have caused sickness and death among their neighbors by occult means."[47] Ritual use of these figures was undertaken by qualified experts (*nganga*) who, on behalf of an individual or community, empowered the figures with the addition of mineral, vegetable, and animal materials known as medicines or *bilongo* (in this case partially sealed in a packet on the figure's head), and drove one or more nails or blades into the figure, while making incantations to direct the figure to its task. *Minkisi* figures "could be used to deflect sorcerous intent, protect against misfortune and illness, regulate disputes, create treaties or swear oaths."[48] Nails driven into these figures may thus represent oaths taken under the auspices of these powerful figures or perhaps also offerings of thanks for tasks completed by the *minkisi* rituals. Much scholarship has been devoted to *minkisi* figures—their styles, makers, and uses—reflecting their continued fascination and power.[49]

Ashanti *Akua Ma* Figurines

Produced in great numbers by the Ashanti (Asante) and other west African cultural groups, *akua ma* (or *akua 'mma*) figurines are often described by the misleading term "dolls" (see Figure 8.8). While the use of this term is not wholly inaccurate, these objects were not intended as toys or playthings but rather as powerful vehicles to promote female fertility. They are generally carved of wood and typically have enlarged, round, flat heads, stylized facial features of long straight noses and prominent eyebrows, long necks, and small bodies (with or without horizontally projecting arms.)

Akua ma figurines were created to be cared for, and carried by, women hoping to have children (and thus fulfill their primary social role of childbearing). The carved figures, after having been consecrated at a shrine, were customarily carried by young women, tucked into their garments on their backs, in the fashion real babies are often carried. The practice continues today. "Thought to have the power to make women conceive [they] are carried around and treated like a real child by the Asante women. After use, they are placed in a domestic shrine."[50] *Akua ma* means "Akua's children" in reference to the Ashanti legend of a woman named Akua who was "the first woman to own and care

Figure 8.8 Ashanti *Akua Ma* figurines, wood, Ghana. The Art Archive / Paris: Musée des Arts Africains et Océaniens / Gianni Dagli Orti.

Figure 8.9 Kota *Mbulu-Ngulu* figure, metal and wood, Gabon. The Art Archive / Paris: Musée des Arts Africains et Océaniens / Gianni Dagli Orti.

for a consecrated human figure on instruction from a priest. Barren, and mocked for carrying a surrogate baby made of wood, Akua is said to have gotten pregnant nevertheless, eventually giving birth to a healthy baby girl. Female children are preferred among the matrilineal Akan, and *akua ma* are almost always carved as female."[51]

Kota *Mbulu-Ngulu* Figure

The Kota people live in the west African region of Gabon bordering the Republic of Congo. Among their most distinctive forms of art are objects known as *mbulu-ngulu* (or *mbulungulu*) (see Figure 8.9). Although these objects are often called "reliquary figures," it might be rather more accurate to describe them as "guardian figures." These objects were tied to cloth bundles or baskets of relics (known as *bwete*) and served to protect the relics while also providing a focus for prayers and rituals honoring the prominent ancestors whose bones were contained in the *bwete* bundles. The practice of honoring ancestors is a shared feature of many traditional African religions. Of course, the practice of collecting and venerating the bodily remains of important figures is common to many of the world's religious practices as well as the custom of creating objects of art to contain or signal the presence of relics.

There are a number of regional forms and variations of *mbulu-ngulu*. Traditionally, these figures are made of wood and covered with metal (copper or brass) sheets. They have enlarged, flat, oval, or shovel-shaped faces with stylized features indicating eyes, nose, and mouth. Many examples show a variety of hair styles, different degrees of elaboration with flat projecting flanges to the top or sides incised with decorative patterns, and indications of jewelry, such as earrings and neck bands. The enlarged heads customarily sit atop tall necks and are fixed to a minimally represented body (of V or diamond shape) symbolizing a human figure.

The *bwete* bundles/baskets and their *mbulu-ngulu* figures were intended to be kept safely in shrines dedicated to the veneration of ancestral figures, whose power and efficacy guided the fortunes of the people. Divorced from their original settings and presented as objects of art—or of ethnographic interest—the *mbulu-ngulu* figures lack their full context. Nevertheless, these are among the objects of African art forms most prized by collectors, and response to this market has also generated the lively production of recent examples of this traditional art form.

Yoruba *Iroke Ifa* Divination Wand

The complex system of divination known as Ifa is characteristic of the Yoruba peoples of southwestern Nigeria, Benin, and Togo, and continues to be practiced by many adherents today in various regions of the world.[52] Divination systems, in general, represent means to communicate with and learn the will of spirit forces and may be employed in any number of life stages and decision-making situations.

Ifa divination is undertaken by specially trained practitioners or priests known as *babalawo*, who employ a variety of consecrated ritual objects in the ceremonies. Among these are tappers, or wands, known as *iroke ifa,* which are used to invoke the oracular spirits and powers and guide the divination process (see Figure 8.10). Most often made of wood or ivory, *iroke ifa* are tapped, by the priest, against a wooden divination tray (known as *opon ifa*) on

Figure 8.10 Yoruba *Iroke Ifa* wand, wood, Nigeria. Private collection. Werner Forman / Art Resource, NY.

which wood dust or powder has been sprinkled. Invocations are chanted and the process continues through a series of stages in which markings are made in the powder on the divination tray based on the number and order of palm nuts (or shells) that are successively drawn from a special container by the priest. It is a highly orderly, complicated, and multifaceted ritual in which consecrated objects play a critical role.

Wands or tappers are often elaborately carved with important and complex symbols, such as the wooden example illustrated here. The conical projection at the top is said to represent the inner head or *ori inu* of the supplicant(s) for whom the divination is performed. This symbolizes "a person's past, present and future and the essence of his/her personality."[53] The middle section of the example shown depicts a kneeling, nude female figure holding her breasts. A frequent figure on *iroke ifa*, she serves as an intermediary and symbolic carrier of life force. Her prayerful, kneeling position (also associated with childbirth) represents "the most appropriate way to salute the orisa or divinities, who are known as Akunlebo ('the-ones-who-must-be-worshiped-kneeling-down'). Her nudity is evidence of the solemnity of the moment."[54]

As sculptural carvings, *iroke ifa* may be greatly admired for their styles, materials, formats, and fine details. However, an understanding of the function and purpose of these objects greatly enhances this comprehension. *Iroke ifa* functioned as one critical element in complex rituals involving a plethora of other objects, actions, and attitudes. Seeing "art and ritual as integral to each other" is essential to understanding the complete context.[55]

NOTES

1. See, for example, Tom Phillips, curator (with essays by Kwame Appiah, Suzanne Blier, Ekpo Eyo, Henry Gates, and Peter Mark), *Africa: The Art of a Continent* (New York: Guggenheim Museum, 1996); Monica Visonà, Robin Poyner, Herbert Cole, and Michael Harris, *A History of Art in Africa* (New York: Harry N. Abrams, 2001); and John Mack, ed., *Africa: Arts and Cultures* (New York: Oxford University Press, 2000).

2. Ekpo Eyo, "Putting Northern Africa Back into Africa," in *Africa: The Art of a Continent*, curated by Tom Phillips, 9–14.

3. Rosalind Hackett, *Art and Religion in Africa* (London: Cassell, 1996), 1–21.

4. Peter Mark, "Is There Such a Thing as African Art?" *Record of the Art Museum, Princeton University* 58, no. 1 (1999): 7–15.

5. Hackett, *Art and Religion in Africa*, 4.

6. For example, see the section titled "African Culture and Western Attitudes toward African Religion" in Douglas Thomas, *African Traditional Religion in the Modern World* (Jefferson, NC: McFarland, 2005), 43–82.

7. Many scholars have addressed these issues extensively. See Monni Adams, "African Visual Art from an Art Historical Perspective," *The African Studies Review* 32, no. 2 (1989): 55–103; Paula Ben-Amos, "African Visual Art from a Social Perspective," *The African Studies Review* 32, no. 2 (1989): 1–53; Suzanne Blier, "Words about Words about Icons: Iconologology and the Study of African Art," *Art Journal* 47, no. 2 (1988): 75–87; and Jacqueline Chanda, "Alternative Concepts and Terminologies for Teaching African Art," *Art Education* 45, no. 1 (1992): 56–61.

8. "The word 'primitive' of course is Protean in its meanings. Its basic sense is 'primary in time,' and by extension undeveloped, simple, crude, unsophisticated. . . . An attempt is sometimes made among art historians to justify the use of the term 'primitive art' on the grounds that 'we know what we mean by it.' . . . Art historians may think that they know what they mean by the term, though they have failed to produce a working definition. . . . Even as used by art historians the term has several distinct meanings." Frank Willett, *African Art: An Introduction* (New York: Thames and Hudson, 1993), 27–28. See also the lively and detailed discussion in Marianna Torgovnick, *Gone Primitive: Savage Intellects, Modern Lives* (Chicago, IL: University of Chicago Press, 1990).

9. For an excellent sampling, see: William Rubin, ed., *"Primitivism" in Twentieth-Century Art: Affinity of the Tribal and the Modern*. 2 vols. (New York: Museum of Modern Art, 1984); Charles Harrison, Francis Frascina, and Gill Perry, *Primitivism, Cubism, Abstraction: The Early Twentieth Century* (New Haven, CT: Yale University Press, 1994); and Patricia Leighten, "The White Peril and L'Art Nègre: Picasso, Primitivism and Anticolonialism," *The Art Bulletin* 72, no. 4 (1990): 609–30.

10. Hackett, *Art and Religion in Africa*, 5.

11. For example, Jean-Baptiste Bacquart, *The Tribal Arts of Africa* (New York: Thames and Hudson, 1998).

12. Terence Ranger, "The Invention of Tradition in Colonial Africa," in *The Invention of Tradition*, ed. Eric Hobshawm and Terence Ranger (Cambridge: Cambridge University Press, 1983), 211–62, especially 247–62.

13. Hackett, *Art and Religion in Africa*, 6–7.

14. Hackett, *Art and Religion in Africa*, 9.

15. Huston Smith, *The Illustrated World's Religions* (San Francisco: Harper San Francisco, 1994), 230–43.

16. Hackett, *Art and Religion in Africa*, 11.

17. See, for example, Rowland Abiodun, "Understanding Yoruba Art and Aesthetics: The Concept of Ase," *African Arts* 27, no. 3 (1994): 67–78, 102–3.

18. Geoffrey Parrinder, *African Mythology* (London: Paul Hamlyn, 1967), 18–19.

19. Parrinder, 66.

20. Mary Nooter, ed., *Secrecy: African Art That Conceals and Reveals* (New York: Museum for African Art, 1993); and Mary Nooter Roberts and Allen Roberts, eds., *Memory: Luba Art and the Making of History* (New York: Museum for African Art, 1996).

21. Rosalind Hackett, "Women in African Religions," in *Religion and Women*, ed. Arvind Sharma (Albany: State University of New York Press, 1994), 61–92.

22. John Matthews, ed., *The World Atlas of Divination* (Boston: Bulfinch Press, 1992), 93–108

23. The terminology used to describe these practices is often rather problematic and laden with cultural biases. Terms such as "magic," "witchcraft," and "sorcery" often imply Western-based notions of primitive superstitions, and many Westerners encountering the arts and beliefs of Africans in the colonial period especially tended to use these terms in a highly pejorative fashion.

24. A plethora of sources address these issues; see Sally Price, *Primitive Art in Civilized Places* (Chicago, IL: University of Chicago Press, 2001).

25. Hackett, *Art and Religion in Africa*, 5.

26. Ena Heller, "Religion on a Pedestal: Exhibiting Sacred Art," in *Reluctant Partners: Art and Religion in Dialogue*, ed. Ena Heller (New York: Gallery at the American Bible Society, 2004), 122–41; Chris Arthur, "Exhibiting the Sacred," in *Godly Things: Museums, Objects and Religion*, ed. Crispin Paine (London: Leicester University Press, 2000), 1–27.

27. Hackett, *Art and Religion in Africa*, 15.

28. John Mack, "African Masking," in *Masks and the Art of Expression*, ed. John Mack (New York: Harry N. Abrams: 1994), 33.

29. Maria Kecskési and László Vajda, "I Am Not Myself," in *African Masks: The Barbier-Mueller Collection*, Iris Hahner, Maria Kecskési, and László Vajda (Munich, Germany: Prestel, 2007), 14.

30. Kecskési and Vajda, 14.

31. Robert Thompson, *African Art in Motion: Icon and Act in the Collection of Katherine Coryton White* (Los Angeles: University of California Press, 1974), and Herbert Cole, ed., *I Am Not Myself: The Art of African Masquerade* (Los Angeles: University of California, Los Angeles, Museum of Cultural History, 1985).

32. This raises some excellent terminological issues again, "with expressions of the body in motion—we are far from the habitual terrain of art historians. . . . does dance become an object of the art historian's attention only at the moment the dancers wear masks?" Peter Mark, 13.

33. John Nunley and Cara McCarty, *Masks: Faces of Culture* (New York: Harry N. Abrams, 1999), and Gary Edson, *Masks and Masking: Faces of Tradition and Belief Worldwide* (Jefferson, NC: McFarland, 2005).

34. Mack, "African Masking," 35.

35. Kecskési and Vajda, 33.

36. See the useful diagrams in Kecskési and Vajda, 15–16.

37. Hans Silvester, *Natural Fashion: Tribal Decoration from Africa* (London: Thames and Hudson, 2008).

38. Monni Adams, "Women and Masks among the Western Wè of Ivory Coast," *African Arts* 19, no. 2 (1986): 46–55, 90; and Elizabeth Tonkin, "Women Excluded? Masking and Masquerading in West Africa," in *Women's Religious Experience*, ed. Pat Holden (London: Croom Helm, 1983), 163–74.

39. Mack, "African Masking," 43.

40. Pascal Imperato, "The Dance of the Tyi Wara," *African Arts* 4, no. 1 (1970), 8.

41. Monica Visonà, "Mande Worlds and the Upper Niger," in *A History of Art in Africa*, Monica Visonà, Robin Poyner, Herbert Cole, and Michael Harris (New York: Harry N. Abrams, 2001), 117.

42. Imperato, 8.

43. Imperato, 8.

44. Imperato, 72.

45. Imperato, 73.

46. Wyatt MacGaffey, catalogue entry no. 50 , in *Africa: The Art of a Continent*, curated Tom Phillips, 106.

47. MacGaffey, 106.

48. Mack, *Africa: Arts and Cultures*, 147.

49. Ezio Bassani, "Kongo Nail Fetishes from the Chiloango River Area," *African Arts* 10, no. 3 (1977): 36–40, 88; and Wyatt MacGaffey, "The Eyes of Understanding Kongo Minkisi," in *Astonishment and Power*, ed. Wyatt MacGaffey and Michael Harris (Washington, DC: Smithsonian Institution Press, 1993), 21–103.

50. Bacquart, 32.

51. Herbert Cole, "Akan Worlds," in *A History of Art in Africa*, Monica Visonà, Robin Poyner, Herbert Cole, and Michael Harris, 211.

52. John Turpin and Judith Gleason, "Ifa: A Yoruba System of Oracular Divination," in *The World Atlas of Divination*, ed. John Matthews, 101–8.

53. Hackett, *Art and Religion in Africa*, 124.

54. Hackett, *Art and Religion in Africa*, 125.

55. Hackett, *Art and Religion in Africa*, 126.

BIBLIOGRAPHY AND FURTHER READING

Abiodun, Rowland. "Understanding Yoruba Art and Aesthetics: The Concept of *Ase*." *African Arts* 27, no. 3 (1994): 67–78, 102–3.

Abiodun, Rowland, Suzanne Blier, Henry Drewal, and Adrian Gerbrands. *African Art Studies: The State of the Discipline*. Washington, DC: National Museum of African Art, 1990.

Adams, Monni. "African Visual Art from an Art Historical Perspective." *The African Studies Review* 32, no. 2 (1989): 55–103.

Adams, Monni. "Women and Masks among the Western Wè of Ivory Coast." *African Arts* 19, no. 2 (1986): 46–55, 90.

Arthur, Chris. "Exhibiting the Sacred." In *Godly Things: Museums, Objects and Religion*, ed. Crispin Paine, 1–27. London: Leicester University Press, 2000.

Bacquart, Jean-Baptiste. *The Tribal Arts of Africa*. New York: Thames and Hudson, 1998.

Bassani, Ezio. "Kongo Nail Fetishes from the Chiloango River Area." *African Arts* 10, no. 3 (1977): 36–40, 88.

Ben-Amos, Paula. "African Visual Art from a Social Perspective." *The African Studies Review* 32, no. 2 (1989): 1–53.

Ben-Amos, Paula. *The Art of Benin*. London: British Museum Press, 1995.

Bibliography on African Traditional Religion, http://www.afrikaworld.net/.

Blier, Suzanne. "Words about Words about Icons: Iconologology and the Study of African Art." *Art Journal* 47, no. 2 (1988): 75–87.

Brett-Smith, Sarah. *The Making of Bamana Sculpture: Creativity and Gender*. Cambridge, UK: Cambridge University Press, 1994.

Chanda, Jacqueline. "Alternative Concepts and Terminologies for Teaching African Art." *Art Education* 45, no. 1 (1992): 56–61.

Cole, Herbert. "Akan Worlds." In *A History of Art in Africa*, Monica Visonà, Robin Poyner, Herbert Cole, and Michael Harris, 194–226. New York: Harry N. Abrams, 2001.

Cole, Herbert, ed. *I Am Not Myself: The Art of African Masquerade*. Los Angeles: University of California, Los Angeles, Museum of Cultural History, 1985.

Cole, Herbert. *Icons: Ideals and Power in the Art of Africa*. Washington, DC: Smithsonian Institution, 1989.

Edson, Gary. *Masks and Masking: Faces of Tradition and Belief Worldwide*. Jefferson, NC: McFarland, 2005.

Ekpo Eyo. "Putting Northern Africa Back into Africa." In *Africa: The Art of a Continent*, curated by Tom Phillips, 9–14. New York: Guggenheim Museum, 1996

Ezra, Kate. *Royal Art of Benin: The Perls Collection in the Metropolitan Museum of Art*. New York: Metropolitan Museum of Art, 1992.Hackett, Rosalind. *Art and Religion in Africa*. London: Cassell, 1996.

Hackett, Rosalind. "Women in African Religions." In *Religion and Women*, ed. Arvind Sharma, 61–92. Albany: State University of New York Press, 1994.

Hahner, Iris, Maria Kecskési, and László Vajda. *African Masks: The Barbier-Mueller Collection*. Munich, Germany: Prestel, 2007.

Harris, Nathaniel. *Great Works of African Art*. New York: Smithmark, 1996.

Harrison, Charles, Francis Frascina, and Gill Perry. *Primitivism, Cubism, Abstraction: The Early Twentieth Century*. New Haven, CT: Yale University Press, 1994.

Heller, Ena. "Religion on a Pedestal: Exhibiting Sacred Art." In *Reluctant Partners: Art and Religion in Dialogue*, ed. Ena Heller, 122–41. New York: Gallery at the American Bible Society, 2004.

Heller, Ena, ed. *Reluctant Partners: Art and Religion in Dialogue*. New York: Gallery at the American Bible Society, 2004.

Hobshawm, Eric, and Terence Ranger, eds. *The Invention of Tradition*. Cambridge, UK: Cambridge University Press, 1983.

Holden, Pat, ed. *Women's Religious Experience*. London: Croom Helm, 1983.

Imperato, Pascal. "The Dance of the Tyi Wara." *African Arts* 4, no. 1 (1970): 8–13, 71–80.

Johnson, Barbara. *Four Dan Sculptors: Continuity and Change*. San Francisco: The Fine Arts Museums of San Francisco, 1986.

Kecskési, Maria, and László Vajda. "I Am Not Myself." In *African Masks: The Barbier-Mueller Collection*, Iris Hahner, Maria Kecskési, and László Vajda, 11–36. Munich, Germany: Prestel, 2007.

Leighten, Patricia. "The White Peril and L'Art Nègre: Picasso, Primitivism and Anti-colonialism." *The Art Bulletin* 72, no. 4 (1990): 609–30.

MacGaffey, Wyatt. "The Eyes of Understanding Kongo Minkisi." In *Astonishment and Power*, ed. Wyatt MacGaffey and Michael Harris, 21–103. Washington, DC: Smithsonian Institution Press, 1993.

MacGaffey, Wyatt, and Michael Harris, eds. *Astonishment and Power*. Washington, DC: Smithsonian Institution Press, 1993.

Mack, John, ed. *Africa: Arts and Cultures*. New York: Oxford University Press, 2000.

Mack, John. "African Masking." In *Masks and the Art of Expression*, ed. John Mack, 33–55. New York: Harry N. Abrams: 1994.

Mack, John, ed. *Masks and the Art of Expression*. New York: Harry N. Abrams: 1994.

Mark Peter. "Is There Such a Thing as African Art?" *Record of the Art Museum, Princeton University* 58, no. 1 (1999): 7–15.

Matthews, John, ed. *The World Atlas of Divination*. Boston: Bulfinch Press, 1992.

Meyer, Laure. *Black Africa: Masks, Sculpture, Jewelry*. Paris: Terrail, 1992.

Meyer, Laure. *Art and Craft in Africa: Everyday Life, Ritual, Court Art*. Paris: Terrail, 1995.

National Museum of African Art, Smithsonian Institution, http://africa.si.edu/.

Nooter, Mary, ed. *Secrecy: African Art That Conceals and Reveals*. New York: Museum for African Art, 1993.

Nunley, John, and Cara McCarty. *Masks: Faces of Culture*. New York: Harry N. Abrams, 1999.

Okpewho, Isidore. "Principles of Traditional African Art." *The Journal of Aesthetics and Art Criticism* 35, no. 3 (1977): 301–14.

Paine, Crispin, ed. *Godly Things: Museums, Objects and Religion*. London: Leicester University Press, 2000.

Parrinder, Geoffrey. *African Mythology*. London: Paul Hamlyn, 1967.

Perry, Gill. "Primitivism and the Modern." In *Primitivism, Cubism, Abstraction: The Early Twentieth Century*, Charles Harrison, Francis Frascina, and Gill Perry, 2–85. New Haven, CT: Yale University Press, 1994.

Phillips, Tom, curator (with essays by Kwame Appiah, Suzanne Blier, Ekpo Eyo, Henry Gates, and Peter Mark). *Africa: The Art of a Continent*. New York: Guggenheim Museum, 1996.

Price, Sally. *Primitive Art in Civilized Places*. Chicago, IL: University of Chicago Press, 2001.

Ranger, Terence. "The Invention of Tradition in Colonial Africa." In *The Invention of Tradition*, ed. Eric Hobshawm and Terence Ranger, 211–62. Cambridge, UK: Cambridge University Press, 1983.

Roberts, Mary Nooter, and Allen Roberts, eds. *Memory: Luba Art and the Making of History*. New York: Museum for African Art, 1996.

Roberts, Mary Nooter, and Allen Roberts. *A Sense of Wonder: African Art from the Faletti Family Collection.* Phoenix, AZ: Phoenix Art Museum, 1997.

Roberts, Mary Nooter, and Allen Roberts. *The Shape of Belief: African Art from the Michael R. Heide Collection.* San Francisco: The Fine Arts Museums of San Francisco, 1996.

Rubin, William, ed. *"Primitivism" in Twentieth-Century Art: Affinity of the Tribal and the Modern.* 2 vols. New York: Museum of Modern Art, 1984.

Sharma, Arvind, ed. *Religion and Women.* Albany: State University of New York Press, 1994.

Silvester, Hans. *Natural Fashion: Tribal Decoration from Africa.* London: Thames and Hudson, 2008.

Smith, Huston. *The Illustrated World's Religions.* San Francisco: Harper San Francisco, 1994.

Teuten, Timothy. *The Collector's Guide to Masks.* London: Random House/Bracken Books, 1996.

Thomas, Douglas. *African Traditional Religion in the Modern World.* Jefferson, NC: McFarland, 2005.

Thompson, Robert. *African Art in Motion: Icon and Act in the Collection of Katherine Coryton White.* Los Angeles: University of California Press, 1974.

Tonkin, Elizabeth. "Women Excluded? Masking and Masquerading in West Africa." In *Women's Religious Experience,* ed. Pat Holden, 163–74. London: Croom Helm, 1983.

Torgovnick, Marianna. *Gone Primitive: Savage Intellects, Modern Lives.* Chicago, IL: University of Chicago Press, 1990.

Turpin, John, and Judith Gleason. "Ifa: A Yoruba System of Oracular Divination." In *The World Atlas of Divination,* ed. John Matthews, 101–8. Boston: Bulfinch Press, 1992.

Vansina, Jan. *Art History in Africa.* London: Longman, 1984.

Visonà, Monica. "Mande Worlds and the Upper Niger." In *A History of Art in Africa,* Monica Visonà, Robin Poyner, Herbert Cole and Michael Harris, 106–29. New York: Harry N. Abrams, 2001.

Visonà, Monica, Robin Poyner, Herbert Cole, and Michael Harris. *A History of Art in Africa.* New York: Harry N. Abrams, 2001.

Vogel, Susan. *Baule: African Art, Western Eyes.* New Haven, CT: Yale University Press, 1997.

Wassing, René. *African Art: Its Background and Traditions.* New York: Portland House, 1988.

Werness, Hope. *The Continuum Encyclopedia of Native Art: Worldview, Symbolism, and Culture in Africa, Oceania, and North America.* New York: Continuum, 2000.

Willett, Frank. *African Art: An Introduction.* New York: Thames and Hudson, 1993.

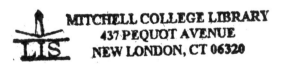